MW00414440

TWO ERRORS: 1. to take everything literally
2. to take everything spiritually

Pascal

The Ordinary
Transformed

KARL RAHNER AND THE
CHRISTIAN VISION OF
TRANSCENDENCE

R. R. Reno

WILLIAM B. EERDMANS PUBLISHING COMPANY
GRAND RAPIDS, MICHIGAN / CAMBRIDGE, U.K.

For my wife

© 1995 Wm. B. Eerdmans Publishing Co.
255 Jefferson Ave. S.E., Grand Rapids, Michigan 49503
P. O. Box 163, Cambridge CB3 9PU U.K.

All rights reserved

Printed in the United States of America

00 99 98 97 96 95   7 6 5 4 3 2 1

Library of Congress Cataloging-in-Publication Data

Reno, Russell, R., 1959-
The ordinary transformed: an inquiry into the Christian vision of transcendence /
R. R. Reno.
p.   cm.
Includes bibliographical references.
ISBN 0-8028-0784-4 (pbk.: alk. paper)
1. Transcendence of God — History of doctrines — 20th century.
2. Transcendence (Philosophy). 3. Rahner, Karl, 1904 — Contributions in
doctrine of transcendence.   I. Title.
BT124.5.R46 1995
231'.4 — dc20   95-33948
                                                      CIP

Contents

Chapter Six • Transcendence and the Christian Form of Life

In light of Kerr's challenge, attention turns to the senses in which the transcendence implied in a dynamic view of pilgrimage is necessary from within the Christian frame of reference

understood is intrinsic to created and divine reality • The
grammar of Christian faith propels the reader into the
strangeness and depth of mystery • Since God is fully and
finally mystery, the Christian pilgrimage is the eternal form of
our relation to God

Acknowledgments

This project was born out of a desire to come to terms with the individualism which is both the blessing and curse of modernity. As a graduate student, I was deceived by the blossoming literature on "communitarianism" into thinking that I could get to the heart of the matter by investigating the relation of the individual to the community. Anxious about the absorption of the self into communal practice, I set about writing a dissertation on that very topic, as exemplified in the thought of Karl Rahner. That dissertation was a conceptual failure, for the vision of transcendence that funds modern individualism, and the corresponding communalist reactions, do not map onto a simple individual vs. community grid. Both the tyranny of freedom, which gives Rousseau his frenzied energy, and the ironies of community, which Rahner knew so well, refused my strategy of setting the individual against the community.

With kind indulgence the Yale University Department of Religious Studies conferred a degree; however, my continued perplexity forced me to begin again from scratch. Our fate as late moderns has to do far more with the parties of purity — pure immanence and pure transcendence — than labels such as "liberals" and "communitarians." And in the tangles of Rahner's essays, I have come to see that the alternative to these perennial parties of purity is the vision of transcendence that takes as its point of departure the Cross upon which is revealed the God who is love. This attempt to clarify Rahner's account of the Christian vision of transcendence seeks, then, to give the reader some small sense of how we might make our way through the perhaps protracted dusk of modernity.

This project owes a great deal to two Yale professors. Gene Outka guided me into the intricate, interlocking claims and commitments of modern moral theory and traditional Christian morality. More than anyone, Gene Outka taught me to avoid the parties of purity which brutalize the details. His was a lesson in how to think "amphibiously." I take this to be the key to a humane intellectual life. The fingerprints of George Lindbeck are all over this project. Whatever else the "cultural-linguistic" approach to theology might be, it is at least a distinctive habit of thought which penetrates into the language of theology without trying either to get beyond or to do without the words. By teaching me this habit of thought, George Lindbeck has shown me that theology is a discipline in which love of the tradition (cultivating the words) is, at the same time, a call to freedom (penetrating the language), and this combination makes theology the most serious and most joyful of sciences. I hope that I have done George Lindbeck justice by treating Karl Rahner lovingly and freely, seriously and joyfully.

This project has not suffered from loneliness. A number of colleagues both near and far have contributed significantly to my thinking on the question of transcendence. David Kelsey and Richard Fern both read the misbegotten dissertation out of which this project grew, and their comments directed me toward the enigmatic notion of transcendence. Kendall Soulen read the entire manuscript at various stages. His comments and encouragement were of great value. David Wisdo and David Yeago were incalculably helpful conversation partners, and both read the manuscript with generous hearts. Michael Brown and William Stephens read select chapters and provided philosophical resistance to my theological aggressiveness. Stanley Hauerwas and Bruce Marshall helped me navigate the passage from manuscript to publication with both encouragement and practical advice.

If readers take any pleasure in the art of this study, they owe a debt of gratitude to Peggy Troy. Her expert pencil corrected the entire manuscript, saving me from verbal error and ugliness, and encouraging me toward clarity and whatever elegance of which I might be capable. Her ear for the music of words has set high standards for me, and I am a far better writer for her good company as reader and critic.

The Graduate School of Creighton University provided much appreciated support with a Faculty Research Fellowship in the summer of 1992. The Theology Department of Creighton University sustains a warm and supportive context for my theological work, and my Chair has been kind enough to absorb my not insignificant long distance bills into the department budget. For three years my freshman students in Theology of Human Existence have bent themselves to the task of reading Hume's *Dialogues Concerning Natural Religion*. Chapter One of the present volume is in part a product of their patience with and interest in my interpretation of Hume. Finally, the folks at Eerdmans, especially the boss, have been lots of fun. Their good and his offbeat humor are a pleasant antidote to the high seriousness of academic publishing.

Introduction

"To transcend" simply means to step over, climb beyond or surmount. We might transcend a river or a mountain range on our travels. We could say that a criminal transcends the law. We might regard an overreaching politician as someone who transcends the limits of his or her office. In each instance, use of the concept of transcendence simply denotes a movement, a change in location or status. No philosophical theories or metaphysical commitments are entailed. When crossing streams or mountains, the transcendence is purely geographical. The criminal's transcendence is statutory. The politician's transcendence is constitutional. In none of these instances does transcendence denote a departure from the temporal realm, a release from bodily existence, a limitless, "transcendent" existence. These metaphysical assumptions may describe the point of departure and goal of certain movements of transcendence, but in no way are they a necessary part of every use of the term.

This is not to say that the philosophical or metaphysical uses of the term "transcendence" are wrongheaded. When a philosopher speaks of transcending the limitations of prejudice to attain a universal point of view, or transcending the fallibility of our senses to reach a state of certainty, the notion of surmounting and overstepping is entirely appropriate. We need to recognize, however, that the intelligibility of transcendence in all these cases stems from the fact that the concept refers to a process, not a specific content. This process may be very formally described. In each case — transcending rivers, transcending the law, transcending prejudice, transcending the senses — one state of affairs is replaced by another. We were formerly on the eastern side of the river; now we are on the western side. The criminal was formerly within the law; now his actions are outside the law. Prejudice formerly governed our beliefs and actions; now universal principles shape our identities. We formerly reasoned according to the deliverances of the senses; now we ground our knowledge in the certainty of clear and distinct ideas. Thus, to say that we transcend simply means that by virtue of a significant change our original situation no longer has the same status for us. The nature of our situation — within the law, on the eastern side of the river, conditioned by prejudice — and the means by which we transcend it — moral choices, physical acts, mental discipline — are important questions, but they are not analytic to the concept of transcendence. Recognizing the quite formal meaning of transcendence is important, for this study shall attempt to shed various assumptions about the material content of transcendence in order to show how the concept of transcendence is appropriate to Christianity.

1. The Conceptual Goal of the Inquiry

A GLANCE AT the structure of Christianity indicates the crucial role of transcendence. The basic Christian story is one of differences, and moves across three decisive "rivers" or "mountain ranges." A first divide separates creation and consummation. Even in our integrity as natural creatures, we are not what we are destined to become as children of God. In order for God to realize His eternal purposes for us and the entire created order, we must change. Abraham provides a poignant illustration of this need for change. He receives a promise from God which alters his standing in the created order. No longer is Abraham defined by his creaturehood. What God had done on the sixth day is transcended, and the Lord's promise for the future now shapes Abraham's identity. This transcendence is sealed by the mark of circumcision — a very direct and dramatic alteration of Abraham's creaturely form. In this way a process is begun which leads toward God's consummating purposes.

The change entailed in the transcendence — the "surmounting" or "overstepping" — of the divide which separates creation and consummation is complicated by a second "mountain range" across which the Christian story is told — the divide between sin and righteousness. At present, we are not just creatures awaiting consummation. We exist in a state of active alienation from God. This alienation corrupts our very creaturehood, distorting our identities. However, by God's gracious intervention on our behalf we are restored to right relation with God. The way is made clear for us to find our ultimate purpose in God. The transformation of the persecutor Saul of Tarsus into the Apostle Paul represents a striking instance of this transcendence. No longer does he breathe fire against the followers of Jesus. Instead, he becomes the most zealous of servants. On the road to Damascus, Paul has "overstepped" or transcended the condition of slavery to sin and has begun to move toward righteousness.

The third divide is the most central and dramatic: the difference between God and creature. This difference gives direction to our journey towards consummation. This division gives pathos to the frightening depths of our alienation. In the Christian context, the creature is utterly incapable of bridging this chasm, traversing this mountain range. Instead, the whole drama of the Christian story flows from the fact that this difference and division between creature and Creator is transcended by God. In the election of Israel and in the incarnation of the Son of God, the Lord of all creation transcends the widest of rivers, that which separates the Creator from his creature. This deepest of divides is "overstepped" by God. Only he has the power for such a journey. As such, the central Christian claim is that God's transcendence takes place in the life of that particular first century Palestinian Jew, Jesus of Nazareth. In this transcendence we find the possibility of our own transcendence — the offer of forgiveness of sin and the invitation to the heavenly banquet. Only in God's transcendence does our transcendence of sin and creaturely nature, each in a quite different way, become a real possibility.

The logic of the matter dictates, then, beginning a study of the Christian vision of transcendence with God's transcendence in Jesus Christ. Our redemption and consummation, like Saul's transformation into Paul and Abraham's new identity as father of the chosen people, follows from God's initiative, God's "going over" or transcendence to our side of the divide between God and humanity. However, "beginning" is a thick notion which means far more than making Christ the first word of the first chapter. Given our tendency to reject the particular form of God's transcendence in Christ, this kind of beginning might be prudent, but it is not necessary. For the crucial sense of beginning with Christ has to do with the forces and pressures which shape theological language, not the mechanical order of the words. Indeed, we can speak first and often of Christ, yet never allow the transcendence of God to control the deeper structures of our thought. To avoid such an outcome, we must seek a beginning in Christ which allows our language to be formed by the distinctive shape of God's transcendence in Christ.

Though the first word of this study of the Christian vision of transcendence is about *our* transcendence, I have attempted to begin in this deeper sense with God's transcendence in Christ. The structure of the study will not be like that of a building. I shall not lay the Christological foundations first, then build upwards to our situation. Instead, the Christological control of this study is like that of a field of forces which has a distinctive center. One may enter this field of forces at any point and identify lines of stress and pressure which cross in many complex ways. Then, with sufficient patience, one can find the point from which the forces originate. To that end, the purpose of this study is to investigate the "plate tectonics" of the concept of transcendence, and to bring the reader to see that these "geological pressures" have their beginning and end in the transcendence of God in Christ which is summarized in the Johannine proposition that God is love (*cf.* Chapter Three, Sections 3 and 4).

2. The Polemical Purpose of the Inquiry

BEGINNING WITH our transcendence in order to explore God's transcendence in Christ has two distinct advantages, both usefully polemical. The first involves showing the distinctively theological failure of the modern, crypto-Gnostic philosophical accounts of transcendence. These accounts of transcendence have so distorted our vision that the watchwords of modernity, freedom and truth, have become empty gestures. A theology which flirts with this "transcendence," to say nothing of matrimony, can rarely proceed in obedience to God's transcendence in Christ. The second polemical advantage rests with the present constitution of the theological discipline. Against preoccupations with method (or "hermeneutics" or "epistemology"), this study hopes to strike a material rather than methodological blow for Christocentric governance, and to do so with the very conceptual tools used by those who find such governance either impossible or unnecessary. Both advantages deserve further scrutiny, since they supply the polemical harmonies to the main conceptual melody.

Crypto-gnostic failure

The cultural manure which has fertilized the growth of the importance of the term "transcendence" is intimately bound up with the philosophical "turn to the subject." Modernity's preoccupation with *our* powers and faculties, hopes and aspirations, gives rise to the very loaded connotations which surround all appeals to transcendence. For modernity, transcendence entails breaking the chains of tradition, overcoming the fallability of the senses, and leaving behind the prejudices of society. At every turn, the particular and concrete features of our lives are regarded as limitations to be transcended. In theology, this modern urge for transcendence all too often involves rooting out the particular authority of that first century Palestinian Jew, Jesus of Nazareth. Most of what passes for Christian theology is simply a variation on this theme, where our transcendence is juxtaposed to Jesus' recalcitrant and unfortunate identity as a particular, historical person. This is why my observation that God transcends in the Word made flesh sounds so crazy. Becoming a particular person would seem, thinks the modern, exactly the opposite of true transcendence, which entails becoming a universal mind, an autonomous will, an authentic feeling. Under the sway of this assumption about transcendence, much of current theology is simply a biblically literate form of modernity's alienation from all particularity.

When confronting this legacy, we are faced with a choice. We may either avoid the term "transcendence" and thus set aside its troubling associations, or we can confront its connotative legacy. I have opted for confrontation. My goal throughout is to wrest the notion of transcendence away from the modern context and recover for the concept a properly Christian meaning. My hope is to so gain control over the concept that the reader is able to see transcendence simply as the form of our relation to the God who is the communion of love as Father, Son, and Holy Spirit. If I am successful, then the reader will find it not at all awkward or illogical that while I begin this study with our transcendence, I end with God's mystery.

Wittgenstein's influence on theology confirms this strategy of confrontation. Theologians have read Wittgenstein as providing good reasons for avoiding (if not directly demolishing) the concept of transcendence. If modernity's control of the concept of transcendence and the attendant alienation from particularity is unassailable, then surely theologians must follow Wittgenstein and escape the influence of the concept of transcendence. For theology must find a way to regard the particular form of God's transcendence in Christ as a gift rather than a burden. However, the Wittgensteinian approach to modernity's control over transcendence involves a fundamental reorientation of the theological project. As such, Wittgenstein's significance may eventually match that of Plotinus. Where Plotinus bequeathed to Christianity a vocabulary for expressing the depth of God's love, a depth which might utterly transform who we are, Wittgenstein provides the resources for understanding the breadth of God's love, a breadth which has the power to embrace all that we are. These Wittgensteinian resources represent a perhaps indispensable recovery of a the fullness of grace. Nonetheless, where Plotinus tempts us to leave ourselves behind in our journey to God (I call this radical transcendence), Wittgenstein tempts us to so nurture the cultural and linguistic texture of our identities that we never depart (I call this pure immanence). Both are temptations worth avoiding. Thus, in cultivating the concept of our transcendence for theological use, not only shall I set aside the radical transcendence implicit in much of the modern reference to the subject, but I shall also provide an extended argument against the pure immanence which is latent in the post-modern reaction. In this way, I wish to provide a framework for redeeming, rather than rejecting, modernity's watchwords of truth and freedom.

Preoccupation with method

My second reason for using the anthropological point of departure rests on an assessment of the way in which the theological milieu of the late twentieth century handles modernity. Methodological questions, as in the past, continue to dominate. On the one side, theologians ask: Must not theology begin with human experience in order to be authentic, free from empty conformity? Should not theology settle questions of justified true belief in order to speak about truth, rather than simply reiterate traditional pieties? These questions direct us toward the human condition as the criterion for theological reflection. This approach characterizes the liberal or revisionist agenda. On the other side, opponents to this immersion in the human ask: Should not theology begin with Christ in order to be faithful? Must not theology take revelation as its criterion of truth rather than simply project human norms and values as the standards of the divine? These questions point towards the distinctiveness of the Christian story as the framework for theological reflection. This approach has been associated with Karl Barth.

As I have indicated, this study in the deepest sense begins with Christ, and as such, is fundamentally opposed to any theological program which either proscribes the Barthian approach or makes the Christocentric strategy unintelligible. However, opposition is not the same as diagnosis or cure. The methodological *Auseinandersetzung* which characterizes the way in which so much of modern theology discusses the question of "priority," "criteria," "foundations," and "beginnings" is often little more than sloganeering; and the eager efforts to outflank the enemy on either side has led to perverse mirror images in which the afflictions of modernity take on intensified, if inverted, form. As a result, I have rejected the methodological form of the struggle against our perennial tendency to find ourselves, rather than God, in theology.

In the place of methodological formulations, my strategy is to carry the battle against anthropocentrism into the enemy territory precisely by treating the question of human transcendence. As I shall argue, the logic of our transcendence is strictly "grammatical," and that which shapes the grammar of our transcendence is the communion of love which is Father, Son, and Holy Spirit. In other words, though the words I speak refer to our situation, the grammar is formed by God's offer of love in Christ. Discovering this grammar and the way it must shape interpretations of our own existence makes anthropocentrism impossible. Yet, this discovery is independent of any distinctively Barthian strategies or methods. As a result, not only is this study set against the theological liberalism of our age, but also, my approach cuts against the grain of contemporary presumptions about method.

The theological guide of this study, Karl Rahner, fits delightfully into both reasons for concentrating on our transcendence. First, he is an undercover agent working amidst the modern "turn to the subject." According to my reading, Rahner does not begin with human experience in anything like a foundational sense. Rather, he turns to our condition in order to explore the conceptual shock waves which result from the discovery that in Christ we are blessed by a God who is love. These shock waves shape every aspect of the created order, especially the human dimension. Rahner's treatment of our situation simply seeks to render ex-

plicit the effects of those shock waves. Based on this reading, the Rahner
who emerges on these pages will be a theologian who uses the philosophical
milieu of modernity as an instrument for doxology. Thus, as I use Rahner
to explore the logic of the question of transcendence, the reader will take
an important step towards a reading of Rahner as a non-foundational
theologian who takes Barthian liberties with philosophical conceptualities.

Not only is Rahner a fitting vehicle for my strategy with the philosophers, but he also provides an opportunity to confute the methodological
assumptions of the present age by allowing me to address theological
liberalism on its own terms. In contemporary theology, Rahner is a pivotal
figure. His work gives sophisticated theological expression to the mid-century Catholic move out of the cultural eddies of neo-scholasticism and
Italian church politics, and into a broad engagement with the modern
world. These particular details of Rahner's Catholic milieu are important
for interpreting his work, but they do not limit the scope of his influence,
for the tenor of his work is characteristic of any theological struggle to
make the Christian vision reach outwards to do justice to the distinctive
shape of the human condition. In this sense, Rahner's theology is motivated
by concerns similar to those which govern the liberal or revisionist agenda.

Two Rahnerian conceptual innovations — the supernatural existential
and the anonymous Christian — are typical of both the spirit of Rahner's
work and the nature of his influence. The supernatural existential, a
concept about which I shall say a great deal more in later chapters, serves
as the anthropological intersection of God's purposes and our situation.
As Rahner tries to express in this concept, and throughout his work, to
be Christian is intimately bound up with what it means to be human.
This study of transcendence is in large part an investigation of the structure
of this being "intimately bound up." The notion of anonymous Christianity simply adds nuance to the concept of the supernatural existential.
In this notion, Rahner speculates about the relationship between God's
purposes, our situation, and the particular form of life called Christianity,
in order to speak coherently about those who live outside the proclamation
of Christ. In both instances, Rahner gives a determinedly ambitious reading to the broad embrace of the Christian vision. Far more can be included
into the Christian frame of reference than the older, pinched neo-scholastic
approach would allow. The fullness of human experience, even outside the
influence of Christianity, can be absorbed, thinks Rahner, into the conceptual structure of Christian theology. As a result, the spirit of Rahner's

theology is that of a triumphant exploration of new territory. Christ's banner is planted on any number of anthropological promontories.

Many explorers have been naive; claiming a new discovery for Christ on the beach or from the mountaintop is not a substitute for a real transformation of the ordinary lives of the inhabitants. If we are to judge Rahner by his influence in contemporary theology, then surely we must say he was naive. For where Rahner writes in the spirit of ever widening circles of conquest on behalf of the Christian vision — even the experiences of non-Christians come under the eventual Lordship of Christ — Rahnerians consistently signal retreat. All too often, concepts such as the supernatural existential do not serve as the means for injecting the particular shape of the Christian vision into the fullness of human life, but rather, these Rahnerian innovations become the rationale for redefining and recasting Christianity so that it will better conform to the modern banalities of subjectivity, autonomy and authenticity. Where Rahner evidences a perhaps foolhardy boldness on behalf of the tradition, Rahnerians and liberal theological programs which scavange from Rahner's work nearly always apologize for the constraints and demands of the tradition. Through the notion of our transcendence, the modern alienation from particularity returns to dominate what, for Rahner, has been claimed for God's transcendence in Christ. As such, though the words are often nearly identical, the spirit of the projects are quite different.

My immediate purpose is not to wrest Rahner away from the Rahnerians. This would entail a full scale interpretation of Rahner's theological project. Instead, I shall pursue a more focused strategy. My goal is to use Rahner to probe the question of transcendence and to show that this question cannot be handled adequately unless the particular form of Christian revelation controls the analysis. This shall reveal the distinctively theological shape of modernity's failure to grasp transcendence. Further, such a conclusion shall demonstrate the wrongheadedness of the liberal theological agenda on material rather than methodological grounds. I certainly regard such results as properly "Rahnerian," but this is really secondary. What is important is that the reader see that a boldness on behalf of the revelation in Christ that God is love is the only way we can make sense out of the field of forces which constitutes our transcendence.

3. The Thesis of the Inquiry

LET US TURN, THEN, to the question of our transcendence. When Abraham is chosen, what happens to his creaturehood? When Paul is made a servant of Christ on the road to Damascus, what happens to the man Saul of Tarsus? Clearly, Abraham is no longer Abram. Paul is no longer Saul. Yet, what is the nature of this "no longer"? Has Abraham left behind Abram? Is the new man Paul nothing like the old man Saul? I shall not answer these questions exegetically. Instead, this inquiry abstracts from the specific biblical instances of transcendence and asks this question about the logic of transcendence in the following way: What is the role of the ordinary stuff of life in a Christian vision of transcendence? What is the fate of the worldly context which defined Abraham before he was chosen, the way of life which defined the Pharisee Saul before he became the apostle Paul, the situation which defines us as we are called to become servants of Christ?

Perhaps we should view the worldly context as *the* impediment to be overcome and left behind in the drama of Christian transcendence. A great deal of the mystical and ascetical tradition seems to give that impression. Paul himself suggests as much when he appears to completely separate the old life according to the flesh from the new life according to the Spirit (cf. Romans 7:13–8:17). Are we to say, then, that Christian transcendence is radical and absolute, where walking in the ways of the Spirit involves leaving behind earthly life altogether? Such a view is troubling, for it sees no role for ordinary life in the difference which God makes for us in Christ. Our destiny in God is extrinsic, and in that sense unrelated and dangerously irrelevant to the kinds of practices and relations which constitute life for us now. This view of transcendence makes it difficult to see how our destiny in God *matters*.

Paul's themes are rarely univocal. Not only does he seem to repudiate earthly life, but he also appears to affirm it as the beginning, middle and end of God's eternal purpose. Writing to the Colossians, Paul pictures Christ as the first-born of all creation (Colossians 1:15-19). God's redemptive and consummating initiative includes and affirms the created order. Far from denying the givenness of ordinary life, not a few Christian humanists have read such a passage as commending the worldly context as the proper focus, even the primary task, of the Christian pilgrimage. We are to intensify our involvement in the world as we participate in God's fulfillment of all creation. Embracing our createdness serves, then, as the *telos* of our relation to God. A view of pure immanence emerges. The condition in which we find ourselves is the condition for which we are destined. Here we find consequences which are as troubling as the discontinuous or radical view. This account treats our destiny in God as already intrinsic to the activities which constitute life for us now. Yet, if that is the case, how can we regard our destiny as a real *difference* which God makes for us?

My argument in this study will be that neither a repudiation nor an embrace of the givenness of life expresses the proper form of Christian transcendence. The worldly context is neither the impediment to be overcome, nor the ultimate purpose of God's initiative for us. Instead, the view I shall defend includes both discontinuity — there really is something new in our new life in Christ — and continuity — this newness includes the givenness of ordinary life. This "mixed" view is Paul's underlying vision. Immediately after dichotomizing life into two spheres, the flesh and the Spirit, Paul turns to make observations about the fate of the created order. He writes to the Romans that in Christ "creation itself will be set free from its bondage to decay and obtain the glorious liberty of the Children of God" (Romans 8:21). The very "stuff" of life, paradigmatically (but by no means not exclusively) our bodies, which Paul regards as redeemed in Christ, will be taken up into the difference which God chooses to make for us. The upshot is an account of transcendence which implies neither a repudiation nor an embrace of the "stuff" of life. Instead, the givennness of the worldly context is transformed. Here we find a difference which is both real and relevant. Christian transcendence is real because it implies change, perhaps radical change, and in that respect the Christian view opposes the singular emphasis on the continuity characteristic of pure immanence. This mixed transcendence is also relevant because that change penetrates rather than ignores or denies the world as would the univocal emphasis on discontinuity which characterizes radical transcendence. Thus, the Christian view of transcendence is of the ordinary transformed.

Three features of this view of transcendence guide this inquiry. First, the Christian commitment to the ordinary transformed is perennial. In spite of the metaphysical and skeptical assumptions which vie for control of philosophical accounts of transcendence, the Christian, or mixed view, consistently reemerges. Showing the perennial appeal of the mixed view gives this study its distinctive apologetic coloring. Second, though Christian transcendence exerts a remarkable charm over philosophical discourse, this mixed view is incoherent outside of the particular Christian revelation that God is love. As I indicated above, God's transcendence is prior to our transcendence. Seeing this priority is crucial if we are to grasp the "grammatical solution" and escape the extremes of radical transcendence and pure immanence. This second feature produces loud Barthian echoes throughout the study. Third, the relatively abstract and formal notion of transcendence serves as a conceptual figure for the quite particular and substantive life of Christian pilgrimage. Once subsumed into the grammar of divine love, the concept of transcendence can serve as a useful pivot point upon which to reorder the partial gestures of modern and post-modern philosophy so that they may be redeployed to give depth and texture to our accounts of the distinctively Christian form of life. This third feature proposes a new reading of Rahner and through his work suggests a broad tropological strategy for handling troublesome cultural notions such as transcendence.

4. An Overview of the Inquiry

IN THE FIRST CHAPTER I take Hume, a thinker noted for his opposition to Christian dogma, and show how his faithfulness to the ebb and flow of religious argument leads him in the direction of the Christian or mixed view of transcendence. My conceit is that I give the most compelling possible reading of Hume's *Dialogues Concerning Natural Religion,* which is also the most Christian. In this way, I implicitly indicate for the reader what will become clearer as the study develops — that the Christian view of transcendence is perennial. However, Hume does more than illustrate the durable appeal of mixed transcendence. Throughout the *Dialogues,* I trace the ways in which the combination of both discontinuity and continuity in our mixed aspiration for transcendence generates conceptual difficulties. I characterize discontinuity as the "extraordinary" element of our destiny, that part which does not "fit" and may even conflict with our current form of life. The continuity rests in the fate of the "ordinary" element. I provide a reading of Hume's *Dialogues* which shows the conceptual perplexity of saying, as I read Paul and the Christian tradition as a whole to be saying, that Christian transcendence requires a mixture of both the extraordinary and ordinary. This Christian mixed view tends toward either an extreme discontinuity (radical transcendence) in which the extraordinary is exalted and the ordinary denigrated, or a complete continuity (pure immanence) in which the extraordinary is absorbed into the ordinary. The goal of this first chapter, then, is that the reader see the Christian vision of transcendence as perennial, but deeply puzzling.

Chapter Two gives an account of the Roman Catholic response to the challenges of modernity. My survey of nineteenth century Roman Catholicism attempts to plant the seeds of doubt in the cocksure assumption that ecclesiastically strong and doctrinally serious Christianity is "archaic" and "regressive." Where my reading of Hume's *Dialogues* gives the reader a sense of the strange persistence of the mixed view of transcendence — a persistence through seemingly devastating conceptual objections from the sides of radical transcendence and pure immanence — in this second chapter, the reader should gain a respect for the historical resilience and appeal of the peculiar Christian mixture of both the extraordinary and ordinary throughout an epoch when the two extremes of radical transcendence and pure immanence were such obvious temptations. The Christian view of transcendence is not just an alluring and perplexing concept; it is a durable and appealing form of life.

In telling this story of the career of the mixed, or as I often call it, "amphibious" view, I gather background for a sustained demonstration of the second feature of the Christian view of transcendence: that its intelligibility depends upon Christian revelation. In Chapter Three I turn to Karl Rahner, and develop his arguments to show the logical impossibility of accounting for the Christian vision of transcendence as anything other than a "grammatical" concept arising out of the distinctively Christian proposition that God is love. Not only does this argument show that the combination of extraordinary and ordinary, discontinuity and continuity, is woven into the Christian way of thinking, it also shows that the philosophical pressures of pure immanence and radical transcendence can only be tamed by purely theological formulation. If one understands what is meant by "grammatical" necessity, two conclusions follow. First, the mixed view of transcendence no longer appears as conceptually confused. Second, the truth of our condition is theological; the concept of transcendence falls under the Lordship of Christ.

Chapters Four, Five and Six both reinforce the conclusions drawn in Chapter Three and turn to a patient illustration of the need for a proper account of transcendence in our characterization of the Christian life. Chapter Four raises what I regard as the most important objection to

Rahner's (and my) approach to the problem of Christian transcendence. Here, Fergus Kerr deploys characteristic Wittgensteinian insights to show that the confusion of the mixed view of transcendence is not merely conceptual. A disposition towards radical transcendence cuts all the way down into our basic attitudes towards our bodies and the shared world of language. Regardless of the "grammatical" solution, the legacy of radical transcendence so powerfully overdetermines the Western philosophical and theological tradition that any suggestion of the extraordinary inevitably decays into a neglect (if not outright repudiation) of the ordinary. Kerr regards this neglect as dehumanizing, and more importantly, tries to show that any and all views of transcendence, even the "mixed" view, *must* fail to do justice to the distinctively Christian form of life. For Kerr, the proper solution to the "problem" of transcendence is not the purely "grammatical" mixed view, but rather a very real and tangible immersion in the givenness of life. After rendering the full force of this objection to my strategy of recovering a properly theological sense of transcendence, I demur from Kerr's conclusions and suggest the dangers of simply rejecting the concept of transcendence.

Chapter Five seeks to refute Kerr's assumption that the legacy of radical transcendence *inevitably* overdetermines theological reflection. Rahner's metaphysics of knowledge serves as a counterexample. I try to show that Rahner's philosophical writings are (at least in significant part) governed by the mixed view of transcendence. In this way, I am able to argue two points, one explicit and the other implicit, and to suggest a third. First, the "grammatical" solution has a real effectiveness in our efforts to puzzle out the actual forms of our relation to the worldly context. Far from a debilitating confusion which plays into the hands of a metaphysical prejudice, the mixed view seems to have a heuristic usefulness. The second and implicit claim is that philosophical notions can be controlled theologically. The source of theological discourse is sufficiently powerful to control even the most troublesome philosophical concepts. As a result, theology is free to use whatever resources it chooses to articulate the structure and logic of the life of pilgrimage towards God. Finally, Chapter Five suggests to the reader that modernity's passion for truth, a passion which too often leads to a disdain for the ordinary, can be redeemed under proper theological governance.

Chapter Six reinforces the conclusions drawn in Chapter Three by developing the "necessity" of the mixed view of transcendence in a more informal way. Kerr's affirmation of the givenness of life, especially as he develops this givenness in terms of language and tradition, is accepted. I apply this Wittgensteinian insight to the givenness of the Christian tradition. The upshot is not, however, as Kerr suggests, an embrace of the "stuff" which constitutes Christianity. Instead, an immersion in the ordinary forms of Christian language and practice seem, of their own logic, to engender the need for transcendence. Rahner expresses this logic in his account of theological method. As both an indirect method and a *reductio in mysterium,* our intellectual participation in the ordinary "givenness" of Christianity reaches for the extraordinary as an *ad hoc* "idea" of the object of faith (indirect method) and as a pilgrimage into the hiddenness of the Subject of faith *(reductio in mysterium).* The Christian form of life, then, seems to require something like the mixed form of transcendence, and this amphibious vision makes intelligible the striking freedom of that particularity which is our destiny in Christ.

CHAPTER ONE

⁊⁊   ⁊⁊

The Ordinary and Extraordinary

Yet let him keep the rest
But keep them with repining restlessnesse:
Let him be rich and wearie, that at least,
If goodnesse leade him not, yet wearinesse
May tosse him to my breast.[1]

RADICAL TRANSCENDENCE involves an exaltation to the extraordinary. Pure immanence entails an immersion in the ordinary. These two visions give direction to our fate. They represent opposing assessments of human destiny, which, though rarely found in their purity, seem to serve as the basic choice upon which the many philosophies of life are founded.

The commitment to immanence is found when we face life and conclude that our destiny is not bound up with anything recognizably different. The ancient skeptical dictum, "Live by appearances!" is an economical expression of this commitment to immanence. By no means does skepticism exhaust the embrace of the immanent. In fact, logical positivism's program of certainty is directly opposed to many of the epistemological doctrines of skepticism. Yet, logical positivism's repudiation of human aspiration in ethics, metaphysics, and religion betrays a similar commitment to immanence. The logical positivist is clear-minded. Certainty is possible only if we repudiate the extraordinary. What is decisive, then, is not a shared set of specific philosophical doctrines; instead, central to the

---

1. George Herbert, "The Pulley."

immanent vision is a distinctly modest aspiration, a putatively realistic and accessible view of human flourishing which sets aside desires for the extraordinary. Against the anxiety and frustration of seemingly unquenchable aspiration, the immanent vision formulates a plan: life is to be made sane by keeping ordinary things ordinary.

In contrast, the approach of radical transcendence comes to the fore when we declare that a complete transformation is necessary in order to achieve human excellence. We must set aside the dross of the ordinary in order to reach the true promise of the extraordinary. For the radical utopian, this repudiation of the ordinary serves a fundamentally new future. Life as it is now lived bears no positive or continuous relationship with the new, extraordinary form of life which will, finally, satisfy true human needs and purposes. For the mystic, the ordinary is forsaken in the moment of apophasis. The extraordinary truth is only known by virtue of a negation of all that we normally and ordinarily see and understand. For both the radical utopian and the mystic, a plan of life which is the opposite of that promoted by the commitment to immanence emerges: life is to be made significant by overcoming the ordinary.

The difference between these two assessments of our destiny is clear. The direction of immanence is this-worldly, that of radical transcendence is other-worldly. Yet, what is crucial is their similarity. In their pure forms both are characterized by all or nothing affirmations, and this, in turn, yields the security and serenity of closure. Both function as real *solutions* to the problem of the ultimate direction of human life. In their opposing ways, the ambiguities of the inexplicable extraordinary and the recalcitrant ordinary are resolved. The immanent vision concedes no transcendence, and in this way eliminates the anxiety born of aspiration.[2] Happiness is found in a life made ordinary through and through. The alternative demands complete transcendence, leaving behind the turmoil of the imperfect present.[3] For the pro-

---

2. Sextus Empiricus gives concise expression to the immanent vision: "[The skeptic] does not exert himself to avoid anything or to seek after anything, and hence he is in a tranquil state" (*Outlines of Pyrrhonism,* trans. Sanford G. Etheridge [Indianapolis: Hackett Publishing Co., 1985], Book I, chapter XII). For Sextus, skeptical happiness is to be found in the absence of the anxiety born of inappropriate and unrealistic epistemic ambition.

3. Boethius provides an account of the tranquility gained by radical transcendence. Speaking in the voice of Philosophy, he explains the proper response to the pressures, demands and difficulties which worldlings place upon those who participate in the

ponent of radical transcendence, happiness is found in a life made fully and completely extraordinary. So both options are linked in their willingness to choose sides in the dichotomy between the ordinary and extraordinary: neither admits the possibility of partial movements, both abhor the thought that the ordinary and extraordinary might mix in some way.

What is interesting about this companionship in conceptual purity is a shared static and attenuated view of the self.[4] As an illustration, consider

---

eternal: "When their forces attack us in superior numbers, our general conducts a tactical withdrawl of his forces to a strong point, and they are left to encumber themselves with useless plunder. Safe from their furious activity on our ramparts above, we can smile at their efforts to collect all the most useless booty: our citadel cannot fall to the assaults of folly" (*The Consolation of Philosophy,* trans. V. E. Watts [New York: Penguin Books, 1969], p. 40). Here, Boethius speaks only of a tactical withdrawal. However, without compelling reason for return to the dangerous realm below (and his comment about the useless booty to be found among the worldly leaves little doubt that Boethius will be hard pressed to find such reasons), permanent residence in the impregnable citadel would seem an obvious choice. The tactical withdrawl becomes, then, a long-term strategic commitment.

4. This shared commitment yields other interesting alliances between these two seemingly antithetical views. For example, Stanley Cavell explores the connection between a kind of passionless acquiescence to things as they are and an interest in metaphysics. As he reads Wittgenstein, "metaphysics would be seen as one more of the false or fantastic excitements that boredom craves" (*In Quest of the Ordinary* [Chicago: University of Chicago Press, 1988], p. 7). Keeping in mind the ways in which the modern conditions for skeptical life differ from the classical context, this observation can be understood in light of the advice which Sextus gives the prospective skeptic. Aware that human life requires practical activity, even if reason is impotent in its quest to justify such activities, Sextus allows that the skeptic should develop a skill in a practical art, thus giving him something with which to occupy himself in his state of skeptical tranquility. It may well be that metaphysics is a "practical" art which enjoys a limitless potential for entertaining (but, of course, for the skeptic, inconsequential and undisturbing) distraction, making it the perfect vocation for the well trained skeptic. A commitment to the ordinary might cultivate, then, a fascination with the extraordinary.

The contrast and peculiar alliance between skepticism and metaphysics does not exhaust the larger contrasts and links between commitments to immanence and radical transcendence. In fact, in the person of Auguste Comte, we find a perspicuous vacillation on this very question. Comte's positivism certainly involves a steady repudiation of the many traditional forms of the extraordinary in morality, philosophy, and religion. However, Comte is very ambitious on behalf of the ordinary. In fact, he sees the embrace of his positivism as a first step towards the radical transformation of human life on purely scientific grounds. Thus an embrace of the ordinary — things as they really are in their "positive" or scientific aspect — serves the purpose of radical transcendence.

in more detail the ancient skeptical view.[5] For the skeptic, the self is simply one aspect of a vast world, no part of which may be identified or privileged as a locus of truth or meaning. We are part of a seamless web of events, firmly bound to the homogeneity of all that is. In this world of the purely ordinary, the individual is but a convention which serves as the vessel for mental and intentional events. As individual members of the human race, we have a certain uniqueness, but this sense of individuality is minimal. Things happen to me, I do and think things, they add up to the "me" that I am; but this "me" is no more significant than any other aggregate of characteristics and events which might be found in the cosmos.[6] To use the language of classical skepticism, my mental and physical existence is nothing other than one appearance, or better, a series of appearances among the many that constitute the world. I have nothing at my disposal to resist my immersion in the ordinary. In light of the equipose of many possible visions of life, the skeptic takes note that my life, as it simply appears and in whatever form it happens to take, is at least no worse (no less authentic, no less happy, no less pure, no less pious) than any other hypothetical possibility. Thus, the only reasonable approach to life is obvious: accept individual existence for what it is, purely immanent.[7]

5. In any interpretation of the skeptical tradition, Terence Penelhum warns against importing post-Cartesian assumptions into the ancient skeptical treatment of appearances. Although the classical tradition included epistemological conundrums created by the differences between thought, sense and object, the injunction to live by appearances has a much broader meaning. It means, simply, "Take things as they are." For Sextus Empiricus, there is no attempt to organize experience along distinctions such as good or bad, ultimate or proximate, true or false, for none of these distinctions survives the skeptical tropes. Instead, all arguments and assessments are equally weighted. No proposition strikes the skeptic as special, extraordinary or transcendent, worthy somehow of affirmation, assent or action. As a consequence, the skeptic embraces everything as ordinary. Experience flows over the self with a tranquillizing ordinariness, rather than, as for Descartes, an occasion for anxiety. For Penelhum's helpful discussion, see God and Skepticism (Dordrecht: D. Reidel, 1983), pp. 3-13.

6. In this respect, Rousseau begins his Confessions with a far more minimal sense of individuality than he ends. In the very first sentence, he writes, "I am not like any of those I have ever seen; I venture to believe that I am not made like any of those who are in existence. If I am not better, at least I am different." This degree of individuality can be found in the purely ordinary. Of course, Rousseau is far from unwilling to affirm a stronger sense of self, and as his account of the development of his consciousness progresses, his individuality becomes much more multifaceted.

7. Again, skeptical doctrines are but one way to arrive at a commitment to immanence. Freud illustrates a quite confident approach to the possibilities of scientific knowledge

The commitment to radical transcendence leads to a similarly thin account of our existence. From the outset, a happy immersion in the ordinary is denied. As a result, a decisive struggle is enjoined, a struggle to achieve release from the ordinary. This feverish activity would suggest a rather fulsome view of the self. For the other-worldly view, there is nearly always a struggle for transcendence. However, the quest is the means and not the end of radical transcendence. In this approach, the self may have a current solidity which the immanent view denies, but this rich view of the self need not be permanent. In fact, in its purest form, the ideal of radical transcendence makes my individuality an impediment to be over-come. Consider Rousseau's hopes for humanity. Free and equal, it would seem that Rousseau is a patron of the indispensable and inviolable dignity of the self. However, as he turns to the problem of achieving true freedom and equality, he identifies the defining feature of our individuality, our *amor propre*, as the impediment to be overcome. And how is this to be overcome? For Rousseau, the failures of civilization are transcended by the unequivocal identification of the will of the many with the general will of all. As in Rousseau's political philosophy, so also in the neo-platonic mysticism of the ancient world, to lose our individuality — our own distinctive quest for knowledge, our singular powers of discernment and capacity for action — is part of our happy destiny in the peaceful security of radical transcendence.

Ordinary and extraordinary — appealing is a view which allows the self to rest in either one or the other. However, in this respect, as in so many others, the Christian frame of reference fails to please. Christianity refuses the simple dichotomies of ordinary life or extraordinary otherworldliness, and instead cultivates some strange hybrids. To put the matter in its most elementary form, Christianity repudiates both pure immanence and radical transcendence. Against immanence it contends that *something* is in store for us, *something* which will raise us to a new relation, a decisively better and truer relation, to existence, is within our reach, however inconclusive our experience might remain. For Christianity, life is not submerged in a endless flux of events. Certain events are clearly privileged, certain expe-

---

about the human psyche. Indeed, it is the full force of that knowledge which leads him to conclude that among "normal" adults, unhappiness results from unrealistic aspirations. Transcendent goals cause anxiety. To deal with this anxiety, Freud develops a therapeutic model of culture. The goal is to accommodate oneself to the way things are.

riences affirmed. One man's history is identified as indispensable, and we are called as human creatures to recognize and affirm these events. Creedal claims are offered as true and decisive, and we are urged to shape our identities in light of these claims. But this raising to a new relation, this call to recognition, affirmation, and action, cannot entail a complete departure. Against the vision of radical transcendence, Christianity claims that the extraordinary does not annihilate the ordinary. The real difference between the extraordinary and ordinary does not involve the discontinuity of radical transcendence. There is no escape to a remote, extra-human citadel. The life transformed in Christianity is still the same life. Many things change, but we still have the same human address. In the most preliminary of terms, then, this is the Christian view of transcendence: something extraordinary awaits us in the midst of the ordinary.

This combination of ordinary and extraordinary is one of the conceptual oddities of Christianity. It contains the kernel of any number of metaphysical antinomies which characterize Christian theological discourse, e.g., time and eternity, the finite and the infinite, God and man. Moreover, although the connection is more ambiguous, the combination of the ordinary and extraordinary sets the stage for what might be called the moral antinomies of power and weakness, lordship and obedience, life and death, hiddenness and revelation, defeat and triumph. Our interests here, however, are not to explore these peculiar juxtapositions on their own terms, but rather to see how a certain view of transcendence is entailed by this impure vision, this "hypostatic union," if you will, of the extraordinary and the ordinary.[8]

8. Pascal identifies Christianity's strange view of the self in moral terms which presuppose and intensify the dualities indicated at this point. Echoing the two extremes of immersion in the ordinary and radical transcendence toward the extraordinary, which seem the two logical alternatives, he writes, "Christianity is strange; It bids man to recognize that he is vile and even abominable, and bids him to want to be like God" (*Pensées,* Lafuma numeration, #351). Not merely the metaphysical strangeness of the creature made Godlike characterizes Christianity. Pascal continues with the exclamation, "What sort of freak is man! How novel, how monstrous, how choatic, how paradoxical, how prodigious! Judge of all things, feeble earthworm, repository of truth, sink of doubt and error, glory and refuse of the universe!" (#131). In every sense humans are fully invested in the ordinary and extraordinary. And Pascal thinks fittingly so, since "without such a counterweight [man's] exaltation would make him horribly vain or his abasement horribly abject" (#351). This remark suggests an important apologetical strategy. For Pascal, the Christian view of the self is conceptually strange, a contradiction perhaps, but it is nonetheless more humane than the alternatives.

If Christianity does indeed reject the choice between other-worldly transcendence and this-worldly immanence, then the life envisioned is mongrel, one of partial half-steps, neither accepting a strictly immanent existence nor pressing forward towards some supra-human state. Faced with both the irreducible extraordinary and the inescapable ordinary, the Christian view affirms a destiny for us which is both immanent in the world and transcendent. We are, then, beasts both in the water and out, creatures which are dynamic. Try to drag us fully down into the immanent world of appearances and out we climb. Pull us out of the world and we protest for return. Betwixt and between, we enjoy an amphibious form of existence which resists strict categorization within this world or the next, refuses labels such as material and immaterial, sets aside the conceptual clarity which follows from clear distinctions between temporal and eternal, finite and infinite.[9] In contrast to the transcended and immanent selves, the amphibious self is not static, resting in either the ordinary or extraordinary. Instead, this categorical free-spirit, thematic wanderer and metaphysical vagrant is dynamic, a creature of movement, a pilgrim. Taking seriously the mixture of the ordinary and extraordinary and the dynamism which it entails must be the point of departure if we

9. I take the term "amphibious existence" from C. S. Lewis's observation in *The Screwtape Letters* (New York: Collier, 1982), p. 36. Lewis quite likely derives this term from Sir Thomas Browne, who writes, "We are onely that amphibious piece betweene a corporall and spirituall essence, that middle forme that links those two together, and makes good the method of God and nature" (*Religio Medici* i.34).

Basil Willey suggests that the "metaphysicals," among whom he ranges Browne, are amphibians in the sense that they stood between the nascent world of Baconian experimentalism and pre-modern supernaturalistic belief. As Willey observes, "Many different worlds or countries of the mind then lay close together — the world of scholastic learning, the world of scientific learning, the worlds of classical mythology and of Biblical history, of fable and fact, of theology and demonology, of sacred and profane love, of pagan and Christian morals, of activity and contemplation; and a cultivated man had freedom of them all" (*Seventeenth Century Background* [New York: Columbia University Press, 1967], p. 42). In each instance, the metaphysicals achieved a synthesis which, though unsystematic, wove disparate features of human life, the western cultural legacy, and Christianity into an imaginative whole. Willey suggests that this synthesis was possible because the "metaphysical mind" was not fully or finally committed to any one world. I shall argue (and Lewis would as well, I think) that Willey is right about the imaginative results of the "metaphysical mind," but he is wrong about its internal constitution. The amphibian vision results from a full commitment to the Christian world, a world of both Baconian bodies and scholastic souls.

are to say anything about transcendence from the Christian frame of reference.[10]

1. Natural Religion and Amphibious Debate

PRIOR TO DRESSING UP amphibious existence and the dynamic self in theological clothing, no small amount of attention needs to be paid to the oddity or strangeness of this view of transcendence committed to both the ordinary and extraordinary. For the goal is not only to understand the texture of Christianity's investment in such a combination, but also to have a sense of the pressures which assail this view and persistently threaten to collapse the duality of existence and to tame the wanderlust of the pilgrim life. To this end, Hume's *Dialogues Concerning Natural Religion* represents an excellent opportunity to explore the instability of amphibious assumptions about the union of the ordinary and extraordinary. Although Hume does not set out to discuss the matter in these "speculative" terms, he is guided in this direction by the very nature of the topic around which he builds the debate. For the term "natural religion" is an oxymoron which participates in the same confusion of categories which characterizes the Christian view of transcendence.[11]

---

10. Although my interest as a theologian is specifically Christian, the idea of amphibious existence and the dynamic self is by no means limited to the followers of Jesus. Indeed, Platonic philosophy yields a detailed picture of a self both ordinary and extraordinary. And this picture has been extremely influential in the western world, especially as mediated through the Christian tradition. As Arthur O. Lovejoy explains, "The most notable — and the less noted — fact about [Plato's] historic influences is that he did *not* merely give to European other-worldliness its characteristic form and phraseology and dialectic, but that he also gave characteristic form and phraseology and dialectic to precisely the contrary tendency — to a particularly exuberant kind of this-worldliness" (*The Great Chain of Being* [Cambridge: Harvard University Press, 1936], p. 45). These contrary emphases are evident in the figure of Socrates, as he is portrayed sympathetically (cf. Symposium) and unsympathetically (cf. Aristophanes' *The Clouds*). In both instances, Socrates, neither a man of this world nor the next, floats in between. Thus, in this as in so many other ways, to speak from the Christian frame of reference is not to speak merely in a Christian way.

11. We need to be sure to read this relationship carefully. The fact that natural religion shares an amphibious view with Christianity should not lead to the spurious inference that natural religion is the same as, or is the essential content of, Christianity, even on the limited question of the nature and role of transcendence. All that is here implied is that natural religion exhibits tensions also found in the Christian view of transcendence. Mere fortuitous resemblance is all that is assumed at this juncture.

Natural religion, or more specifically, natural theology, the intellectual underpinnings of a piety which exists without supernatural revelation, is a tradition of thought which encompasses conflicting impulses. On the one hand, natural religion claims to be grounded in the immanent world of human affairs. A promise is made to promote beliefs and practices which extend no further than ordinary human powers allow. In the broadest sense, then, there is a commitment to the ordinary. For the "natural" aspect of natural religion is its acceptance of the human locale as the base of operations for the religious life. In the case of the intellectual strand of the tradition, which interests Hume, the general stance within the human is specifically rational. The commitment to the ordinary is worked out in terms of a full investment in the principles of reason. This is, moreover, intensified in Hume's approach. His greatest contribution to philosophy is his insight into the ways in which "principles" of reason are but generalizations about the persistent regularities of ordinary epistemic practices. In this respect, then, a Humean treatment of natural religion will accentuate its already deep immersion in the ordinary or natural, an immersion so deep, that, to his mind, there can be no escape. However, what Hume considers is more expansive than what he concludes, and the former is of greatest interest in this case.

What concerns Hume in the *Dialogues* is that natural religion assumes that ordinary rational powers yield a degree of transcendence. The expectation is that the "natural" point of departure will yield conclusions of decisive religious or "supernatural" significance.[12] The upshot of natural theology is a type of knowledge unlike that found in other sciences. The conclusions arrived at are special. The beliefs commended have a significance beyond that normally associated with epistemic activities. In other words, natural religion sees itself as reaching towards the extraordinary. Specifically, the extraordinary goal is knowledge about the ultimate origin and purpose of the natural world and the human place in it. Something,

---

12. Regarding the term "supernatural," the reader must be disabused of any parapsychological or spiritualistic connotations. For my purposes, it is important that the reader take a more strictly literal view of the term. Just as "extraordinary" is paired as the opposite of "ordinary," the word "supernatural" simply denotes that which is other than the "natural." At this juncture, questions of content may be set aside. The simple opposition is sufficient. For an economical etiology of the theological use of the term, see Henri de Lubac, *A Brief Catechesis on Nature and Grace* (San Francisco: Ignatius Press, 1984), pp. 9-54.

then, may be said *sub specie aeternitatis,* even while our feet remain firmly rooted in the comings and goings of this world. In this way, natural religion presupposes that we may traverse the ground from the ordinary world of natural phenomena and natural human capacities to the extraordinary world of ultimate and universal truths.

Hume is alive to the dual commitments of natural religion — on the one hand a full investment in the ordinary, and on the other a promise of the extraordinary — and he flags them for the reader in the student Pamphilus's introductory remarks to the *Dialogues.* There, Pamphilus observes that the dialogue form is by no means universally recommended as the vehicle for presenting arguments. Some topics, especially those which require systematic development, are best handled in a didactic manner. However, two kinds of issues are especially well suited to the give and take of dialogue. First, notes Pamphilus, "Any point of doctrine, which is so *obvious,* that it scarcely admits of dispute, but at the same time so *important,* that it cannot be too often inculcated, seems to require [dialogue]. . . ." That is to say, some issues are so ordinary as to be pre-theoretical, if you will, and in this respect a systematic development would strike the reader as mere tedious exposition of what is already taken for granted. Yet, at the same time, that which is taken for granted is quite often of absolute importance, and conversation is able, by originality of expression and creativity in spontaneous exchange, to bring to the fore the importance which is so often unexpressed and overlooked.[13] This twin quality of obviousness and importance is then paired by Pamphilus with another twofold aspect of matters suited to dialogue. As he continues, "Any question of philosophy . . . which is so *obscure* and *uncertain* that human reason can reach no fixed determination with regard to it . . . seems to lead us naturally into the style of dialogue and conversation."[14] Here the unsystematic approach of dialogue makes clear sense, since the obscure and

13. More Humean than Hume in so many respects, Wittgenstein in *On Certainty* builds a case for the claim that what is taken for granted, what is simply assumed to be the case, is always the most important part of the structure of our understanding, since it constitutes certainty. Wittgenstein differs from Hume (at least in this instance when Hume speaks through the character of Pamphilus) insofar as he rejects the idea that the obvious ought to be discussed or even admits of conversation. More often than not, Wittgenstein suggests that bringing matters into the realm of argument undermines rather than reinforces.

14. Both quotes from *Dialogues,* ed. Richard H. Popkin (Indianapolis: Hackett Publishing Co., 1980), p. 1.

uncertain will not admit of didactic treatment, and nothing is lost in the less than perfect logical development of ideas which usually characterizes conversation.

The message of Pamphilus's digression into the purposes of dialogue is that natural religion is a topic which combines matters quite obvious and certain with those which are obscure and uncertain. Like the question of justice, the question of God enjoys an interesting combination of immediacy and distance. On the one hand, nearly everyone assumes that there is a standard of justice. We cannot do as we please. We take it as obvious that some actions are right, while others are wrong. And this conviction is so important that at the slightest provocation we are likely to express our commitment to justice, to exhort others to heed the call of justice, to bemoan the present lack of justice. And yet, when the general panegyric is over and we ask ourselves the question "what *is* justice?" the second half of Pamphilus's characterization is quite relevant. For the question is eminently contestable since the font of justice is so obscure and the upshot of competing principles so uncertain. For Hume, our disposition towards the divine is parallel to that of justice. We assume that God exists, or more generally, that religious questions are sensible, meaningful, and centrally important; but we have little certainty about the nature of the divine. In this respect, then, though we take our religious interest for granted, the satisfaction of that interest is not at all evident. Hence, religion is the most ordinary of things, assumed and accepted as are so many aspects of everyday life. Yet, the content and consequence of religion are unsettled. Our religious interest presses for some kind of additional dimension which is far from the everyday or ordinary, and this casts the whole issue into a very uncertain light.

These remarks by Pamphilus underline the peculiarity of natural religion. Religious questions are not a normal assignment for the natural faculty of reason. Natural religion is not a simple exploration of our surroundings. Hume is quite aware that a religiously interested use of reason is not concerned with an expansion of our knowledge in the manner of scientific exploration, a project which is quite well suited to didactic presentation.[15] Instead, as Pamphilus's remarks hint, the conversation between the characters of the dialogue, Demea, Philo, and Cleanthes, will

15. *The Natural History of Religion* constitutes Hume's treatment of religion in scientific terms, and, appropriately, the text is strictly didactic.

concentrate on extremes — that which is most immediate and evident, the very center of our existence, and that which is very remote and non-evident, very difficult to interpret as in any way even part of our lives. In this way, Hume forewarns us that the debate which extends through the *Dialogues* will range from the ordinary to the extraordinary, from that which is central to our self-understanding to the hazy perimeters.

Of course, one of the crucial questions is whether we are up to the task. Are we capable of such a volatile mixture? In classical terms, are humans *capaces infinitatis?* More to the tune of Enlightenment concerns with epistemology, are humans capable of transcendent knowledge? If natural religion is to make good its dual commitments, then we *must* enjoy this capacity. Without the ability to reach across the divide suggested by the oppositions of ordinary and extraordinary, immanent and transcendent, natural and supernatural, the human creature cannot make a claim to citizenship in both realms. And in that case, one side of the equation must be foresaken, and an exclusive residence established on one side or the other of this great divide.

The richness of Hume's *Dialogues* is his refusal to argue solely for one conclusion or another with respect to this crucial question. Testimony, perhaps, to the fertility of conversation which Pamphilus praises, the issue is treated with a fruitful indeterminacy. Hume never uses the dialogue to disguise the didactic. Conclusions about the proper address of the human creature are abjured. Some of the arguments make the typically empiricist assumption that the ordinary world of experience is nonproblematic, and the challenge lies in showing that we are genuinely capable of the extraordinary. However, this is not always the case, for sometimes Hume reverses the problem, showing how difficult it might be to accept the ordinary.[16] Perhaps the difficulty lies in showing that humans are *capaces finitatis!* By allowing the interlocutors to play across the full spectrum of possibilities, Hume is then able to pose the question of the human capacity for transcendent knowledge in a way which brings into the sharpest possible focus the oddity of the Christian amphibious view.[17] For the *Dialogues*, as we

---

16. Part of the radical spiritual message implicit in Wittgenstein's later philosophy is precisely this reversal of assumptions.

17. J. C. A. Gaskin suggests this focus when he observes that the themes of Hume's *Dialogues* are not simply reworked Enlightenment concerns about the rational justification of religion. More than philosophical issues are at stake. The ebb and flow of argument is

shall explore in some detail, concerns itself less with with the questions of which realm — the immanent or transcendent, the natural or supernatural, the ordinary or extraordinary — constitutes the true human home, than it does with the more interesting question of whether the human creature might maintain *both* as legal residences.

2. The Temptations of Purity

HUME PREPARES THE READER for the problem of dual citizenship by introducing the topic through a preliminary discussion of the role of religion in education. For our assumptions about how the mind should be prepared to encounter religious teachings reveal our views of human rational capacities. For example, a prevailing contemporary assumption is that religion is a form of indoctrination which is fundamentally at odds with the educational process. For proponents of this position, the claims of religion are clearly beyond (or more likely, below) our rational capacities. If religion is to have any human significance, then it must address something other than our natures as rational creatures. Here, the possibility of amphibious existence, at least in its rational aspect, is denied. What is interesting is that many who support religious education often harbor the same assumptions about our rational capacities. Hume exposes this similarity at the outset.

One of the surprising features of the *Dialogues* is that Philo the skeptic and Demea the dogmatist express unanimity about the place of religious instruction in the education of youths. Both agree that religious truths should be introduced at the end of the educational process. This is because both see religion as fundamentally alien to reason. Unlike twentieth century secularists who draw the immediate inference that what is alien to reason has no place in human life, Philo and Demea draw the opposite conclusion. Instead of ruling out religion because of its offense to reason, the two join

---

also controlled by pressures internal to religious belief, most particularly, the tension between a God ordinary enough to be accessible to the believer, but extraordinary enough to really be God. As Gaskin puts the matter, "This tension between a personal God and ineffable Majesty pervades Christianity. Hume was perhaps the first significant philosopher to point out that it also pervades the design argument as it could be used by a Christian" (*Hume's Philosophy of Religion* [London: MacMillan Press, 1978], p. 33).

hands in interpreting the entire purpose of education as a preparation of the mind for the acceptance of the alien teachings of religion.[18]

For Philo and Demea, proper preparation involves training the intellect towards a realization of its own impotence. Here, the dichotomy between the ordinary and extraordinary plays a decisive role. Both assume a radical discontinuity between the scope and force of human rational activity and religious claims. Therefore, training in doubt is necessary. This approach disposes the individual to discount the mind's initial repulsion from religious teachings and allows traditional doctrines to be accepted on the basis of authority. As Demea explains, when his students consider various disciplines he underlines "the uncertainty of each part; the external disputations of men; the obscurity of all philosophy; and the strange, ridiculous conclusions which some of the greatest geniuses have derived from the principles of mere human reason." This prepares the students for faith, since the pedagogy of uncertainty eliminates "any danger from that assuming arrogance of philosophy, which may lead them to reject the most established doctrines and opinions."[19] By undermining confidence in our powers of discernment and judgment, by calling into question all our own

18. The opening observations about the unified aspiration of the commitment to immanence and the proponent of radical transcendence for the tranquility of absorption into a singularly consititued world have already provided some suggestions for understanding the surprising allegiance between Philo and Demea, as has the note of Stanley Cavell's interpretation of Wittgenstein's interest in both skepticism and metaphysics. However, a far fuller development of the shared assumptions which underwrite the united front between Philo and Demea may be found in Terence Penelhum, *God and Skepticism*. There, Penelhum identifies two religious uses of skepticism. The first he calls Conformist Fideism, a position which concludes from the uncertainty of all things that it is not irrational (or better, no less irrational) and not inappropriate to conform oneself to prevailing religious practices. Penelhum links Erasmus, Montaigne and Bayle as representatives of this type of skeptical affirmation of religion. Where the Conformist Fideism uses skepticism to justifiy the *acceptance* of religion, the Evangelical Fideist uses skepticism to generate a deep religious *passion*. For the Evangelical Fideist, the uncertainty generated by skeptical arguments yields a despair so serious that it may be cured only by a passionate act of faith. The depths of doubt are conquered by the heights of faith. Although neither Philo nor Demea belongs unequivocally in either camp — Philo actually presents arguments against conformity to religious practice in any form in Part XII (only to contradict them at the very end of the dialogues) and Demea never articulates the need for passion in faith — we may usefully range Philo among the Conformists and Demea among the Evangelicals.

19. Both quotes from *Dialogues,* ed. Richard H. Popkin (Indianapolis: Hackett Publishing Co., 1980), pp. 3-4.

independent attempts to answer ultimate (or even proximate) questions, the path towards faith is made smooth. Or more accurately, the way of reason is made so bumpy that the lurch across the divide which separates religion from ordinary life is accepted as one epistemic jolt among many. In concert, then, Demea the dogmatist and Philo the skeptic deny our capacity for rational knowledge of God in order to secure a specifically and strictly doctrinal affirmation of faith.

The role of the individual in this educational process is telling. In terms developed above, the goal of this pedagogy of doubt is a staying of the dynamic self. By training the individual in doubt, confidence in the powers of discernment and judgment are undermined. As a result, the individual can have no role to play in the formation of her own belief. Since the "arrogance of reason" has been tamed, the individual is disposed simply to accept religious teaching by authority. The mind conforms itself to traditional doctrines, and this conformity cannot be questioned since the entire educational process has been designed to extinguish confidence in reason. As a consequence, the individual is passive, charged only with the task of accepting the teachings of religion. The upshot is a propositional form of absorption. The self, undermined by the pedagogy of doubt, is absorbed into the brute givenness of traditional religious doctrines.

The fate of the self in this absorption is especially evident if we consider the rationale which Philo might have for defending religious education. For Philo, a deep, consistent skepticism allows for an "affirmation" of religion, because as the skeptic discovers the dialectical impotence of reason, he realizes that there is no rational defense against the epistemic transformations wrought by culture. In the particular case of the cultural force of religion, the skeptic has no reason to resist conventional forces of religious indoctrination, since, after all, the true skeptic suspends judgment as to whether the teachings of religion are true or false. In Hume's day, it simply was the case that an attenuated Christianity was part of the furniture of the culture. Thus, Philo accepts his fate of being absorbed by this religious givenness, just as he conforms to other appearances, be they naturalistic (he makes free use of experimental observation) or rational (he conforms himself to the linguistic and argumentative practices which prevail).[20] The self, rendered passive by the pedagogy of doubt, is a recep-

20. Penelhum summarizes Montaigne's reasoning on this matter: "Man, placed in-dividually in history, is unable to rise above the relativities that derive from this, must

tacle into which is poured the customs and practices which constitute the prevailing traditions. Unlike Philo, Demea may hold out for some activity on the part of the student. The hope is not that the pedagogy of doubt will render the self completely passive, but rather that it will weaken the self-will of reason sufficiently to allow for the affirmation of faith. In spite of this important difference, however, both place an emphasis on the need to still the rational efforts of the self.

Cleanthes, the defender of natural religion, rejects this approach. He will have nothing of a pedagogy which tries to sidestep the rational dimension of faith by denying our ability to reason. He rejects the notion that we can be led to believe by default. From the outset he attacks the skeptical assumptions which Philo and Demea share. Is it possible, he asks, to build one's life around doubt? He issues a clear challenge to Philo. Is it not the case that when he departs, he will use the stairs like the rest, knowing that departure through the second story window will result in injury? The answer, of course, is that Philo will use the stairs. But if this is so, reasons Cleanthes, then should we not reject attempts to cast doubt on *all* of knowledge? Can Demea's and Philo's pedagogy of doubt be anything more than partial? Does the self not retain the capacity to identify and affirm *some* claims as true? And is this capacity, on closer inspection, not broader than simply an acceptance of the commonplace facts of ordinary existence? Cleanthes' answers are clear. He contends, "In vain would the skeptic [as well as the dogmatist] make a distinction between science and common life, or between one science and another." Cleanthes notes that in a post-Copernican world, educated individuals are very willing to ascribe a high degree of certainty to the teachings of modern astronomy. The strength of the evidence is sufficient to overcome our absence of everyday, "hands-on" knowledge of the solar system as such. Since we are willing to affirm claims about the extraordinarily large and distant world of planets, Cleanthes concludes that the very same principles of reason might well obtain in the extraordinary realm of religion. If doubt is defeated in both ordinary life and the distant science of astronomy, then

---

recognize his inability to do so, and should submit to the religious forms and teachings that surround him, rather than try arrogantly to assert or deny them from an objective standpoint that is impossible for him" (*God and Skepticism*, p. 23). Hume, well aware of Montaigne's work, was no doubt influenced by this line of argument in the formation of the character of Philo.

why may not doubt be defeated in religion? As he observes, "The arguments employed in all, if just, are of a similar nature and contain the same force and evidence."[21] We cannot assume, then, a fundamental dichotomy between reason and religion, the ordinary and the extraordinary.

Although Cleanthes' strong arguments in favor of a mixed vision of transcendence and an amphibious view of the self emerge later in the dialogues, at this point he clearly states his commitment: we cannot cordon off religious beliefs from the principles which guide our assent to other forms of belief. Our beliefs constitute a whole which must be subject to the same principles of reason. To admit of the possibility of genuine knowledge in one aspect of life is to allow for the *possibility* in every dimension. This claim is central to Cleanthes' position. In the broadest terms, for Cleanthes our rational participation in the extraordinary world of religious belief, whatever that might entail, is not, in principle, distinct from "common life." Religion cannot come on the scene *deus ex machina* after reason has exhausted itself in skeptical self-doubt. For reasons which will become clear as our analysis of the debate develops, for Cleanthes, if the religious life holds out any promise, it must encompass, not exclude, our capacity to reason. Thus emerges a necessary presupposition of Cleanthes' defense of natural religion: at the very least, both aspects of our lives, the secular and religious, the natural and supernatural, the proximate and ultimate, fall under the same principles of argument and evidence.

At this point, Cleanthes has not committed himself to the claim that we actually do have the capacity to secure religious knowledge on the basis of rational principles, the ability to travel the distance from the immediacy of experience to the distant knowledge of the divine. To do so he must show that we have access to religious belief under the ordinary principles of reason and evidence. To make good that commitment, Cleanthes gives voice to the Argument from Design. The argument proceeds *a posteriori;* it entails reasoning out of the thick of things by drawing attention to a specific feature of ordinary perception, our experience of order throughout the natural world. This experience of order is evident to all, claims Cleanthes, and this natural order calls to mind the kind of order created by human intelligence. In light of this resemblance, Cleanthes concludes that by the principle of analogy — similar effects suggest similar causes — we may rationally believe that just as the

21. Both quotes from *Dialogues,* pp. 9-10.

order of human creations is caused by human intelligence, the cosmic order was created by a divine intelligence. In this way Cleanthes satisfies the dual commitments of natural religion, arguing that the self may move from common life (our experience of natural order and our acquaintance with the order of human designs) to the quite extraordinary state of knowledge of the divine (the conclusion that the world was created by an intelligent being) while remaining the very same rational creatures — this is indeed a dynamic possibility and the very definition of the mixed or amphibious view of our condition.

3. The Pull of Radical Transcendence

DEMEA, LIKE PHILO THE SKEPTIC, confronts and rejects Cleanthes' *a posteriori* argument regarding the being and nature of God. However, unlike Philo, Demea finds that the Argument from Design rings true. For him, the appeals to order in the cosmos, the analogy of design, and the conclusion that the divine must be an intelligent being have a *prima facie* plausability. Cleanthes' conception of an Intelligent Designer and the evidence he marshals on its behalf strike Demea as appropriate. Moreover, as a believer, Demea recognizes that Cleanthes' arguments in favor of a Supreme Being ought to be congenial to his religious loyalties. Surely any argument which shows the rationality of religious belief is on the side of the angels. But Demea rejects Cleanthes' argument. Demea dismisses the idea that we might have a rational grasp of the divine. How is this possible? How could the representative of traditional theism who admits to the persuasive force of the Argument from Design reject its conclusions?

Demea's reasons for rejecting what he admits are good arguments are bound up with his theological commitment to a dogmatic form of radical transcendence. He draws away from the entire line of thinking involved in the Argument from Design. He is repulsed not by the conclusion, since he too affirms the divine as intelligent, but by what might fairly be called the religious logic of the argument, the presuppositions about the relationship of the ordinary and extraordinary, as well as the human role in the religious project. For Demea, Cleanthes' approach draws the world of human experience too near the world of the divine. The ordinary and extraordinary are woven together all too closely. This yields two negative consequences. First, the argumentative strategies vest too many divine qualities in the human creature — exaltation by association. Second, the elevation of the human compromises the distant majesty of the deity, and for Demea this undermines the drama of transcendence by turning the leap across a chasm into an easy step across a modest divide between the divine and human.

Demea is alive to the logic of Cleanthes' position from the very outset. Immediately following Cleanthes' articulation of the Argument from Design, Demea objects, "I could not approve of your conclusion concerning the similarity of the Deity to men; still less can I approve of the mediums by which you endeavor to establish it." The mode of argumentation is the source of Demea's repulsion. Demea warns Cleanthes that he will not be an ally in spite of the fact that they both seek to affirm theism. In fact, Demea suggests that Cleanthes may present a greater danger to religious orthodoxy than the ancient skeptical tradition. Demea observes, presciently, "You give advantages to the atheists which they never could obtain by the mere dint of argument and reasoning."[22] For Demea, the wrongheadedness of Cleanthes' argument cuts to the deepest level since it empowers the self in a way which, Demea suspects, cuts against the agenda of radical transcendence. For as Cleanthes draws down the capital of the extraordinary to fund his Argument from Design, Demea recognizes an impoverishment of the divine.

In his brief outburst immediately following Cleanthes' first articulation of the Argument from Design, Demea does not elaborate on the "mediums" of which he so disapproves. Demea falls largely silent, and it is not until after a storm of skeptical objections raised by Philo, followed by Cleanthes' valiant responses, that Demea returns to the debate to explain the full force of his initial objection. At the end of Part III of the *Dialogues,* Demea expresses a confidence that Cleanthes has defeated Philo's skeptical objections. This makes crystal clear the fact that Demea can have no strictly rational objection to Cleanthes' approach. Only the "mediums" of his argument will be called into question. And the logic of the Argument from Design is exactly what Demea attacks.

In light of Cleanthes' bold claims on behalf of the human capacity to form judgments about the nature of the divine based on the evidence of design, Demea formulates his basic worry: "May it not render us presumptuous, by making us imagine we comprehend the Deity and have

22. Both quotes from *Dialogues,* p. 15.

some adequate idea of his nature and attributes?"[23] To Demea's mind, this presumption has pernicious theological consequences. Foreshadowing the controversies of the nineteenth century, Demea specifies his concern about the "mediums" of Cleanthes' argument. He observes, "By representing the Deity as so intelligible and comprehensible, and so similar to a human mind, we are guilty of the grossest and most narrow partiality, and make ourselves the model of the whole universe."[24] The religious logic of Cleanthes' approach is anthropocentric. The pivot on which the Argument from Design turns is the analogy of design, and the analogy, in turn, depends upon our familiarity with designs as *human* phenomena. The key to the strength of Cleanthes' argument, then, is the way in which it is grounded in the familiar or ordinary. Yet, for Demea, this argumentative gain is a religious loss. Demea recognizes that if *we* and *our* designs are the model of the whole universe, then what possible significance could God have? If beauty is in the eye of the beholder, then is not transcendence in the mind of the reasoner? Do we really *need* a supreme being when the rational force of Cleanthes' argument — the analogy of design — grows out of the distinctively human point of view?

Demea's insight is that knowledge of God, based on empirical reasoning in general and analogy in particular, entails a religiously troubling familiarity with the divine. Cleanthes' argument invites us to consider immediate phenomena, and through the use of analogy to shape our conceptions of the divine into the same form and structure as the ordinary. In more poetical terms, Cleanthes asks us to read the book of nature so as to discern the mind of its author. Demea is deeply troubled by the effect of this reflective strategy on our understanding of transcendence. He notes, "When I read a volume, I enter into the mind and intention of the author; I become him, in a manner, for the instant."[25] Demea may be overstating the case. Cleanthes does not suggest that our knowledge of order and purpose in nature allows us to *become* the divine, but Demea is correct insofar as Cleanthes' argumentative strategy certainly requires us to enroll our thoughts about the extraordinary object of our religious interest into the evidential patterns of thinking which characterize our epistemic relations to ordinary and familiar objects and events. Since the Argument

23. *Dialogues*, p. 26.
24. *Dialogues*, p. 27.
25. *Dialogues*, p. 26.

from Design pivots on the concept of analogy, its rational strength rests on its ability to accentuate the similarity between the divine act of creation and the human act of invention. The "medium" or logic of Cleanthes' approach is one of convergence. The divine and human are shaped into the same familiar form by the powerful pressures of analogy.

This convergence of our apprehension of the extraordinary and our thinking about the ordinary is intolerable in the religious world occupied by Demea. For Demea, the immediate context of existence — in this case the physical world which provides evidence of design but which could well be the inner world of intuition or feeling, just as it might be the context of historical development, the world of social custom, or the structure of ordinary language use — *cannot* be the realm of the spiritual drama of transcendence. His intuition here is characteristic of the vision of radical transcendence: surely that worth striving for, that worthy of worship and veneration, must be far beyond the familiar, must be quite extraordinary indeed. After all, our lives are shaped by transient passions and sentiments, shot through with doubts and uncertainties, buffeted by impersonal forces and events. Do we wish to drag God down into *this* condition, as Cleanthes' argumentative strategy seems to do? If God and our attachment to Him in faith are to have any allure or significance, Demea assumes, the extraordinary must be distanced from the familiar, the ordinary, the worldly. Given the Newtonian world which informs Cleanthes' Argument from Design, this means specifically that the divine must be utterly separated from the knowable world of finite causes and finite effects. However, what the divine is distanced from is not important. It might just as well be the internal psychic world of affectivity or the developing drama of history. Without any necessary judgment about the particular form which natural religion might take, the crucial claim is that the divine is wholly other than the familiar world of human experience, however we might describe that world. To say otherwise risks collapsing the extraordinary into the ordinary and draining the drama of transcendence out of the religious life. As a consequence, Demea refuses to accede to the persuasive powers of Cleanthes' argument from design; and he shields himself from further appeals with the traditional claim that God is, above all else, incomprehensible

Cleanthes' response is direct. Whatever might be the dangers of a too familiar, too ordinary and too human diety, the alternative is disastrous. He astutely challenges Demea:

If our ideas, so far as they go, be not just and adequate and correspondent to his real nature, I know not what there is in this subject worth insisting on. Is the name, without any meaning, of such mighty importance? Or how do you *mystics,* who maintain the absolute incomprehensibility of the Deity, differ from skeptics and atheists, who assert that the first cause of all is unknown and unintelligible?[26]

Cleanthes is highlighting much more than an epistemological issue. He is expressing one of the crucial dilemmas of Demea's commitment to radical transcendence: Why would one strive towards something so fundamentally alien to our present condition that we cannot even give its name any meaning? Cleanthes is reminding us that the kind of God envisioned by Demea *cannot* be the goal of our striving. A God of whom we have no knowledge is a supreme being about which we cannot be concerned. Since Demea's God does not touch our epistemic lives, we cannot imagine the significance of such a God's existence. We cannot link such a vision of transcendence to the temporal projects which constitute our lives. We cannot integrate it into the matrix of our experience. The discontinuity between who we are now and our goal in the incomprehensible deity is so extreme that we can say nothing about the purpose and significance of our belief. In short, Cleanthes recognizes an incoherent and ultimately impotent view of transcendence in Demea's exaltation of the divine to a point beyond all human power and beyond all comprehension. In spite of his claims, then, Demea is backing himself into a *de facto* atheism in which the pious world of traditional theism is nothing but a meaningless exercise of the jaw.

Here we have a protean conflict of intuitions, a conflict which shapes our understanding of the relation of the ordinary and extraordinary, and with it our conception of transcendence. On the one hand, in Demea we find a vision of radical transcendence which emphasizes the complete and extrinsic otherness of the goal of human striving. All that is worthy of regard in the present — benevolence, intelligence, beauty — is ascribed to the deity and to an infinite degree, so infinite, in fact, that the perfection of this transcendent being surpasses comprehension. To the degree that we participate in this extraordinary Other we take on a new form, fundamentally discontinuous with the ways of knowing and acting which now characterize our lives as

26. *Dialogues,* p. 28.

natural, social, and historical beings. As a consequence of this discontinuity there is nothing for us to do here and now that has any enduring significance, nothing in our merely human lives which will matter finally. For Demea, we need not be in a state of agitation, for the transcendence suggested is so radical — incomprehensible and beyond human powers — that we cannot anticipate or assist the transformation to be wrought (except, perhaps, in the strictly negative sense of stilling our overreaching desires). On the other hand, Cleanthes presents a vision of transcendence as continuous with the human condition. His appeal to the analogy of human design (indeed, any use of analogy) accentuates the similarities between human projects and activities and the doings of the divine. The ordinary structure of our present existence thus carries over into the extraordinary possibility of knowledge of the divine. For Cleanthes, our relation to the extraordinary must have an enduring this-worldly dimension. By virtue of the already evident presence of the extraordinary in the well-ordered universe, we are called to move towards affirmation and assent. As ordinary rational creatures we are drawn in the direction of the extraordinary, with concrete epistemic and practical changes following in the wake.

Given this conflict of religious intuitions, we should be able to see that Demea's decision simply to set aside the feelings of rational assent stimulated by Cleanthes' arguments is not an expression of a narrow dogmatism.[27] Rather, Demea's position betrays deeper convictions about the

---

27. Where Demea is not completely ignored by commentators, he is too often restricted to the role of representing an uninteresting religious dogmatism. For example, Stanley Tweyman's discussion of the Argument from Design passes over the crucial exchanges between Demea and Cleanthes. He comments only that Demea is engaged in a rather unimaginative exercise of showing the tautology that anthropomorphism is incompatible with the claim that God is incomprehensible. For Tweyman, Demea's role in the *Dialogues* is strictly epiphenomenal. (Cf. *Scepticism and Belief in Hume's Dialogues* [Dortrecht: Martinus Nijhoff Publishers, 1986], p. 67.) Even Gaskin's thorough commentary, *Hume's Philosophy of Religion* (New York: Macmillan Press, 1978), tends to shift attention away from the specifically religious objection with which Demea challenges Cleanthes, and to which Cleanthes provides a religious rather than a purely philosophical reply. Gaskin focuses his analysis on the problems which Demea's comments raise for the possibility of meaningful theological language. This does illustrate the deeper issue which separates Cleanthes and Demea — the conditions under which religion can matter for the human creature — since meaningful language use would seem to be a necessary condition for actually forming one's life around a particular set of religious claims. However, Gaskin does not develop the issue with the breadth suggested by Hume himself.

nature of transcendence. In Demea's other-worldly view, transcendence is radical; our destiny is quite simply beyond the human. No quality or attribute of ordinary life applies directly to the divine. Everything we take to be characteristic of the human condition, even those aspects to which we ascribe intrinsic value, must be radicalized. We might say, then, that all of our ordinary intuitions of value must be run through the mill of the Ontological Argument. For example, we may recognize the deep value of charitable and loving acts. The radical view of transcendence allows us to apply this recognition to our destiny in God, but only in the form greater than that which we can conceive. Likewise, clear thought and reasoned argument, the well crafted verse and luminous painting — Demea's vision of transcendence includes these aesthetic values, but again, in an "incomprehensible" form greater than that which we can imagine.

Throughout this radical vision deep dichotomies dominate. Where our present life is contingent, our goal is necessity. Where our condition is finite and mortal, our destiny is characterized as infinite and immortal. Where we exist in temporal sequence, our ultimate home is the timeless eternal. These are the broadest and most pervasive contrasts, but others crop up according to specific assessments of the human condition. For example, when human knowing is defined as grasping universals through particulars, transcendence is cast as possessing universals directly and immediately. Where human identity is seen as inherently bodily, our proper end is described as immaterial. At every point the accent falls upon the radical *difference* between our present condition and the pull of transcendence.

The radically suprahuman is supremely difficult to articulate. In his challenge to Demea, Cleanthes exploits the way in which the dichotomies characteristic of this view of transcendence tend to descend into incoherence and, as a consequence, undermine the religious intelligibility of radical transcendence. For example, when proponents of the radical view define extraordinary "knowledge," our ordinary sense of what is involved in the practice of knowing is taxed to the point of bankruptcy. With difficulty do we imagine an epistemic state of immediate apprehension as a state of *knowledge*. The dichotomy between human knowing and transcendent knowing is so extreme that it is transformed into a contrast between knowing and some other very different kind of mental state. In which case, notes Cleanthes, "A mind whose acts and sentiments and ideas are not distinct and successive, one that is wholly simple and totally immutable, is a mind which has no thought, no reason, no will, no sentiment, no love, no hatred; or, in a word, is no mind at all."[28] For the proponent of radical and other-worldly transcendence, then, it would seem inappropriate to speak of mind or knowledge on the other side of the temporal. To do so is to wander into a strange use of language.

Later in the *Dialogues,* Cleanthes reformulates this insight. As a representative of a radical and discontinuous view of transcendence, Demea does allow for a specific application of reason to the question of God. Presenting a form of the Cosmological Argument, Demea concludes that God must necessarily exist. No claim is made about the nature of God, and, equally important, the Cosmological Argument requires no *particular* experience as its point of departure. Unlike the Argument from Design, which requires us to entertain specific instances of order, the Cosmological Argument asks us only to observe that there is something rather than nothing, and then reasons that this something must have a cause. Divorced as it is from the particularity of reason's everyday life, distanced from the specific perceptions and judgments which constitute our ordinary epistemic practice, Demea's mode of argument is a fitting complement to his view of radical transcendence.

Cleanthes' reply to Demea's argument parallels his general criticism of radical transcendence. The crucial point for Cleanthes is that our powers of argument cannot be divorced, as Demea would like, from ordinary epistemic assumptions. In the case of the Cosmological Argument, Cleanthes observes that contingency is bound up with the very concept of being. All existence involves the possibility of nonexistence. As Cleanthes notes, "It will be possible for us, at any time, to conceive the non-existence of what we formerly conceived to exist."[29] Necessity, then, cannot apply to existence. The argument that God must be a necessary being descends into nonsense. Not surprisingly, then, Demea's specific application of reason participates in the broader logic of divine incomprehensibility.

In this as in so many other ways, the momentum of radical transcendence carries it beyond the most basic categories by which we understand ordinary life. For Cleanthes, of course, this is a sign of the overall incoherence and existential impotence of Demea's religious presuppositions. His objections show that those who adopt a radical and discontinuous

28. *Dialogues,* p. 29.
29. *Dialogues,* p. 55.

vision of transcendence secure the radical difference of our destiny in the extraordinary only at the price of its intelligibility, and by implication then, its relevance to ordinary human life. Cleanthes' strong claim is that the project of radical transcendence cannot be a real aspiration for those of us who confront existence in the ordinary, contingent way. For Cleanthes, then, Demea's vision of transcendence is a wheel turning with nothing moving. It is a linguistic commitment which can have no practical import since belief in an incomprehensible and necessary being cannot denominate or motivate *anything* in our comprehensible and contingent lives.[30]

These trenchant criticisms of Demea have no effect. Demea departs from the company with his views unchanged. And rightly so. For all the charges of unintelligibility, irrelevance and meaninglessness are, in the mind of the proponent of radical transcendence, evidence *for* rather than against the position. The failures of reason are embraced. Of course, the idea of necessary existence has no meaning. But this is just another illustration of the incomprehensibility of the divine! Even the most basic predication decays upon closer examination, showing the inadequacy of our puny human formulations. So much more, then, do we need to be delivered from this temporal state. So much more do we need to have our impotent reason superseded by divine revelation, our meaningless propo-

30. Although in the voice of Cleanthes Hume emphasizes the irrelevance of a radically transcendent God, in his proto-sociology of religion he does identify practical consequences which flow from the point of view propounded by Demea. There he suggests that a certain correlation exists between the view of radical transcendence and a way of life, just as there is a correlation between Cleanthes' view and a different form of life. Specifically, "Where the deity is represented as infinitely superior to mankind, this belief . . . is apt, when joined with superstitious terrors, to sink the human mind into the lowest submission and abasement, and to represent the monkish virtues of mortification, penance, humility, and passive suffering, as the only qualities which are acceptable to him. But where the gods are conceived to be only a little superior to mankind, and to have been, many of them, advanced from that inferior rank, we are more at our ease, in our addresses to them, and may even, without profaneness, aspire sometimes to a rivalship and emulation of them. Hence activity, spirit, courage, magnanimity, love of liberty, and all the virtues which aggrandize a people" (*Natural History of Religion,* ed. H. E. Root [Stanford: Stanford University Press, 1956], p. 52). Not only does this passage foreshadow Nietzsche's trenchant *practical* criticisms of Christianity, but it also defeats the notion that strong beliefs about transcendence such as those propounded by Demea are "mere" fictions or nonsense. These beliefs have, in spite of the incomprehensibility which Cleanthes exploits (and Demea admits!), a tenacious and powerful relevance.

sitions replaced by divinely sanctioned doctrines. The religious view of Demea is such that every failure in argument (or, for that matter, any failure in human activity), even his own, may be turned to the good purpose of widening the great divide which separates us from our ultimate destiny, thus accentuating our need for total transformation. Radical transcendence enjoys, then, a resiliency found in the pure consistency of its solution to the problem of relating the ordinary world of our existence to the extraordinary world of our religious interest: that of denying any internal or intrinsic relation at all!

Though unable to defeat this incorrigible position, Cleanthes has taken a decisive step towards defining the amphibious view. Against Demea's dichotomous vision, Cleanthes has insisted that our religious interest only makes sense as a *human* interest if it can be satisfied in a way somehow continuous with ordinary life. The difference between the divine and human cannot be so complete that no significant points of contact remain. Although this need not be true for all conceptions of amphibious existence, for Cleanthes these points of contact are specifically rational. Cleanthes thinks that the Argument from Design is capable of constructing a rationally plausible continuity between ordinary life and the extraordinary object of our religious interest. This has the important consequence of enlivening the self. Far from Demea's view of an incomprehensibly distant God, Cleanthes pictures a God sufficiently this-worldly to be the object of legitimate inquiry, and once grasped, a point upon which to orient other aspects of our lives. In short, for Cleanthes the Argument from Design does more than secure the extraordinary proposition that God is an Intelligent Designer. It anchors the extraordinary in the ordinary and gives us a chance to enroll our ordinary lives in the extraordinary. It makes religion a legimate rational, and therefore, *human* interest. However, the strength with which Cleanthes makes his case against Demea will come back to haunt him. For Philo listens well, and he is quick to insist that Cleanthes be true to the ordinary world which he valiantly defends against Demea's affirmation of radical transcendence.

4. The Push of Pure Immanence

THE COMPACT FORM of Hume's exchanges between Cleanthes and Demea is remarkable, and the prescience of his insights into the interlocking network of religious, epistemological and existential commitments at work in the conflict between the two is even more impressive. Much of nineteenth century theology finds itself struggling with these very questions.[31] However, Hume is not primarily interested in exposing the logic of radical transcendence and its claims against the amphibious view. Of greater interest to Hume is the conflict between the purely immanent approach and the form of transcendence suggested by the Argument from Design. Here, the arguments are much more extensive as Hume explores the ways in which Cleanthes' limited vision of rational transcendence can be made to collapse of its own weight into the strictly immanent view propounded by Philo. In terms of the debate we have just surveyed, Philo is able to turn Cleanthes' strongest claim against Demea — that our religious identity, if it is to be of human interest, must be firmly rooted in this world — into the fundamental criticism of Cleanthes' own aspiration towards the extraordinary in the Argument from Design. If the immanent world of experience shapes our interests as human beings, reasons Philo, then why should there be *any* aspiration beyond it, no matter how modest?

31. In his commentary on Hume's philosophy of religion, Gaskin identifies the problems which Hume's theory of knowledge raises for theological claims. The difficulty, as we have seen, is that traditional religious claims use ordinary language (e.g., intelligence) in an extraordinary way (e.g., divine intelligence), and this use stretches language to the point of breaking. As Cleanthes notes, the divine mind as understood by orthodox Christians bears no resemblance to human minds, and might just as well be said to be no mind at all. This difficulty bears out one of Hume's basic and oft repeated principles: we cannot extend our knowledge beyond the limits of common experience. The upshot is Hume's famous conclusion to the *Enquiry:* "If we take any volume — of divinity or school metaphysics, for instance — let us ask, *Does it contain any abstract reasoning concerning quantity or number?* No. *Does it contain any experimental reasoning concerning matter of fact and existence?* No. Commit it then to the flames, for it can contain nothing but sophistry and illusion." Most commentators, including Gaskin, take this observation about the absence of meaning in theology as indicative of the general conflict between faith and reason, a problem which challenges the theological enterprise from the outside. No Hume scholars have observed, however, that the *Dialogues* also indicates the ways in which the problem of meaningful theological statements is a decisive issue of internal theological interest. In fact, the tradition of theological liberalism in the nineteenth century understood itself as an effort to satisfy a *religious* need for humanly meaningful theological statements, not just as an apologetical effort to justify religion before the bar of reason. What has eluded comment is that in its many efforts to address this religious need, the complex and multifaceted liberal tradition in theology never advanced beyond the basic tensions which Hume identifies so effectively in his exchanges between Demea and Cleanthes.

For Philo, our inevitable epistemic commitment to the immanent world of experience continually undermines any claim of transcendence. If one foot is firmly planted in the world, as Cleanthes insists against Demea, then we can never do more than tap randomly with the other. Better to keep *both* feet in the immediate realm of ordinary experience.

Philo's goal, then, is to show that extraordinary things like knowledge of God are beyond the reach of ordinary principles of reason. In this way he seeks to convince us that Cleanthes' amphibious view involves a delusion. Cleanthes *thinks* that his beliefs about the divine are rationally warranted and that the self may gain a degree of transcendence, but he is mistaken. We may *wish* that we were truly amphibious, that we really could draw ultimate conclusions from our ordinary experience, final purposes from proximate events, but this is impossible and is best understood as an artificial urge foisted upon us by the influences of centuries of priestcraft. Philo condemns our aspirations for transcendence with a number of different arguments throughout the *Dialogues,* but the crucial conceptual issue is that of analogy. As we shall see, Cleanthes' use of analogy, like the project of natural theology as a whole, participates in the conceptual vagrancy which characterizes the amphibious view. Philo's dialectical skill exposes the conceptual difficulties which inevitably emerge from Cleanthes' attempt to accentuate the continuity between the ordinary and extraordinary — a continuity which Cleanthes so strongly affirmed in his debate with Demea — while allowing for enough difference to insure that the extraordinary remains just that.

Philo begins his attack on the Argument from Design by immediately identifying the conditions under which arguments from analogy yield solid conclusions. His first move is to state the strongest possible case. As he observes, "That a stone will fall, that a fire will burn, that the earth has solidity, we have observed a thousand and a thousand times; and when any new instance of this nature is presented, we draw the accustomed inference." The principle which he draws from this continuity of experience is that "the exact similarity of cases gives us a perfect assurance of a similar event."[32] With the ideal of similarity in mind, Philo questions Cleanthes' use of analogy. In the Argument from Design, the similarity which motivates the analogy between human and divine intelligence is the similarity between the order created by human fabrications and the order

32. Both quotations from *Dialogues,* p. 16.

found in the cosmos. Yet, comments Philo, this is a similarity which is far from exact. As Philo accurately observes, the kinds of human designs we encounter in life — he gives the example of a house — are quite remote from any design we might detect in the universe. In short, the Argument from Design departs from the exact similarity of cases which is necessary for solid analogical reasoning.

It would seem, then, that Philo objects to Cleanthes' approach because it involves a weak analogy. Philo does say that, but he also says much more. At issue is not just the strength of the analogy of design, but a much wider question about the possibility of using analogy to connect the ordinary with the extraordinary. Behind Philo's principle of exact similarity of cases is an ideal of knowledge (correspondence) and truth (identity) which makes the movement of reasoning (from common experience to uncommon knowledge) entailed in natural religion as conceptually incoherent as Demea's incomprehensible deity. In order to understand how Philo is able to press this much stronger case against Cleanthes, we need to consider in greater detail his claims and Cleanthes' counterclaims.

Philo has opened the debate with the contention that the Argument from Design rests on much less than an exact analogy. Cleanthes' response is to show how the stringent principle of exact similarity fails to account for the full scope of our epistemic practices. He observes, "To prove by experience the origin of the universe from the mind is not more contrary to common experience than to prove the motion of the earth from the same principle."[33] The principle to which Cleanthes refers is a use of analogy which relies on something less than exact similarity. Newtonian theories of motion involve forms of reasoning quite removed from common experience. We certainly do not experience the earth moving in any way like the motion of, say, a falling rock. Yet, Newtonian physics tells us that both the motion of the earth and the rock are essentially the same. And this is convincing, because some rather bold analogies are drawn with mathematical brushstrokes against the background of the principle of gravity. Here, then, is an example of a strong degree of certainty which arises from the comparison of, in many important respects, dissimilar cases.

This is not, however, the last word. From the outset Philo warned that philosophical ideals such as correspondence and identity are not to be confused with actual epistemic practice. These ideals cannot directly guide

33. *Dialogues*, p. 21.

ordinary behavior, epistemic or otherwise.[34] However, such philosophical ideals do condition our habits of reflection. They shape, as it were, the structure of our beliefs; and Philo sees the way in which analogy structures our beliefs so as to accentuate similarity. He exploits Cleanthes' appeal to modern astronomical theories to illustrate this crucial feature of analogy. The point is not the degree of similarity achieved by Newtonian analogies of motion. What is important is the goal, which is, of course, to *reduce* as much as possible the differences between the motion we experience in ordinary life and the seemingly extraordinary motion ascribed to the planets. For example, Philo notes that Galileo was able to gain widespread acceptance for modern theories of motion precisely because through numerous experiments and illustrations he was able to eliminate the traditional distinction between earthly and celestial bodies. As a consequence, observes Philo, "After many instances of this kind, with regard to all the planets, men plainly saw that these bodies became proper objects of experience, and that the similarity of their nature enabled us to extend the same arguments and phenomena from one to the other."[35] Galileo's argumentative practices reveal the ideal of identity. Imperfect analogy is something on which we rely in science as well as everyday life, but what is crucial is that our use always seeks to reduce the differences between cases compared. We are oriented towards the ideal of identity — exactly similar cases — and although we cannot achieve this ideal in practice, we proportion our assent according to the ability of an analogy to move in this direction.

Of course, Cleanthes has committed himself to a degree of convergence between the realm of experience and the divine in his polemics against Demea's vision of discontinuity. Philo exploits this commitment to good effect. At times Philo seeks not to weaken the analogy of design, but rather, he expends every effort to strengthen the analogy to show Cleanthes the

34. Cf. *Dialogues*, pp. 6-7.

35. *Dialogues*, p. 22. What Galileo achieved with his telescope, Newton did with his mathematical representations of the problems of motion. Galileo brought the evening sky down to ordinary experience, exposing the surface of the moon as pocked with rugged features not unlike those found on the surface of the earth — a similarity which the Cardinals were loathe to admit. In contrast, Newton relied on mathematical abstraction. Yet the consequences were the same. All experiences of motion could be subsumed under a single theory by way of a single mode of symbolic representation, and this form of similarity was, in the end, more powerful than that exposed by Galileo's telescope.

true consequences of a commitment to continuity between the ordinary and extraordinary. For example, Philo observes that human designs do not spring from the minds of their creators, but are, in fact, modifications of any number of past efforts which have achieved order by trial and error. A strong analogy, then, would dictate the conclusion that the Great Artificer had to labor long at the task of producing an even minimally functional world. Philo speculates, "Many worlds might have been botched and bungled, throughout eternity, ere this system was struck out; much labor lost; many fruitless trials made; and a slow but continued improvement carried on during infinite ages in the art of world-making."[36] Or, pressing the analogy in other respects, Philo suggests that since human machines have many designers and fabricators, then we ought to suppose that many gods created the cosmos. The requirement of analogy — the greatest possible similarity which the evidence allows — argues in favor of polytheism.

Initially Cleanthes is swept into Philo's line of reasoning, happy that Philo has admitted the principle of analogy rather than trying to refute it with the impossible standard of exact similarity. Yet, this glee is short-lived. What seems like a concession is, in fact, one of Philo's strongest weapons against Cleanthes' position. Philo's use of analogy culminates in a wholesale shift of the argument away from design and intelligence. Accepting now all of Cleanthes' assumptions about our capacity to think analogically, Philo gives a quite different account of the results. He observes:

> The world plainly resembles more an animal or a vegetable than it does a watch or a knitting loom. Its cause, therefore, it is more probable, resembles the cause of the former. The cause of the former is generation or vegetation. The cause, therefore, of the world we may infer to be something similar or analogous to generation or vegetation.[37]

Cleanthes' response to Philo's alternative Argument from Generation or Vegetation is telling. He finds himself stumped. He has no arguments to counter Philo's suggested strengthening of the analogy between ordinary experience and our extraordinary conclusions about the origin of the cosmos. Cleanthes' dilemma is that the Argument from Design *cannot*

36. *Dialogues*, p. 36.
37. *Dialogues*, p. 45.

move in the direction of greater similarity and remain an argument of religious or transcendent significance. Cleanthes is as committed to the *difference* between the divine and human as he is to the similarity. And this is inevitable, for the entire project of natural religion is to secure some kind of extraordinary knowledge: as it is variously expressed, knowledge of the infinite, knowledge of the transcendent, knowledge of the divine. In the particular case of the Argument from Design this means that the difference between the design of nature and the designs of human creation cannot be minimized, for this would yield a similarity of designers which, in turn, would produce one of two conclusions: one, "god" is very nearly human, or two, we are very nearly "gods." Cleanthes' only response, then, is a query: "You must be sensible that common sense and reason are entirely against you, and that such whimsies as you have delivered may puzzle but never can convince us."[38]

We must recognize that although Philo rightly identifies a suppressed premise in Cleanthes' use of analogy — that the kind of God to be discerned in the application of analogy must be suitably divine — Cleanthes' appeal to common sense is not mere sophistry designed to extricate himself from a difficult situation. To be sure, Philo has strengthened the analogy used by Cleanthes, drawing conclusions which should be acceptable in the terms made explicit by the Argument from Design as initially presented. To resist this development involves putting an external check on the logic of analogy. But, suggests Cleanthes, common sense does just that. He thinks there is something in us which will reject Philo's arguments as resting on comparisons *too* common, *too* familiar. Implicit in Cleanthes' appeal to common sense is the assumption that the idea of a vegetative or generative demiurge will stimulate no religious interest in us. In spite of the very fanciful conceptions imagined by Philo, a strengthened use of analogy can yield nothing but *ordinary* conclusions. And such knowledge offers us nothing. Philo's cosmogony is religiously uninteresting; it can have no extraordinary edge which would influence our self-understanding and behavior. In this respect Cleanthes' objection to Philo parallels Cleanthes' rejection of Demea's radical transcendence. Both develop conceptions of the relationship of the ordinary and extraordinary which undermine our capacity for religious interest. Demea defeats our religious aspirations with the supposition of radical discontinuity. Philo takes the drama out

38. *Dialogues,* p. 48.

of the Argument from Design by accentuating similarity. Just as Cleanthes rejects Demea's position, so also he sets aside Philo's approach. For Cleanthes, the convergence suggested by analogy — and necessary to defeat Demea's other-worldly transcendence — has a common sense limit, and that limit is the difference which must be preserved between the ordinary and extraordinary in order to sustain the allure of transcendence.

Though not sophistical, Cleanthes' appeal to common sense is problematic. Cleanthes assumes that it is a rational, or at least human, interest which checks Philo's revised Argument from Design. Hume gives no direct explanation of Cleanthes' supposition of a religious or common sense interest in difference. However, a peculiar juxtaposition emerges in Part XII which helps to highlight the nature of Cleanthes' position. At the outset of this enigmatic conclusion to the *Dialogues*, Philo claims that he presupposes the very principle of common sense which Cleanthes has used to excuse himself from the troublingly persuasive arguments from vegetation and generation. Philo comments, "I can never . . . corrupt the principle of any man of common sense . . ." when deploying such arguments.[39] It would seem that Philo joins Cleanthes in assuming that we are conditioned by a certain religious sense which trumps the reductive and purely immanent pressures of arguments from analogy. However, as the discussion develops, this apparent agreement disintegrates.

Thinking Philo to have joined him, Cleanthes gives his first clear account of the wider religious role of the Argument from Design. He notes, "One great advantage of the principle of theism is that it is the only system of cosmogony which can be rendered intelligible and complete, and yet can throughout preserve a strong analogy to what we every day see and experience in the world."[40] Here Cleanthes admits what his appeal to common sense presupposes. We have certain religious sentiments — a common interest in the uncommon — which stand independent of the Argument from Design. In view of this independent sense, arguments become useful not as proofs, but serve instead as strategies for articulating a religious vision that can actively enroll our ordinary lives by accentuating the rational threads connecting common epistemic practices to the extraordinary realm of our religious aspirations. For our purposes the actual content of Cleanthes' "intelligible and complete" cosmogony is not sig-

39. *Dialogues*, p. 77.
40. *Dialogues*, p. 79.

nificant. What is decisive and what defines Cleanthes' overall position is his dual commitment: on the one hand to the extraordinary, even as this leads him to overreach the possibilities of analogy and presuppose a new organ of knowledge, a common (religious) sense; on the other hand, to the ordinary as embodied in our capacity to present rational, persuasive analogies which really do matter, even if they are underdetermined by the actual evidence.

As we have seen, Philo exploits Cleanthes' commitment to the ordinary when he observes that if we accentuate the similarity between human and divine fabrication, then we might conclude that the cosmos was created by many gods, since all humanly constructed complex machines are planned and built by many individuals. Or we might conclude that the Great Artificer is a cosmic spider, generating the order of the cosmos by instinct. But if conclusions such as these emerge, then Cleanthes has failed to secure what he sought at the outset, genuinely religious knowledge. For our religious interest is oriented towards the uncommon, the extraordinary, the suprahuman. The problem is that analogy, when grounded in ordinary experience, leads away from just such a realm.[41] The argumentative practice which Cleanthes adopts has exactly the opposite valence from our aspirations for transcendence, and for that reason Philo's arguments cannot help but succeed.

The contrast with Philo is telling. Where Cleanthes holds out the promise of religiously significant affirmations, Philo concludes with what may fairly be called a more accurate use of analogy: "That the cause or causes of order in the universe probably bear some remote analogy to human intelligence." And although his conclusion here retreats from the radical possibilities of his earlier attempt to strengthen analogy in arguments from vegetation and generation, the upshot is the same. This affirmation, accurate though it may be, "affords no inference that affects human life, or can be the source of any action or forebearance."[42] In this respect, and in spite of the fact that he is affirming a proposition as true, Philo's position retains the ethos of the commitment to immanence. Though the possibility of transcendent knowledge is admitted, it has no

41. Hume is very much alive to this inevitable tendency in analogy, and Philo's affirmation in Part XII, of the by then ennervated Argument from Design, testifies to the way in which analogy is unable to sustain a religiously interesting form of transcendence.
42. Both quotes from *Dialogues,* p. 88.

practical significance. Religious arguments may be entertained, but their consequences are so remote and inconclusive that they will not disturb Philo's skeptical tranquillity. The self remains firmly planted in the everyday world. The ordinary triumphs by default.

Or does it? Philo concludes his remarks in Part XII with a surprising return to the position which he articulated at the outset of the *Dialogues*. Echoing his initial alliance with the departed Demea, Philo declares that the self with no capacity to discern religiously significant principles under the guidance of reason "will fly to revealed truth with the greatest avidity."[43] So it would seem that Philo reverses himself. He seems to be advocating an acceptance of traditional Christian doctrine. However, the reversal is not as dramatic as it would seem. His ultimate location is unimportant. Whether firmly enmeshed in the inconclusive world of common experience, admitting only of the vague possibility of a deity which might have certain characteristics, or "flying" to the encompassing realm of revealed truth, Philo is offering a form of monistic closure and with it a view of epistemic futility, and with this closure and futility, a fundamentally passive view of human destiny. We should not be surprised, then, that Cleanthes' rejection of Philo has been the same as his polemic against Demea. In both cases, Cleanthes senses that the pure immanence of skepticism and the radical transcendence of dogmatism cannot sustain our religious interest in genuine pilgrimage. A purely ordinary world, just like a purely extraordinary world, is incapable of stimulating us to engage religious questions. In the purely ordinary world, we find nothing which would make the kind of *difference* necessary to motivate striving for transcendence. For the strictly extraordinary, our destiny is so remote from the ordinary conditions of existence that it becomes impossible to see how an aspiration might influence or direct *our* inescapably human aspirations for transcendence. Thus, Cleanthes feels himself threatened in essentially the same way by both Demea and Philo. Both seek to quell the aspiration for transcendence with the purities of either the ordinary or extraordinary. Neither will admit the combination of the ordinary and extraordinary which Cleanthes presupposes is the necessary condition for the enlivening and dynamic project of transcendence.

43. *Dialogues,* p. 89.

5. The Appeal of Impurity

HUME'S LETTERS and his other works on religion make clear the fact that he found the unstable mixture of the ordinary and extraordinary problematic at best. Philo is rightly seen by most readers as the dialectical victor in the *Dialogues,* and the notion that his paper-thin "affirmation" of the divine in Part XII stimulates no religious interest would, most likely, be taken as a compliment by Hume. So much the worse, Hume might be heard concluding, for our putative religious interest. However, Philo's surprising alliance with the departed Demea at the very end of the *Dialogues* raises interesting questions. Perhaps this peculiar twist reveals doubts in Hume's own mind about whether Philo's dialectical triumph can be sustained in practice. Perhaps, though driven from the scene by argument, Demea finds his way back again, and inevitably so. Perhaps Philo's account of "flying to revealed truth" expresses Hume's sense of the impotence of skepticism, a dangerous weakness, for though doubt is capable of destruction, it knows no satisfaction and leaves the field open to all manner of "incomprehensibilities" and any number of "unspeakable" possibilities. Perhaps, in this respect, the victorious Philo is a "traitor" to his skeptical reasoning in precisely the way Hume must have realized that we all are "traitors" to the limits of reason, lusting as we do after something more, aspiring for the extraordinary which, if unattainable by reason, we will embrace by some other means. Is it possible, then, that given Philo's final leap to concurrence with Demea and his suggestion of a flight from skeptical ordinariness to the heights of radical transcendence, Cleanthes might ironically have lost the arguments but won the debate? Could we not say that, though his arguments are defeated, at least he was more forthright insofar as he took seriously at the very outset our desire for flight rather than leaving it until the end as an unintelligible leap? Could Cleanthes have come nearest to the truth, at least descriptively, when he would not foresake our persistent (if perhaps irrational) efforts to reach for a margin of transcendence? Was he, perhaps, more humane when he tried to give these efforts towards transcendence both a workable basis in ordinary life and a satisfying goal in the extraordinary possibility of knowledge of God? Might we conclude, then, that the final words uttered by Pamphilus which draw the *Dialogues* to a close, words which proclaim Cleanthes victor, are not concessions to an intolerant age, but rather speak the mind of the author — an author who, though he honored the deliverances of his rational inquiries, was no worshipper of reason, and who was very much aware of the fact that the truth about human beings contained much that could not be explained?

Interesting though these questions are, they cannot here be our concern. The success of Cleanthes' position may be decisive from an apologetical point of view, but we have not yet reached the point where we know the Christian position regarding transcendence well enough to defend it. What is important at this stage is simply an appreciation of the basic features of Cleanthes' view. We may shift our concentration away from reason (as we will in the next chapters); however, the balancing act between the ordinary and the extraordinary which Cleanthes tries to sustain will carry through all our considerations, since this balancing act is central to the Christian view of transcendence. On the one hand, the emphasis falls on the this-worldly drama of human life. On the other hand, our expectations are other-worldly; they involve extraordinary new possibilities. Both commitments are entailed in the affirmation of a God who matters. The God of Demea cannot matter for us because such a God so transcends this life that belief has no practical consequences. Philo's God does not matter because we are grounded in the ordinary and our minds can detect so little about such a being that belief also has no practical consequences. For Cleanthes, neither approach provides a vision ambitious enough to make a difference or comprehensible enough to matter. Against the radical alternatives represented by Demea and Philo, Cleanthes reaches for a mixed or amphibious vision — transcendence within the knowable world of human existence. Human existence must be characterized by the possibility of genuine commerce between the human and divine.

The vision of a difference between the ordinary and extraordinary which is real enough to resist Philo's collapse into immanence, but not so rigid as to lead to Demea's position of radical transcendence, is conceptually unstable. The Christian view is always afflicted by projects of purification: "Away with the idols created by the hands of mere mortals! Away with conceptions of the divine formed by finite minds! Anthropomorphites all! You claim to desire the extraordinary, but you know nothing other than corruption. Give up your partial transcendence. The only way to preserve the extraordinary is to abjure of the ordinary." As if strident foes such as these are not problem enough, the Christian view of transcendence must also deal with more reasonable voices from the opposite corner: "Come now, be honest, if it is the ordinary that you seek to preserve against the tirades of my other-worldly companion, then surely you cannot hold onto the extraordinary. The words of transcendence which you preserve are like a child's comforting stuffed animal, a useful talisman, reassuring but of no real power. It is time now to grow up. You must follow through to the logical conclusion. Break with radical transcendence and embrace the ordinary as your true and final home. Give up your silly, fantastical aspirations. Let go of your bootstraps. You tire of constructing the rational scaffolding of partial transcendence, and I tire of deploying the inevitable arguments of demolition. Come now, soberly accept your fate and just be human."

Whatever "victory" for Cleanthes we might conjure out of the enigmatic conclusion to the *Dialogues* offered by Hume, it is not the sort of triumph that will overcome the arguments from above and below. There is no way to silence the sirens of pure immanence and radical transcendence. The conceptual purity of their views and the fact that this purity accentuates legitimate dimensions of the amphibious view which we are attributing to Christianity ensures continuing appeal. Henri de Lubac gives effective expression to the way in which Philo and Demea are at work continuously within the Christian vision of transcendence:

> We should like a truth that was not abstract and a reality that was not empirical; a fact that had all the characteristics of a law; a verification which would at the same time be an answer to a need; an ideal satisfaction which was also a real possession. . . . But in fact we always swing between the two poles. The duality is insurmountable to our divided nature. Unity always slips the grasp of that compound of sense and reason. No sooner do we think we have seized it on the wing than it falls apart. . . . What in fact we attain is not merely, because of its inadequacy, the starting point of a new inquiry: it is always a fresh disillusionment.[44]

The pressures of immanent ordinariness and the extraordinary possibilities of radical transcendence cannot be eliminated. They are endemic to the Christian attempt to affirm both the ordinary and the extraordinary. Thus, the questions inevitably arise: Why struggle to sustain this unstable vision of transcendence? Why set out on a path which leads only to one disillusionment after another? Why commit Christianity to this strange middle position? To answer these questions requires us to grasp the centrality of the amphibious view for the Christian way of thinking.

44. *The Discovery of God* (New York: P. J. Kenedy & Sons, 1960), pp. 47-48.

CHAPTER TWO

❧ ❧

Rahner's Inheritance

The sole work and deed of universal freedom is death, *a death too which has no inner significance or filling, for what is neglected is the empty point of the absolutely free self. It is thus the coldest and meanest of deaths, with no more significance than cutting off a head of cabbage.*

G. W. F. Hegel, *Phenomenology of Spirit*, para. 590

U P TO THIS POINT, my bold appeal to the "Christian frame of reference" or the "Christian way of thinking" has floated safely above the diverse and sometimes conflicting theological voices which constitute the Christian tradition. This cavalier use of the term "Christian" has been, I think, a justifiable risk in the direction of generalization. Sometimes we must speak carelessly in order to speak clearly. Nonetheless, now that I have established the broad context of the debate about the possibilities of transcendence, the time has come to take another and very different kind of risk. Instead of floating above the theological conversation of the tradition, I will submerge our inquiry in the very rich detail of a single theological vision, that of Karl Rahner. Through this immersion I hope to provide a sense of why the Christian view of transcendence so consistently frames a view of our situation as amphibious.

Throughout, my concern with Karl Rahner is interpretive in the strongest sense. That is to say, my desire is to use Rahner's thought as a guide through some of the complex twists and turns of the Christian tradition in order to gain a deeper understanding of our place amidst the ordinary and extraordi-

nary. This rules out a narrow enumeration of Rahner's direct pronouncements on the nature of existence and the possibilities of transcendence. In
Rahner's view, we would fail as readers if we limit ourselves to these writings
and fall back upon a "compendium" approach which catalogues and com-
pares without probing the deeper rationale for his positions. Consider
Rahner's own description of his study of Aquinas: "Our procedure here
cannot be that of gathering together everything and anything that Thomas
ever said, as though all were of equal weight, and organizing it to some
extrinsic principle."[1] Instead, when a historical figure is engaged with an eye
toward insight, analysis is pursued with an emphasis on the underlying
patterns of thought. The interpreter is forced to think with the author. As
Rahner understands this approach, such an inquiry "joins [with the author]
in looking at the matter itself."[2] And the "matter itself," to the degree that it
is in fact a potent and compelling force, has its own trajectory, its own
directive and illuminative power.

My treatment of Rahner's theology seeks precisely this form — to enter
with the author into an examination of the "matter itself," the relationship
of that which is near at hand, the familiar and ordinary, to that which is our
final purpose, the elusive and extraordinary. To do so, we must join Rahner
in considering the classical loci of the relationship between nature and grace,
as well as the status of philosophy, theological method, the Christian form
of life, and the reality of mystery. These efforts to think with and through
Rahner cannot be easily separated, for they fuel each other both in principle
and in practice. But the effort will, I hope, be repaid by a deeper and more
explicitly theological understanding of the role of the ordinary and extraordinary. Through that understanding we may well come to a clearer conception of the logic of Christian transcendence.

An objection emerges to this plan of action. It dwells upon Rahner's
unequivocal Roman Catholic identity. This *Roman* Catholic identity would
seem to be parochial rather than representative. Such parochial idiosyncrasy
seems all the more the case when the emphasis falls on the question of the
relationship between nature and grace, for this locus is distinctive to the
Catholic scholastic tradition, and its terms and concerns have fallen into
disrepute. In light of my interest in mixed transcendence, this parochial
Catholic approach would seem inherently uncongenial to amphibious exis-

1. *Spirit in the World* (New York: Herder and Herder, 1968), p. xlix.
2. *Spirit*, p. xlix.

tence. After all, does the Catholic tradition not "solve" the problem of the ordinary and the extraordinary by appeals to supernatural and infallible authority? Does Catholicism not overcome the oddity of amphibious existence with a form of Demea's radical transcendence in which the sacramental community is separate from ordinary life? Is Catholicism not, then, the religion of the triumphant Church rather than the pilgrim self? To answer these questions and meet this objection, we must consider the nineteenth century background which formed Rahner's inheritance.

1. Clearing Away a False Antithesis

ONE ASSUMPTION which shapes our assessment of Rahner's background is a contrast between Protestantism and Catholicism. Such a contrast tends to paint the differences between Protestantism and Catholicism as social and political. Protestantism is regarded as the religion of individuality, emphasizing the role of the individual believer in relation to God. In light of this emphasis, the antithesis assumes that Protestantism advocates a type of transcendence which devalues the institutions and structures of society, including the ecclesiastical structures of the church, and exalts the individual as a solitary soul on the pilgrimage to the extraordinary. Political consequences are taken to follow. Individual rights emerge to protect this pilgrimage from heteronomous contamination. Various freedoms are defended to give full rein to the potency and sanctity of the individual. Equality triumphs over now irrelevant worldly distinctions, and democratic participation is justified in light of the fact that all individuals possess an unmediated relation to God.

Over and against this vision of transcendence, Catholicism is seen as a religion of community which tends toward an absorption of the self into the tradition. Whether conceived of juridically, sacramentally, or sociologically, the Church serves as the decisive locus of the interaction of the ordinary and extraordinary. The succession of bishops in Rome functions so as to guarantee the presence of the extraordinary, and the individual must obey the authority of the ancient tradition and its representatives. This obedience carries forward into all human affairs. Given the location of the extraordinary in the structures and authority of the church, the Christian life becomes training in submission. The direction of pilgrimage is into the brute givenness of the tradition.

Early in the nineteenth century, Schleiermacher put the matter clearly. He characterizes the antithesis between Protestantism and Catholicism as essentially a matter of the role of community in the believer's relation to Christ. "The antithesis," he observes, "may be conceived thus: the former makes the individual's relation to the Church dependent on his relation to Christ, while the latter contrariwise makes the individual's relation to Christ dependent on his relation to the Church."[3] As a Protestant, Schleiermacher assumes that the drama of transcendence takes place within the individual. The Catholic, in contrast, must depend wholly upon the institutional Church as the mediator of his relationship to the divine. Thus does a modern interpretation of the Reformation propagate characteristic dichotomies.

Although Schleiermacher's formulation contains some important insights into the real differences between Protestantism and Catholicism, nineteenth century intellectual culture raised this dichotomy to the level of an eternal verity. Polemicists both Catholic and Protestant adopted the antithesis.[4] For example, the Catholic Restorationists continually appealed to this antithesis to explain the terrors of modernity. Untethered from altar and throne, they argued, the "liberated" Protestant individual gives full expression to a furious selfishness and destructive pride. In this way, all the ills which afflicted the nineteenth century — wars, riots, industrial exploitation, unemployment, poverty and autocracy — were laid at the door of the

---

3. *The Christian Faith,* 2nd ed., §24.

4. In fairness to Schleiermacher, in the polemical use of this antithesis the subtlety of his assessment of the essential difference between Catholicism and Protestantism was neglected. For Schleiermacher, the contrast between the two is not one of experience opposed to authority, feeling opposed to obedience. Instead, his theory of religion presupposes that all religious forms are grounded in the feeling of absolute dependence. The difference between Catholicism and Protestantism is to be found in the way in which the respective traditions shape that feeling. For the Protestant, the New Testament picture of the man Jesus stimulates and structures the feeling of absolute dependence. In contrast, for the Catholic, the tradition of the Church serves as the point of orientation. Thus, Schleiermacher sees the doctrinal divide of the Reformation as irrelevant. The particular shape of the feeling of absolute dependence in Catholicism is alien to Protestantism, but "we feel we may leave it standing alongside of our own religion, as being of a different formation but equally Christian" (§24). As a result, the significance of the antithesis between Catholic and Protestant is not polemical. Instead, it serves the heuristic "task of bringing to clear consciousness the distinctive character of Protestantism" (§24). The goal of dogmatics, then, is not a defense of the apostolicity of Protestantism. Rather, the purpose is to render an authentic account of the "spirit of Protestantism." Indeed, far from attacking Catholicism, Schleiermacher thanks Catholicism for providing a clear antithesis to his own self-consciousness as a Protestant. For the depth of the antithesis helps "to provide against un-Protestant matter creeping in unawares" (§24).

Reformation.[5] As late as the middle of this century, an eminent Catholic theologian could deploy the contrast to good apologetical effect. Henri Daniel-Rops writes, in the Catholic vision "a communal notion is opposed to Protestant individualism, the principle of authority to anarchism."[6]

In light of this consensus, how can we possibly appeal to Rahner, theologian of the Church of Community, as a defender of the amphibious vision? He might, perhaps, echo Cleanthes' odd mixture of the ordinary and the extraordinary, but only in order to place the Church rather than the self into the role of amphibian. In the end, surely the Roman Catholic view is allied with Demea and seeks to absorb the individual into the Christian community. Therefore, my agenda seems to misrepresent Rahner: either he does not defend the reality of amphibious personal or individual existence in any significant way, or he is not a true Roman Catholic theologian.

Should we, however, accept the assumption that a contrast between individual and community defines Protestant and Catholic identity? One factor in the dominance of this contrast is that the Protestant point of reference in the antithesis has been characterized by theological liberalism. Here we find a fully individualized conception of the relation of the ordinary to the extraordinary. For the theological liberal, our relationship to the extraordinary in focused solely on the subjective powers of the self. The surrounding world of ordinary life does not constitute our ultimate destiny unless validated by the inner promptings of the spirit. This, then,

---

5. Faced with the ascendency of a liberal Protestant *reductio* of Catholicism to the moral and political crimes of intolerance and persecution, the translator of Joseph de Maistre's unrepentant defense of the Spanish Inquisition prefaced de Maistre's *Letters on the Spanish Inquisition* with this blanket condemnation: "Innovation, the daring offspring of selfishness and pride, flung a worse than Gothic gloom over an immense portion of the European mind, and, cooperating with the prince of darkness, cruelly sought to establish the empire of libertinism by emancipating the tyrannic passions of the human heart from the mild and light yoke of the cross" ([Boston: Patrick Donahoe, Catholic Bookseller, 1843], p. 3). Linking the innovations of the Reformation to the innovations of the Enlightenment, the young Lamennais issues a similar assessment. Of modern man, he writes, "His reason — that is his law, his truth, his justice. To seek to impose on him an obligation he has not previously imposed on himself by his own thought and will is to violate the most sacred of his rights. . . . Hence, no legislation, no power is possible, and the same doctrine which produces anarchy in men's minds further produces an irremediable political anarchy and overturns the bases of human society" (*Oeuvres complètes* [Paris, 1836-37], vol. IX, p. 17, cited from Lukes, *Individualism* [Oxford: Basil Blackwell, 1973], p. 5).

6. *The Catholic Reformation,* vol. I (New York: Image Books, 1963), p. 143.

is clearly at odds with a Catholic vision of the indispensibility of the Church. Liberal Protestantism was well aware of this clear conflict and exploited the contrast to show the putative authoritarian and (worse!) anti-modern character of Catholicism.

In his widely popular set of lectures *What is Christianity?* Adolph von Harnack provides an illustration of this attack upon Catholicism, an attack all the more significant because of the wide cultural authority he wielded as a historian of Christianity. Harnack does give credit to Catholicism for nurturing a legitimate Christian sensibility, but his overriding assessment is that Catholicism has in recent centuries been a reactionary force out of step with modernity. Where Harnack values purity, sincerity, and freedom, Roman Catholicism is characterized by artifice, hypocrisy, and hierarchy. Thus, Harnack states what he assumes is obvious to his listeners, "The time, of course, is well since past since it was a leader; on the contrary, it is now a drag."[7]

In contrast, Protestantism is the key to progress. For Harnack, Luther is decisive because he rejected hierarchy, external authority, and ritualism, substituting the equality of the priesthood of all believers, the spiritual freedom of justification by faith, and the unadorned integrity of the Word. Of course, Harnack's responsibilities as a historian force him to admit that Luther was not an univocal spokesman for progress. He notes Luther's "failures" — his affirmations of trinitarian and Christological dogmas, his concern for theological precision, his reliance upon the authority of scripture, and his defense of the apostolic integrity of the Reformation Churches. These "failures" involve, notably, "a risk of Protestantism becoming a sorry double of Catholicism."[8] Such a regression would be sorry because Protestantism will always lack the baroque splendor of Rome. Further, Luther's affirmations of dogmatic, scriptural, and ecclesiological commitments call into question the pure "inwardness and spirituality" which Harnack takes to be the essence of Protestantism and, of course, Christianity as well.

Harnack's two-step with Luther on this score is not surprising. For from the orthodox Protestant perspective, the easy individual-versus-community contrast is never possible. The Reformation's actual debate with Catholicism was conducted in terms of the question of who might claim true allegiance to the Apostolic community. Protestant apologists sought to

7. Harnack, *What is Christianity?* (New York: Harper & Row, 1957), p. 247.
8. *What is Christianity?* p. 247.

uncover Papist innovations, and Roman polemicists focused on the Protestant break with tradition. Owen Chadwick characterizes the typical controversy as follows:

> Where do you find in the tenth century or the thirteenth, cried the Counter-Reformation, your teaching about the Eucharist or about justification by faith alone? The extant documents are rare and infrequent, answered the reforming defence, because the others were suppressed and destroyed by persecuting and un-Christian inquisitors. Where do you find in the second or third century, cried the Protestants in riposte, your teaching about transubstantiation or papal authority? The extant documents are rare and infrequent, replied the conservative defense, because the others were suppressed and destroyed by persecuting and un-Christian emperors. Can you find your faith in the Bible or the Fathers? asked the Protestants. Was there a thousand years at which God winked? retorted the Counter-Reformation. "Though we, or an angel from heaven, preach any other gospel unto you than you have received, let him be accursed" — how can the Council of Trent justify itself before the Pauline text? "Upon this rock I will build my Church and the gates of hell shall not prevail against it" — how can the Lutherans and the Reformed justify themselves before this text when *ex hypothesi* their doctrine vanished out of historical record for centuries?[9]

The debates addressed what was to be considered true and Godly doctrine and polity. These questions, to be sure, entailed differing assessments of the role of the individual believer as interpreter of scripture and tradition, as well as the ultimate significance of ecclesiastical structures, but the question of the priority of one or the other was not at the center of the issue in any direct or immediate way.

Such a question could not become central because of the distinctively communalistic features of traditional Protestantism. Much of the focus of the generations of and after the Reformation was on achieving confessional clarity and unity, evidencing a strong concern for the communal dimensions of the life of faith. Further, at the practical level, Protestantism developed a great sensitivity to the requirements of religious training for children, and Puritan communities have, as a result, come under some

---

9. *From Bousseut to Newman,* 2nd ed. (Cambridge: Cambridge University Press, 1987), pp. 2-3.

heavy fire as harbingers of totalitarian society — hardly a criticism to be
leveling against the denomination of putative individualists! Finally and
perhaps most significantly, Protestant orthodoxy sustained a consensus
about biblical interpretation which insured a widely shared *Weltanschauung*
based upon the scriptural stories.

Thus, when we consider a study such as Max Weber's *The Protestant
Ethic and the Spirit of Capitalism,* we must recognize that the ideal type
which emerges, the individual set adrift in a de-sacralized world without
essential attachment to others, may not do justice to the real texture of
the Reformation frame of reference. The point is not to deny that Protestantism has an individualistic emphasis. Here, one may well find Weber's
account of the spiritual loneliness of the Protestant soul convincing. Of
the Doctrine of Predestination, he writes:

> In its extreme inhumanity this doctrine must above all have had one
> consequence for the life of a generation which surrendered to its mag-
> nificent consistency. That was a feeling of unprecedented loneliness of
> the single individual. In what was for the man of the age of the Refor-
> mation the most important thing in life, his eternal salvation, he was
> forced to follow his path alone to meet a destiny which had been decreed
> for him from eternity. No one could help him.[10]

Theologically, Weber is certainly correct. The doctrine of predestination
expresses the sense in which the Christian vision of salvation involves a
decisive disruption of the ordinary. God's decree emerges according to its
own logic and for its own purposes, quite independent of ordinary human
affairs. In this sense, the extraordinary can never be collapsed into the
ordinary. It challenges and judges, drawing the self out along a previously
unseen and unexpected path.

Foregoing the supposed "inhumanity" of such a vision, the question
remains, is this vision of a self forced to follow the path out of ordinary
life and into the extraordinary decrees of eternity uniquely Prostestant or
Calvinist? Perhaps the doctrine of predestination is but one of a number
of theological expressions of a deeper Christian consensus about the destiny
of the self in grace. Indeed, can *any* affirmation of prevenient grace help
but render the soul lonely, or at least lonely until he realizes that it is not
the case that *no* one can help him, but that there is only One who is,

10. *The Protestant Ethic and the Spirit of Capitalism* (New York: Scribners, 1958), p. 104.

finally, there for him? Can an affirmation of the purely and truly extraordinary offer of grace yield anything but a challenge to ordinary life, a challenge which could often alienate us from our common assumptions about what really and finally "counts"? These questions cut across Reformation divisions. The disposition of the Calvinist before the eternal decree need be no less lonely than that of the Catholic receiving the Holy Sacrament who feels an utter solitude before God as the wafer touches his tongue. Surely this is a moment when "no one could help him."[11] For both, Christian identity involves an engagement with something extraordinary — an eternal decree, a sacrament — which calls into question the familiar form of ordinary life and demands movement down a new path. After all, the dynamism of amphibious transcendence entails a moment of alienation even as it affirms the ongoing significance of the ordinary.

In part, the ways in which the Christian understanding of the role of grace cuts across the distinction between Protestant individualism and Catholic communalism have remained unexamined by observers such as Schleiermacher and Weber because just as Protestant liberalism emphasizes to an extreme certain individualistic features, at the same time nineteenth century Catholicism gave new and heavy weight to communal and institutional factors. The subtle patterns of Protestant community formation and the latent individualism of Catholic piety are virtually invisible in the shadow of the overwhelming institutional presence of the Roman Catholic Church as it has developed over the last two hundred years. Yet, if we entertain the development of nineteenth century Catholicism within the framework of the tensive interplay of the ordinary and extraordinary which we have seen unfolded for us by Hume in his *Dialogues,* this subtlety need not remain invisible. For the drama and appeal of the story of that development, and the crucial background for Rahner's own theological

11. Again, Harnack the historian finds himself raising subtleties which Harnack the Protestant apologist denies. He observes that Catholicism is not a monolithic tradition of communal ascendency. He points out "the 'complexio oppositorum' which we see in Western Catholicism: the Church of rites, of law, of politics, or world-domination, and the Church in which a highly individual, delicate, sublimated sense and doctrine of sin and grace is brought into play" (*What is Christianity?* pp. 260-61). Of course, Harnack finds this tension a mark of the failure of Roman Catholicism to reach the purity of Protestantism ("this has been impossible from the beginning . . ."). We need not draw such a conclusion in order to affirm his insight into the "internal tension and conflict" which marks Roman Catholicism, and Protestantism as well.

vision, is nineteenth century Catholicism's search for the voice of Clean-thes. It is a voice that would preserve the oddity of the Christian view of transcendence from the too often inhumane purities of the modern point of view, a voice which Rahner sought to make his own.

2. The Austerity of Liberty

THE DECISIVE EVENT marking the birth of the modern Catholicism that formed Rahner is the French Revolution. Until the rise of communism in the twentieth century, in the minds of ecclesiastical authorities the policies and practices of the revolutionary and imperial governments in France would be the determining antithesis to the Roman Catholic thesis. And this *Auseinandersetzung* was not unwarranted. The Revolution was anti-clerical, and at its extreme, profoundly anti-Christian. Monastic properties were confiscated, seminaries closed, ecclesiastical principalities abolished, and the governance of the Church clotted. At the height of revolutionary fervor, the utopian delusions of Robespierre resulted in grand festivals designed to supercede Christianity by creating a new civil religion.[12] To this end, in 1793, the cathedral of Notre Dame was reconsecrated to the worship of Reason.

More dangerous to the Church than Robespierre's delusions was the sustained attempt to reconstruct French society on strictly secular prin-ciples. Rousseauian doctrines of the indivisible nature of sovereignty led to the suppression of all corporations independent of the state. This, of course, included the Church. Tithes were eliminated in 1792, and soon thereafter priests who had not taken an oath of allegiance to the Consti-tution were forbidden to celebrate on pain of execution. The suppression of Christianity led a wholesale reconstruction of the basic features of society. A new revolutionary calendar and a new revolutionary ten day week were decreed, complete with an alternative Sabbath, the *decadi*.

12. The efforts to eclipse Christianity culminated in the June 1794 "Festival of the Supreme Being." Focusing on a creed newly invented by Robespierre, its grand scale, mass participation and thinly disguised service of the social order would look comic were it not for the chilling parallels to Nuremberg. To be sure, Robespierre sought a form of devotion which annihilated historical particularity while Hitler sought the deification of German historical particularity. However, in both cases the desire for a religious alternative to the perceived political and social limitations of Christianity was the same.

Worship was prohibited on Sundays, and there were even regulations to prevent the sale of fish on Fridays. The desire was to destroy the influence of the worn-out (and counter-revolutionary) institutions of the *ancien régime,* and to build in their place a new form of life centered around *la patrie.*

Lurid and difficult though the revolutionary times were, they were initially restricted to France itself. Not so in the era of Napoleonic conquest and reform. The Napoleonic era was not nearly so overt in its opposition to the Church. Napoleon established a rapprochement with Rome in order to add legitimacy to his coronation as Emperor (which he eschewed at the last moment by crowning himself!). But this rapprochement seemed, in the end, to be but a fulfillment of Napolean's famous dictum that all one need do to win the people's favor is give them something new every two months. In the end, the successes of his regime both on the battlefield and in the realm of social administration cut very deeply into the fabric of pre-modern Catholicism. The Revolution had been a time of radicalism and turmoil, but its lack of sustained effort in any one direction meant that though its violence was spectacular and far-reaching, the basic structures of pre-Revolutionary society retained the capacity to revive. Shattered though they were, pre-Revolutionary social patterns and expectations endured in large part because the revolutionary acts of destruction were not followed by a consistent and workable reconstruction of society on fundamentally different principles. People needed more than a new calendar to give their lives a new point of orientation.

This task was left to the relative stability of the Napoleonic era. Under Napoleon's tutelage, the idealism of the Revolution was muted, or at least harnessed to deeper imperatives. These imperatives were martial, economic, and institutional. The military and bureaucratic machines of the Napoleonic era made demands upon France and her conquered lands which effected a social revolution that was more sustained and more substantive than that of the 1790s. The revolutionaries had condemned the social forms of the feudal world as archaic and, worse, inefficient. But they had not fully developed the new bureaucracy to administer the law, regulate the economy, and oversee civil life. And more importantly, in both their philosophical abstractions and bitter factional fighting, they failed to inspire Frenchmen with some sense of the value, power, and significance of the new secular state. This Napoleon could do.

In the transformations of the Napoleonic era, to the degree that the

Church was tolerated at all, it was relegated to the periphery of the new order. As a result, not only was the economic wealth and political power of the Church radically curtailed, but its power over men's hearts and minds was diminished. An alternative social structure emerged which required neither the practical assistance (in 1792 registration of births, marriages, and deaths was transferred to civil authorities) nor the ideological legitimation from the Church. For the first time in over a millennium, one could pursue a life of honor and respect in society with no relation to Christianity.

The emergence of an alternative form of life sufficient unto itself and independent of Christianity was no quirk of history. It was implicit in the core ideals of both the Revolution in particular and modernity in general. A State unencumbered by Christianity was recognized by Rousseau as a prerequisite for liberty. Rousseau saw that the theocentric principle undid the unity of ancient society. For him, this loss of unity is the cause of our present social unhappiness. He writes: "Jesus came to establish a spiritual kingdom; this kingdom, by separating the theological system from the political, meant that the state ceased to be a unity, and it caused those intestine divisions which have never ceased to disturb Christian peoples."[13] Rousseau recognizes that Christianity points beyond without leaving the world behind, dividing the allegiance of the soul between the temporal and the spiritual realms. As a consequence, Christianity generates tensions within the concept of authority by propounding a mixture of the ordinary and extraordinary. Christianity takes seriously the political realm, but at the same time will not vest full significance in the State. Thus, the Christian is a worldling who will neither yield full allegiance to the temporal, nor withdraw into the purely spiritual.

The solution to this unruly mixture and its social disturbances is to unify the political and theological; the legitimation of the social order must flow from the social order itself.[14] Robespierre expressed this unity in his apotheosis of the Mob and the dictates of its violence. Napoleon exploited precisely the same quest for unity by proposing that his person

13. *The Social Contract,* Bk. IV, Chpt. VIII.

14. I am strongly influenced in my view of the fundamental imperatives of revolutionary France, as well as modern society, by the complex and stimulating study of the relation of the political and theological in Eric Voeglin's *The New Science of Politics* (Chicago: The University of Chicago Press, 1952).

was the absolute expression of the will of the people, and to no small extent he made that unity a fact by creating a modern civil state out of the need to sustain the success of his military exploits. In both cases, human destiny was absorbed into the State, and in both cases we see a practical echo of Rousseau's unitary view of sovereignty. As Rousseau advises in *The Social Contract,* "[Citizens'] relations among themselves should be as limited, and relations with the entire body as extensive, as possible, in order that each citizen shall be at the same time perfectly independent of all his fellow citizens and excessively dependent upon the republic."[15] The vision is a political form of radical transcendence. We should shed the attachments and encumbrances of ordinary life — family, friends, guilds, and associations — and intensify our attachment to the singular and extraordinary sovereignty of the People.[16] To the extent that the French world at the turn of the century pursued this vision, Christianity was, in principle, a threat to both the task of Revolution and the imperatives of Conquest. For though Christianity expresses some clear sympathies with the redemptive aspirations of Rousseau's *The Social Contract,* the mixed Christian ideal of transcendence resists the purity (and finality) of the solution.

In spite of the effectiveness of the Napoleonic reforms and the rather remarkable ability of France to achieve a high degree of unity and vitality as a military state, the road was rocky. Rousseau was only too right when he observed in *The Government of Poland* that "the laws of liberty are a thousand times more austere than the yokes of tyrants." Benjamin Constant, sometime friend, though more frequently critic, of the Revolution, gives voice to the sense of alienation which was the result of the bold experiment in modern statehood. In *De la religion,* he writes:

> Man looks on a world deprived of protective powers . . . all the previous grounds for his exaltation no longer support him. . . . He is alone on the earth, which will engulf him. On this earth the different generations succeed each other, transitory, fortuitous, and isolated . . . what will man do, without memory and without hope, placed between an aban-

15. Book II, Chapter 12.

16. On its face, the supreme importance of public sovereignty would seem to conflict with classical Rousseauian themes of personal freedom and private conscience. For an attempt to interpret this and other oppositions in Rousseau's thought, see Judith N. Sklar, "Rousseau's Images of Authority," *American Political Science Review,* 1964, pp. 919-32.

doned past and a future closed before him? . . . He has spurned the
support with which his predecessors encompassed him and is reduced
to dependence on his own strength.[17]

The Napoleonic Code, beneficial in its reform of archaic and unjust legal
procedures; the military state, successful in bringing glory to France; the
bureaucratic apparatus, efficient in raising funds and distributing social
benefits; even the new Imperial superstructure, complete with imposing
monuments and regal ostentation — separately and in sum this new order
was unable to give the fullness of life to modern society. Indeed, Constant's
observation calls into question any attempt to set aside the history and
texture of ordinary life in pursuit of an extraordinary revolutionary future.
Human life, it would seem, cannot breathe at the great heights of the
abstractions of Liberty, Equality, and Fraternity. We need aspirations which
can be pursued at the lower altitudes of the ordinary associations, practices,
and traditions of daily life. Otherwise, the radical transcendence implied
in revolutionary aspirations becomes as irrelevant as Demea's incomprehensible deity, and, without even feeling the change, we find ourselves
living Philo's pure immanence, devoid of aspiration even as we continue
to mouth the platitudes of transcendence.

What is decisive for our study is that as the Catholic Church began to
respond to the heavy yoke of revolutionary liberty in the nineteenth
century, it specifically set aside the solution which sought to repudiate the
novelty of modernity with an equal and opposite emphasis on tradition.
To be sure, attacks upon all things new were frequently expressed in the
Catholic reaction against the revolutionary forces of modernity. But
nineteenth century Roman Catholicism was unwilling to let go of the
"conflicts" of the Christian vision of transcendence, so aptly identified by
Rousseau, in the interests of a clearly reactionary traditionalism. The
Roman Catholic Church refused to pursue anti-modernism to the logical
conclusion of denying that our destiny has any extraordinary potential
independent of the customs and traditions of the inherited world. Roman
Catholicism refused to combat Rousseau's absorption of the citizen into
the State with an equal and opposite absorption of the believer into the
Church. Instead of trying to inject its own concerns into the modern vision

17. Quoted from Guy H. Dodge, *Benjamin Constant's Philosophy of Liberalism* (Chapel
Hill: The University of North Carolina Press, 1980), pp. 31-32.

of transcendence, Roman Catholicism sustained Christianity's mixed or amphibious vision of transcendence, and this provided a much more compelling alternative.

3. The Challenge of Renewal

THE CATHOLIC RESTORATIONISTS were among the voices raised against the liberal ideals of the Revolution. Contributing to the antithesis between Protestantism and Catholicism, they coined the term "Political Protestantism" to describe the ideological substratum of the spiritual poverty which, they argued, followed the demise of the *ancien régime.* Impressed by the frightening ability of men to destroy the old without being able to create anything to take its place, Joseph de Maistre and Louis de Bonald led a frontal assault on the revolutionary conception of human flourishing. The enemy of both social peace and religious truth, they argued, was an unfounded faith in the individual and his powers of critical reasoning. This self, they argued, was constrained only by the slender reed of reason. Just as Protestantism had severed the link between the believer and the authority of the Church, modern culture had dissolved the intimate bond between the individual and the vivifying context of tradition.

For the Restorationists, relief was sought in a renewed sense of the universal, impersonal, and divine truth of both social customs and religious institutions. Having every reason to believe that the now independent self would falter at the slightest difficulty and fall to the least temptation, the Restorationists tried to resuscitate the authoritative powers of social and ecclesiastical tradition. Only a restoration of altar and throne could save modernity from the formless ambiguities and potential willful violence of rational autonomy.

The Traditionalism promoted by the Restorationists was eventually rejected by the Catholic Church. Bonald's and Maistre's complete denial of the capacities of reason, a move made in the interest of heightening the contrast between the truth of tradition and the falsity of individual judgment, was unacceptable to a tradition which affirmed the basic goodness of creation and consistently defended the limited, but honorable, powers of the intellect. Catholicism recognized that the Restorationists were, in a way, trying to back themselves into the unity of the political and theological which Rousseau so envied in the ancients. Just as Rousseau envisioned an absorption into the infallible General Will, the Restorationists proposed an absorption of the self into an infallible Church. Both were collective forms of pure transcendence which readily make alliances with pure immanence.

But the authority of the Church could not be defended by simple contrasts between the individual and community or between reason and tradition, only to be settled in favor of the latter in both cases. As Rousseau had noted, such strategies of transcendence are disrupted by the theonomous vision of Christianity which gives rise to a "conflict" between the temporal and spiritual. The authority of the throne, and with it the patrimony of communal tradition which includes Christianity, could not be equated with the deeper imperatives of the altar. Catholicism, of course, insists that there is commerce between these spheres, but it consistently swerves away from the close harmony which both Rousseau and his bitterest enemies so often desire. In this respect, the clear solution to the challenges of revolution which the Restorationists proposed could never be accepted. The matter could not be so easily resolved.[18]

In spite of the official Catholic rejection of the Restorationist approach, the basic worries about the corrosive forces of modern culture continued. Both the individualism engendered by an emphasis on the final authority of individual judgment and the possibility of a fully secular bureaucratic state troubled ecclesiatical authorities. These concerns lay at the heart of Pius IX's rejection of liberalism and democracy, and although the direct path charted by Bonald and Maistre was barred, in the second half of the nineteenth century key developments went a long way toward addressing modernity and forming the distinctively Roman Catholic response.[19]

18. The Catholic rejection of Restorationism raises a number of issues for contemporary critics of the Enlightenment. Maistre and Bonald denounce Enlightenment individualism in terms which are now echoed in the current literature. Both focus on the epistemic authority which the Enlightenment vests in the individual, an authority which threatens to destroy all objective forms of morality and social cohesion. If the nineteenth century saw in Restorationist thought a hidden allegiance with revolutionary thought — the tempting absolute distinction between individual and community with one or the other as saviour, as well as the equally tempting conflation of the theological and the political — then how much more should we see the same in contemporary polemics. For those who join this criticism of the Enlightenment to the service of Christianity, a detailed study of their forgotten brethren, the Restorationists, is very much in order.

19. A concise expression of this rejection was formulated by Cardinal Manning after

The most obvious development was the adoption of ultramontanism as dogma at the First Vatican Council in 1871. In the broadest of strokes, the challenge of individualism was met by a potent claim on behalf of ecclesiastical authority; and the threat of secular society was met by the evolution of an institutional Church which could compete with the State for a significant portion of its members' varied commitments.[20] However, by itself the doctrine of papal infallibility could not have created the imposing institution which was to become the *Roman* Catholic Church. Toward such a purpose the liturgy was reformed in order to insure conformity with the Roman rite. New seminaries and colleges were established in Rome, and the Society of Jesus was revived. All these developments favored the rise of a centralized and unified authority within the Church. Locally, this development was fostered by the renewal of clerically led pilgrimages. Pius Associations were established at mid-century and became bastions of lay support for ultramontanism. These, as well as complex developments in popular piety, all contributed to the process of institutional renewal and growth, of which the dogma of infallibility was but a signal expression. Finally, a whole system of reflection which aided and expressed the character of the modern Catholic Church was developed. Neo-scholasticism triumphed as *the* language of ecclesiastical reflection.

We become victims of Whig history if we think that the Thomistic revival of the nineteenth century was imposed from on high by Leo XIII's

---

Vatican I: "Modern liberalism is the caesarism of the State. Liberalism seems to believe that 'all power in heaven and earth' was given to it — that the State has power to define the limits of its own jurisdiction and also those of the Church. Sin and blasphemy against God is forgiven to Man. There is only one unpardonable sin. Anyone who speaks against the omnipotence of the State is disloyal and shall never be forgiven" (quoted from Harold Laski, *The Problems of Sovereignty* [New Haven: Yale University Press, 1917], p. 196).

20. Evidence of the effectiveness of the Roman Catholic counter to the forces of modern society can be found in the firestorms of controversy which surrounded the revival of Roman Catholicism in England. Even in this comparatively stable and mild of nations in the nineteenth century, the potent challenge of the renewed Church was felt as a definite threat. The Roman Catholic Relief Act of 1829 was the occasion of much breast-beating about the loyalty of Catholic citizens to the English crown. The re-establishment of the Roman hierarchy in 1851 energized fears about foreign domination. And the doctrine of papal infallibility promulgated at the First Vatican Council created one final outburst of public indignation against the efforts of the Church to consolidate its powers as a counterweight to the State.

Aeterni Patris (1879). We might well agree that the intellectual shape of modern Catholicism, like the thought forms of the earlier Church, was influenced and shaped in response to secular and political realities. However, to claim that the ideological character of modern Catholicism, i.e., neo-scholasticism in its many forms and expressions, was strictly subordinated to non-theological, non-philosophical concerns vastly underestimates not only the spiritual needs of the nineteenth and early twentieth centuries, but the real strengths of the "Pian" Church as well, especially its intellectual fruits. We cannot underestimate the intellectual appeal of the neo-scholastic revival of the Thomistic synthesis. This appeal can be broken down into two basic elements: (1) the philosophical power of Thomism, and (2) the capacity of neo-scholasticism to secure the supernatural status of the institutional Church.

In large part, the philosophical appeal of Thomism stemmed from the theological poverty of modern alternatives. As foreshadowed by Cleanthes' philosophical difficulties in the *Dialogues Concerning Natural Religion,* the options of the Enlightenment were developing in directions which became increasingly antithetical to theological reflection. Left-wing Hegelianism and Comtean positivism threatened to reduce Christianity to the social phenomenon of "religion." Within this purely immanent framework, theology becomes anthropology. Other options seemed mired in either a sterile rationalism or moralism, or involved riding the tiger of romanticism. In contrast, Thomistic thought stood as an alternative which could circumvent the various dangers and impasses which were thought to characterize modern philosophy.

This held true for a number of philosophical issues. For example, post-Cartesian philosophy assumed a dichotomy between the thinking subject and the world of nature. *Res cogitans* is utterly separate from *res extensa.* However, the rising historical consciousness of the late eighteenth and early nineteenth century, as well as the nascent human sciences, brought home the decisive formative influence of what Descartes had taken to be the inanimate, merely geometrical reality of the external world. As a result, this dualism became problematic, and not a few scientists, historians, and philosophers sought to overcome it by showing how human subjectivity is grounded in cultural, historical, and biological forces.

Against the background of this play of radical dualisms and potentially equally radical monisms, Thomism seemed to circumvent the problem. In philosophy of mind, Thomas was interpreted as promoting a middle way between an unduly immanent and reductive empiricism and an overly ambitious and dualistic rationalism. Etienne Gilson expresses a typical assessment. For Thomas, "though the proper *object* of the intellect is the sensible, the proper *function* is to disengage the intelligible from the sensible."[21] In this view, Thomism takes seriously what Descartes consigns to the status of mere extension, but it does not fall into the reductive trap of materialism. Like the human person as a whole, the cognitive process is embedded in the created order, but just as the person is destined for more, so also cognition reaches beyond the material to grasp eternal truths. In this and a number of other ways, nineteenth century Thomists were able to present an alternative to the theologically unsuitable philosophies which came to dominate secular and Protestant thought. As a result, Catholic scholars found themselves able to pursue an apologetical program without direct implication in the problematic tendencies of the modern intellectual milieu.[22]

However, Thomism provided more than an alternative to modern philosophy. Its second and historically more important function was to provide modern Catholicism with a form of theological analysis which affirmed the significance of the Church without reducing theology to ecclesiology, as the Restorationists such as Bonald and Maistre threatened to do. The key to this possibility and the crux of Rahner's relation to neo-scholasticism is the distinction between nature and the supernatural. As we shall see in the next chapter, the distinction in neo-scholasticism was clear and firm, and performed an important theological task. A relationship between nature and grace was affirmed, and this closed off the many attempts to translate Catholic anti-modernism into a systematic repudiation of worldliness. Yet, on the whole, this was not a point of great emphasis. Instead, in an intellectual environment which threatened to collapse all interpretation and explanation into naturalistic and anthropological categories, the strict distinction between nature and grace safeguarded the integrity and gratuity of the supernatural.

21. *The Philosophy of St. Thomas* (St. Louis: B. Herder Book Co., 1929), p. 356.
22. One perspicuous example of how the Thomistic system provided this intellectual insulation for Catholic scholars is the way in which the "problem of history" was simply irrelevant to neo-scholastics. It could be ignored not because Thomas offered a solution, as he appeared to do for certain anthropological and epistemological problems, but because the issue is largely alien to the philosophical framework of scholastic thought.

The result of this conception of grace was that when expressing the decisive importance of God's action on our behalf, the field of linguistic options was restricted. Organic metaphors, historical or developmental analogies — in fact, any description which implied an essential continuity between nature and the supernatural — was inadmissable. As a consequence, non-ontological and juridical analogies were dominant.[23] Without any essential relationship between worldly life and the life of grace and glory, emphasis fell on the mediating structures: institutions, rites, and laws which were, so the neo-scholastics argued, established by God and vested in the Church. The relationship between the ontologically separated world of nature and offer of grace came to be expressed institutionally.

George Lindbeck describes this view: "One major Catholic way of picturing the Church within the classical framework is as a hierarchical institution of salvation, hovering between heaven and earth, half human and half divine, which funnels down from the supernatural level the grace which individual men need in order to rise upward." The division of nature and the supernatural as two distinct ontological realms virtually compelled the development of this vision of the Church which, in turn, "leads to an immense exaltation of the ecclesiastical institution."[24] Only an enduring institutional reality with juridical legitimacy could bridge the gap between nature and the supernatural. As a result, basic questions of Christian identity came to rest in seemingly arcane debates about the conditions under which the grace-funneling functions of the Church were "valid."

In addition to structuring its theology around a basic dichotomy which seemed to require a "funnel" for grace or an "ark" to convey souls to their hoped-for destination, neo-scholasticism also provided a philosophical language which gave special weight to descriptions of the Church. It was as if the ontological void created by the division of nature and grace was refilled by an account of the founding and preservation of the Church.

23. In this and a number of other respects, neo-scholasticism shares features of Reformation theology. The forensic doctrine of justification as well as the fiduciary models employed by the federal theologians were motivated by concerns very much alive in neo-scholasticism. Some account must be given of the decisive action by God on our behalf which does not bring grace under the control of human powers and capacities. The models and images used to describe the relationship between the human and the divine must express the "artificiality" of our relationship with God.

24. *The Future of Roman Catholic Theology* (Philadelphia: Fortress Press, 1970), p. 29.

Here neo-scholasticism enjoyed its closest connection to the growing prestige of science. Using the language of causality, the neo-scholastics were able to marshal to their aid the form, if not the content, of scientific explanation.

Consider, for example, a neo-scholastic account of the Church. The divine acts of institution are highlighted and secured as indisputable. Christ is thus shown to be the efficient cause of the Church. With this as a point of departure, neo-scholasticism could then exploit the other features of Aristotelian causality to enumerate the essential features of the Church, trading on the centrality of efficient causality in the increasingly influential world-view of the natural sciences while, at the same time, avoiding a reduction of Christianity to the Church. The Church is causally, but not organically or "essentially," indispensable. Francis Schüssler Fiorenza summarizes the basic moves:

> The material cause is the plurality of believers that make up the Church, whereas the final cause is the sanctification of these members that are now enabled to participate in eternal life. The formal and efficient causes, however, are the most significant categories for understanding the Church. The formal cause — here defined as hierarchy — is that which makes the Church into Church, for only the hierarchical structure provided the formal unity which makes it into a specific entity.[25]

The enduring formative power of Christ's founding acts remains and is made efficacious by the institutional continuity and juridical legitimacy of the Roman Church. Hence, a characteristic concern for clear lines of authority (reaching, in principle, back to Christ) is exhibited, along with anxieties about "validity" which arise out of the inevitable ambiguities regarding the former.

The appeal of this institutionalism was not simply political. Vatican officials surely encouraged any number of political initiatives, rightly perceiving that they would enhance Roman authority over consciences precisely at the time when the Papacy's temporal power was nearly extinguished. However, will to power and "reasons of state" are not sufficient explanations. The perspectives afforded by the Frankfurt School's numerous criticisms of instrumental and bureaucratic rationality should make clear to us how attractive the Church became as a counterweight to the

25. *Foundational Theology* (New York: Crossroad, 1984), p. 73.

modern state. As in recent decades in Poland, allegiance to the Church constituted an act of political defiance. As the organic identities of feudal society were dissolved in the acids of revolutions both political and industrial, the Roman Church grew in response, representing a clearly demarcated institutional identity which could compete with Army, Factory and Civil Service for the souls of the newly created "masses."[26] Rome, unlike Protestant national churches, could go toe-to-toe with the powerful forces of modernity. In this respect, the legacy of Pius IX may be far more positive than "progressive" historians are willing to admit.[27]

In addition to the purely cultural need for an alternative to the modern imperatives of nationalism, militarism and economic growth, the kind of institutionalism which came to define nineteenth century Catholicism addressed a central spiritual need. The antinomies of modern philosophy were a felt reality as well as an intellectual dilemma. The emergence of the social and historical sciences, as well as the complete secularization of the natural sciences, presumed a dichotomy between the ordinary and extraordinary which was as profound as anything found in the neo-scholastic nature/grace scheme. Moreover, this division was all the more powerful for being a practical principle of intellectual life rather than a theological abstraction. Outside the institutional Church the mediating strategies of the nineteenth century either failed to persuade, or if they persuaded, failed to move. The most successful strategy saw the supernatural as immanent within the laws of natural development or the potentialities of the intellect, but its very success threatened to render grace otiose. More than mediation

26. For a detailed study of Catholicism's response and growth as an alternative social identity in post-revolutionary society, see Jonathan Sperber, *Popular Catholicism in Nineteenth Century Germany* (Princeton: Princeton University Press, 1984). Although Sperber restricts his study to western Germany, the basic dynamics of institutional development have substantive overlap with other regions of Catholic influence.

27. Reflecting on the imperatives of Christian living, Rahner gives voice to the insight that in forward-looking, utopian ages, the traditionalist is often the true radical. He writes, "Perhaps we could go so far as to say that today the real non-conformists are to be found in the group of those who have a genuine, calm and loving respect for the religious heritage of the past and the experience of past generations" (*TI* XVI, p. 164). This insight is confirmed by the fact that the popularity of the Roman Catholic Church in historically Catholic regions of the former Soviet Union and Eastern Europe was directly related to the archaism of its liturgical forms. Participation in the very "backwardness" of the traditional forms was construed as a counter-cultural act of dissent against the dominant "progressive" ideology.

was necessary. Some account, some hope of the real presence of grace in this world, a world which was every day becoming more and more "naturalized," was an absolute necessity.

The kind of institutionalism which came to define nineteenth century Catholicism responded precisely to this need. The "Pian Monolith" did not die away as the last words of the sermon were spoken. It did not suffer from the nebulous and often uncertain inner promptings of the Spirit. Within the walls of the neo-scholastic Church, the extraordinary offer of grace was felt as a palpably real possibility in an ever more ordinary world. For a long time, this great ark of grace did not even suffer from the process of historical-critical decomposition which very nearly destroyed the Protestant rock of stability, the Bible. As a result, for a believer now far removed from ancient Palestine, the "formal causality" of the Church, its hierarchical, authoritative structure, was able to preserve Christ's decisive act on our behalf, the act which could make the extraordinary offer of grace a possibility as a "specific entity," something accessible, real and efficacious for those who populate this now exclusively natural and ordinary world.

4. The Dynamic Self Empowered

OPPOSITION BREEDS EXAGGERATION. Although the Restorationists' radical vision was repudiated by the nineteenth century Church, the overwhelming emphasis placed upon the institution throughout the Pian era gave the spirit, if not the letter, of the age a Restorationist complexion. The integrity and dignity of the ordinary self was affirmed, but it was rarely linked to the drama of grace. The view of amphibious transcendence was not repudiated by the purities of either pure immanence or radical transcendence. Instead, it was undermined by an increasingly formal relationship across a rigid separation. Life, then, became divided rather than amphibious, and as a result, alienated rather than dynamic. The institutional solution to the fundamental religious problems of the nineteenth century slid the Church away from the dynamism of a real relation between the extraordinary and ordinary life, and moved Catholicism toward a ghetto in which the characteristic tensions and challenges of amphibious existence could not arise.

Some, however, could speak boldly without distortion. John Henry Newman stands among the most interesting advocates of the potential dynamism of the Christian ideal of transcendence. More than any other figure of his generation, Newman understood the nature of the threat which modernity posed to religion in general and Christianity in particular. Jeremy Bentham's utilitarianism was then entering into a close alliance with science as the structuring network of principles which were beginning to gain control over men's minds and to guide English public life. Although this reformist sensibility was but a pale reflection of the full-blown zeal of continental activists, the upshot was a series of Acts of Parliment which began to erode the traditional ways of Church life.

The events which precipitated the Oxford Movement and thus set Newman's critical intellect and powerful pen into motion seem minor to the modern mind. In Ireland ten Anglican bishoprics were suppressed. This was the occasion of John Keble's inflammatory sermon, "National Apostasy," the catalyst which brought together the like-minded souls who initiated the *Tracts of the Times.* The Irish bishoprics soon receded into the background, and deeper issues emerged. At stake, thought Newman, looking retrospectively in his *Apologia,* was the existence of a rock upon which to found the life of faith. The men of the Oxford Movement concluded that "neither Puritanism nor Liberalism has any permanent inheritance within her."[28] Both, and especially the latter, would deny us our birthright. Neither, and especially not the latter, could speak the word of grace.[29]

A later crucible of ecclesiastical conflict was a dispute over subscription to the 39 Articles upon matriculation to Oxford. More than simply the prerogatives of the Church of England were at stake for Newman. The party demanding the abolition of subscription supported its position by a distinction between the "divine facts" of revelation and the doctrines of the Church, which were but human interpretations and thus not binding upon consciences. Responding to the pamphlet which articulated this position and reflecting on the implications of its crucial supporting distinction, Newman wrote, "While I respect the tone of piety which the pamphlet displays, I dare not trust myself to put on paper my feelings about the principles contained in it; tending as they do, in my opinion, to make a shipwreck of Christian faith."[30] For Newman, the saving truths

28. *Apologia pro vita sua* (New York: Longmans, Green and Co., 1947), p. 93.

29. For a particularly trenchant criticism see Newman's note on Liberalism in the *Apologia,* pp. 259-69.

30. *Apologia,* p. 58.

of Christianity must have a living, tangible, and public reality. The extraordinary offer of grace must have a real solidarity with ordinary life.

In general, the Liberal Camp, thought Newman, gave free rein to an "aggressive, capricious, untrustworthy intellect" which led to the "suicidal excesses" of critical reason.[31] It was a dynamism that could have no home, a self which would neither respect the authority of the extraordinary nor rest in the modest integrity of the ordinary. The Oxford Movement was, in large part, a reaction to this difficulty. It grew out of "the spiritual awakenings of spiritual wants" — most particularly the want of some tangible experience of grace, an assurance that the particular dimensions of this life can be filled with the highest significance. To this end, Newman associated his thought with the romantic poetry of Wordsworth, the literary influence of Scott, and the speculative thought of Coleridge. In each case, these great figures grasped for a vision, a feeling, an imaginative world of medieval spectacle or natural beauty which could give spiritual substance to modern life, which could articulate the interpenetration of the extraordinary in the ordinary. Newman thought them kindred souls, though plowing the wrong fields. For Newman, the obvious answer to the spiritual need for a real, practical, and tangible home for the soul was the Church: her rites and rubrics, her history and tradition. The Church held out this promise, and with his comrades Newman spent a great deal of energy mining the veins of the tradition in order to replace "the dry and superficial character of the religious teaching and the literature of the last generation."[32] In every case the result was an infusion of palpably tangible new material into the life of the nineteenth century English Church.

Eventually, Newman came to believe that the dry and superficial character of his adversaries, both puritanical and liberal, flowed from more than the flaws of the previous generation. As he pressed his theological studies forward, the entire English experiment came to be impugned with what he came to see as the fatal mistake of Protestantism. Proving himself to be as much a Rationalist as Romantic, the combination of which makes him so attractive as both a thinker and a man, Newman maneuvered himself into a position where he was forced to admit that there are only two spiritual options — Atheism or Catholicism. Only the continuous institutional reality of the Church under the guidance of the bishop of

31. *Apologia,* p. 223.
32. *Apologia,* p. 88.

Rome could provide the tangible reality of grace which might tame the "suicidal excesses" of critical thought. Only the very real, and in a sense quite ordinary, fact of authority — something which permeates human life even as modern liberalism tries to deny it — could give worldly significance to the extraordinary offer of grace. To this end, Newman concluded that infallibility "is a supereminent prodigious power sent upon earth to encounter and master a great evil." In Rome and what it represented, Newman found a historical, institutional, and sacramental force powerful enough to subdue reason's tendency to abstract itself away from the particularities which nourish it. The emerging "Pian Monolith" was a tangible reality ample enough, thought Newman, to sustain any soul in the pilgrimage of Christian transcendence.

However, Newman's move to Rome did not entail a rejection of the dynamic powers of the intellect which can be so troublesome to authority. In this way, Newman avoids equating the extraordinary with the institutional, and thus distances himself from the complacency of the ghetto. From his beginnings with the *Tracts,* he saw the Church and her hierarchical authority as the stimulating, vivifying context for the most fruitful and productive exercise of the mind. The Church serves the real purposes of the very human person whom modernity sought to glorify. In an extended passage in the *Apologia,* he gives a description of the interplay of the particularized authority of the Church and the critical and abstractive powers of the intellect:

It is the custom with Protestant writers to consider that, whereas there are two great principles in action in the history of religion, Authority and Private Judgment, they have all the Private Judgment to themselves, and we have the full inheritance and the super-incumbent oppression of Authority. But this is not so; it is the vast Catholic body itself, and it only, which affords an arena for both combatants in that awful, never-dying duel. It is necessary for the very life of religion, viewed in its large operations and its history, that the warfare should be incessantly carried on. Every exercise of Infallibility is brought out into act by an intense and varied operation of Reason, both as its ally and as its opponent, and provokes again, when it has done its work, a re-action of Reason against it; and, as in a civil polity the State exists and endures by means of rivalry and collision, the encroachments and defeats of its constituent parts, so in like manner Catholic Christendom is no simple exhibition of religious absolutism, but presents a continuous picture of Authority and Private Judgment alternately advancing and retreating as the ebb and flow of the tide; — it is a vast assemblage of human beings with willful intellects and wild passions, brought together into one by the beauty and the Majesty of a Superhuman Power, — into what may be called a large reformatory or training-school, not as if into a hospital or into a prison, not in order to be sent to bed, not to be buried alive, but (if I may change my metaphor) brought together as if into some moral factory, for the melting, refining, and moulding, by an incessant, noisy process, of the raw material of human nature, so excellent, so dangerous, so capable of divine purposes.[33]

The insight which pervades is Augustinian. Left to our own devices, we spend our inheritance foolishly. As disordered beings, we must be *re*formed if we are to become capable of the divine purposes to which we are ordained.

What is interesting about Newman is that he espouses a goal of transcendence which cuts across characteristically modern distinctions between reason and authority, subjective and objective, experience and proposition. The saving truths of the gospel come in the ordinary forms of human speech. In relation to these truths the individual cannot go it alone. Authority is the necessary context. Nonetheless, the authority of the Church is not a purely extraordinary power which annihilates our innate cognitive powers. The authority of the tradition presupposes, and even needs, private judgment. In that sense, and in spite of real conflict, the subjective role of the self does not finally clash with the objective role of authority. Our inner purpose as rational creatures requires, even as it resists, the context of an objective and external demand upon us. Nor are "saving truths" miraculous propositions which are to be stored in a place separate from ordinary life. The great doctrines of Christianity are formulated precisely so that the believer might enter into the fray of debate. Dogma is meant to be defended in the marketplace.

In each instance, the extraordinary possibilities which Newman has in mind are a reformatory for the self. He explicitly rules out the dualistic metaphors of hospital and prison. The transformation which he envisions does not involve a denial of the natural self. Instead, he proposes decisive change. The metaphor of the factory highlights the commitment to real

33. *Apologia,* p. 229.

dynamism. We enter into the Christian community in raw form. In that community we are melted by repentance, refined by scripture, and moulded by the holy sacrament into a new form. We emerge as the very human persons we are. We are still constituted by the same willing, thinking, desiring nature. However, we have been formed in a decisively new way, such that the ordinary stuff of life takes on an extraordinary new purpose. In this metaphor we find the amphibious vision which restrained, even as it did not always guide, Catholicism's reaction to modernity.

CHAPTER THREE

⁂ ⁂

Nature and Grace

There is really only one question, whether God wanted to be merely the eternally distant one, or whether beyond that he wanted to be the innermost center of our existence in free grace and self-communication.[1]

ANY NUMBER of factors separate Rahner from Newman. Rahner was educated within the Roman Catholic milieu, whereas Newman transferred his allegiance in mid-life. And more importantly, in Rahner's day, that milieu had taken on its solid, hardened shape, while for Newman, the modern institutional Church was still in a state of flux and change, enjoying all the promise of possibility. This difference is concretized by their respective places with reference to the modernist crisis at the turn of the century. More than any other event, the Church's confrontation with modernism revealed the limitations of the institutional renewal which attracted those such as Newman, and it cut deeply into any optimistic assessment of the life of reason in the Church. After the decree condemning modernism (*Lamentabili,* 1907), the Church no longer held the initiative; its energies were turned toward the defensive, and in this context Rahner's epithet "Pian Monolith" takes on its pejorative meaning.

Rahner's attitude toward the Pian Monolith, however, is complex. He is often claimed as an ally in the attack on "manual theology" and the educational approach which was associated with it. This is certainly appro-

1. *Foundations of Christian Faith* (New York: Crossroad, 1978), p. 12.

85

priate; Rahner led the way in criticizing the "culture" of neo-scholasticism. "Today," he wrote in 1962, "the situation of the Church is still — unhappily is still — one of defensiveness against the powers that threaten her from without, a unity indeed, but a kind of unity that belongs to a faction closed in upon itself so that watchwords are needed to enter it."[2] These are hard words, but many would, and did, say worse about pre–Vatican II Catholic intellectual and ecclesiastical life. That milieu, intimated Rahner and proclaimed others, stifled the Spirit. This charge was developed in a number of different ways: its existentially arid theology stifled personal renewal; its dualism of nature and grace rendered social and historical factors mute; its ghetto mentality failed to respect the broader culture's demand for intellectual honesty; its ecclesiastical structures disenfranchised the laity; its disciplinary mechanism compromised religious consciences.

From the perspective of the middle of the twentieth century, the strengths of nineteenth century Catholicism became its weakness. The authority which Newman identified as a vivifying force came to be seen as stultifying. The baroque splendor of the Church which enchanted Newman and gave a color and texture to life, which he felt altogether absent from the putatively rational world of utility and social progress, became increasingly anachronistic. But most importantly, the Roman Catholic capacity to provide a form of life that was sufficiently independent of and separate from modernity became in the eyes of an increasing number of theologians a spiritual liability. What once created the divisions (which so troubled Rousseau) into which might be poured the possibilities of grace, threatened to become a permanent dichotomy between the worldly and the spiritual. The objectivity of grace rightfully preserved from the aggressive purposes of modern society slowly turned into a remote, carefully guarded treasure, detached from natural life. This tendency was labeled "extrinsicist." At root it involved the alienation of the extraordinary from the ordinary, which, as Cleanthes had warned, condemns the extraordinary to irrelevance.

Extremes often create their own reactions. Opposites attract, and the radical transcendence implied in the extrinsicist view of late neo-scholasticism has managed to create its own counter-image.[3] For many Catholic

2. *Theological Investigations* (hereafter *TI*) VII, p. 76.
3. As Henri de Lubac warns, a theology built upon controversy all too often absorbs into its own fabric the dye of the error it seeks to refute. Lubac observes, "The very conflict between two doctrines nearly always implies certain presuppositions common to

theologians, the dichotomizing tendencies are taken as sufficient reason to repudiate the neo-scholastic tradition *in toto*. Over and against nineteenth century defense of grace a new agenda emerges. To fight the rigid extrinsicism of the old view, an equal and opposite "new" intrinsicism is proposed. This intrinsicism can be quite subtle, as we shall see, but more often than not the reaction to the failures of neo-scholasticism engenders an opposite commitment to immanence which would please Philo were it not so happy-minded and naive.[4]

---

both. Whence arises [a] danger for the theologian who makes too many concessions to the demands of controversy. In his struggle against heresy he always sees the question, more or less, willingly or unwillingly, from the heretic's point of view. He often accepts questions in the form in which the heretic propounds them, so that without sharing the error he may make implicit concessions to his opponents, which are the more serious the more explicit are his refutations" (*Catholicism* [San Francisco: Ignatius Press, 1988]). Although neo-scholasticism is by no means a "heresy," as we shall see, we may well wonder about de Lubac's own ability to avoid "implicit concessions" to neo-scholasticism, especially regarding the role of "human nature" in a theological explication of our relation to God. However, the theologies of experience and subjectivity which populate the contemporary Catholic scene require little deliberation. These theologies are governed almost exclusively by a rejection of "extrinsicism" (often by repudiating the authority of the Magisterium), and as such, "liberal" Catholic theologies do little more than turn the problem of extrinsicism on its head.

4. The Catholic moral theologian Timothy O'Connell provides a fine example of this approach. He recommends a new vision of Catholic morality by juxtaposing the "bad" extrinsicist view with the "good" affirmation of divine immanence. Contrary to the other-worldliness he finds in traditional moral theologies, O'Connell rightly observes that Christianity teaches that "God is to be found in the fabric of human life, in the midst of those tasks and projects that constitute the human experience," or, in other words, "salvation is a human event." However, this radical presence of God in the midst of human life is given an exclusively immanent spin. The observation that God saves us *as* human beings slides toward the proposition that salvation *is* being human. For O'Connell, "It is precisely by struggling with [our] humanness that the Church succeeds in proclaiming the Gospel and sharing the gift of salvation." The upshot for moral theology is an "unconditional humanism." Thus, O'Connell concludes, "Be Human! No more and no less! Christ permits it, and Christ demands it. That is the central conviction of the Christian faith" (all quotes from *Principles for a Catholic Morality* [San Francisco: Harper & Row, 1990], pp. 32-35).

Two features of O'Connell's theology (and the theologies of many other liberal Catholics) disguise the exclusively immanent emphasis. First, the "unconditional humanism" is a legitimate moment in the Christian vision. Indeed, it is a necessary moment over and against the other-worldliness of radical transcendence, and as such, it tethers the drama of amphibious existence to the center of human life. Second, appeals to "the human" are

At his best, Rahner does not conduct his thinking at the level of easy condemnations and even easier solutions.[5] The extrinsicist dangers of

rarely found untinctured with a number of appeals to the "spiritual dimension," "transcendence," "limit experiences" or "conscience" — all concepts which seem to refute that charge of "mere immanence." However, behind the veil of such language is O'Connell's "No more and no less!" And unfortunately, it is the reductive "No more!" which is the defining feature and controlling emphasis. Under such pressure, the necessary moment of "unconditional humanism" becomes the singular and exclusive message of Christianity. Many interpreters regard this conclusion as a natural extension of Rahner's theological project. I intend to argue otherwise.

5. Rahner is not always at his best. In *A New Christology* (with Wilhelm Thusing [New York: Seabury Press, 1980]), he tries to provide a "searching Christology" which will show the "fit" between human transcendence and "Jesus and his self-understanding." The goal of this apologetic strategy is to reject a false dichotomy between unbelief and "mythological credulity." For Rahner, there must be a middle way. Our beliefs about Christ must be, in some decisive sense, integral to our beliefs about life as a whole (and in that respect, "credulous" without being "mythological"), otherwise faith cannot save *us*. However, in pursuit of this admirable goal — a goal implied by the notion of amphibious existence — Rahner begins to transform the "fit" into an equation of human transcendence with the "essential" content of Jesus' life, death, and resurrection. He winds up saying that the mystery of God *is* the mystery of human existence. In a dogmatic context, the line of implication clearly runs from the mystery of God in Christ to humanity, and the identity statement is the *terminus ad quem* of both theological reflection *(reductio in mysterium)* and human destiny *(theosis)*. However, coming as it does in the context of an apologetical exercise, the line of implication is inevitably reversed. The identity statement comes to function as the *terminus a quo* of the theological project. Humanity defines God in Christ. Not surprisingly, then, Rahner is led towards a strikingly reductive definition of faith: "Whoever accepts his humanity completely (and this is inexpressibly difficult to do; it is doubtful whether any of us really ever does it) has at the same time accepted the Son of Man" (p. 17). The platitudes about how "difficult" the mystery of humanity is to accept do not hide the logic of the definition. The reversal is obvious: the mystery of man *is* the mystery of God.

Coming to grips with these moments in Rahner' work is important if we are to assess both his theological achievement as a whole and his influence on contemporary Catholic theology. Neither is directly necessary for the purposes of this study. However, some observations are, perhaps, in order, if only to prepare the reader for further comments in the notes.

Theological achievement is multifaceted. A theologian can attract our appreciation in at least three ways, through: (1) a fecund creativity of expression, (2) evangelical effectiveness, and (3) systematic integrity. (1) It is quite possible for us to find Rahner lacking in the type of biblical imagination we find, for example, in Barth, or the culturally expansive innovation in theological concepts and language so characteristic of von Balthasar. In this respect, Rahner is very much a child of neo-scholasticism. His expressions are technical

neo-scholasticism were not sufficient to condemn it, and the solutions
to the problems created by this view certainly could not be found by
propounding a "corrective" emphasis upon the immanent or intrinsic
presence of grace. Instead, Rahner confronts the matter at its most basic
level: What is the proper understanding of the Christian view of transcendence? To answer that question he reexamines the central systematic
commitment of post-Tridentine Roman Catholic theology, the relationship between nature and grace.[6] And when he finishes with this reex-
amination he produces a striking affirmation of the basic theological logic

---

and he gives the impression of speaking "scientifically" even as he tries to evoke the reality
and depth of mystery. (2) With respect to the second possible appeal, as my observations
above indicate, we might also have serious reservations about the evangelical effectiveness
of Rahner's work as a whole. To a great extent, such effectiveness depends upon correctly
assessing the needs of the moment. Rahner tends to view the spiritlessness of our technological age and a consequent skepticism about religious matters as the greatest challenge
to Christianity. As a result, he views any gain for "transcendence" and "mystery" as a gain
for Christianity — we may worry later about reforming the experience of the Other with
the normative *symbolis* of Christianity. This assumption is, I think, both wrong and naive.
The twentieth century has shocked Enlightenment culture precisely by its powerful (and
seemingly ever more destructive) attachments to the "mysteries" of party, wealth, nation
and leader. Contrary to the assumption that Rahner makes over and over again in his
apologetic writing, unbelief is far less of a problem than "mythological credulities" of all
different and distinctively modern sorts. As a result, the relationship between the mystery
of man and the mystery of God is absolutely crucial from the very outset. The modern
self does not so much need to be convinced of the possibility of mystery as to be directed
toward the *saving* Mystery. (3) This leaves the third and final feature, systematic integrity.
Systematic genius (if I may use the word) does not necessarily mean cramming everything
into a single conceptual framework. Quite the contrary, the integrity of systematic thought
depends upon a willingness to follow the warp and woof of Christian doctrine, to allow
points of emphases to shade off into one another without reductive pressures which distort.
Here, seeing and showing difficulties is, perhaps, more important than "solving" them. In
this respect, I think Rahner's achievement is unquestionable, and not surprisingly, this
aspect of his thought, his ability to give conceptually sophisticated shape to the Christian
vision, is the exclusive emphasis of my use of his work. Unfortunately, this has not been
the main point of interest for those who rely heavily on Rahner in their own work. Instead,
Rahner's influence has primarily been through his rather extended engagement with mistaken assumptions about the apologetic context of contemporary Christianity.

6. Chronologically *Spirit in the World* and *Hearers of the Word* precede Rahner's basic
study of the question of the relationship between nature and grace. However, these works
are still caught up in the very refined question of natural knowledge of God. Only after
these works were completed did Rahner turn to the more basic dogmatic question.

of neo-scholasticism *and* a revolutionary rearticulation of the consequences of that logic.[7]

1. The Strategy of Separation

RECOGNIZING BOTH the futility and heterodoxy of a systematic anti-modernism, nineteenth century Catholicism developed and tried to control a carefully circumscribed relationship with the explosively evolving secular world. The key to that relationship was the concept of *natura pura*. The independence of nature was decisive for the protection of the prerogatives of grace. By separating out a distinct realm of pure nature, the ever more aggressive worldviews of science and secular philosophies could be kept at bay. Through this separation, neo-scholasticism was able to concede enough territory to philosophy and science to account for the growth of knowledge and the experience of progress which characterized the nineteenth century. In this way, the theological agenda of neo-scholasticism was not forced into the impossible position of repudiating the achievements of modernity, achievements which were more and more dominating the ordinary life of the believer. But most importantly, the identification of two distinct realms allowed for a bait and switch approach in neo-scholastic theology. In a world shaped by Enlightenment culture, the natural became ever more real, immediate, and significant. As a result, for a Church trying to survive in just such a world, the designation of "nature" as the appropriate analogue to grace had the salutary effect of infusing theological discourse with what "counts" for the modern mind. If neo-scholasticism chose to talk of nature on its own terms, in large part this was because it hoped to speak in the very next breath about grace, so that

---

7. J. A. DiNoia, O.P., rightly corrects the tendency to overemphasize the "newness" of Rahner's positions. He summarizes Rahner's theological contribution as follows: an emphasis on the concrete and personal significance of Christian Mystery, a defense of grace as gratuitous but not alien to the human condition, a desire to adopt distinctively modern conceptualities whenever appropriate. With respect to this program, DiNoia notes, "The continuities that obtain between these proposals and the neo-scholastic formulations which he sought to correct are as crucial to understanding and appraising his theological program as are the discontinuities" (*The Modern Theologians,* vol. I, ed. David Ford [Oxford: Basil Blackwell, 1988], p. 184). Only when we see how much Rahner preserves can we appreciate how radically he breaks with the theological conceptualities of neo-scholasticism.

what modernity was finding increasingly distant and ethereal, the supernatural, might be thought of as real, immediate, and significant.

One of the central affirmations of the First Vatican Council embodies this multifaceted strategy of separation. "Faith and Reason," Chapter IV of *Dei filius,* the central document of the first Vatican Council, states: "Not only can there be no conflict between faith and reason, they also support each other since right reason demonstrates the foundations of faith and, illuminated by its light, pursues the science of divine things, while faith frees and protects reason from errors and provides it with manifold insights." Here we see the close association of nature and grace. The natural organ of the ordinary — reason — supports and is supported by the supernatural disposition of grace — faith. At its most subtle, this close association is understood in terms of the doctrine of analogy. However, the neo-scholastic tradition rarely found time for subtleties of this sort, and by and large, the interrelationship was grounded in the traditional arguments for the existence of God, hence the emphasis on "foundations of faith."

Yet, how neo-scholasticism understood the role of the intellect and the actual use to which it put the constructs of reason were often quite different. Though the doctrine of analogy was for the most part dormant throughout the nineteenth century, neo-scholasticism involved a particularly profound reliance upon analogy, which was as fundamental as it was unrecognized. This analogical moment is to be found in the conceptual tools of the Aristotelian substance/accident metaphysic which were applied *across* the distinction between the natural and supernatural. At its best and most interesting, the neo-scholastic synthesis involved creative analogical thinking as it analyzed grace in terms of Aristotelian philosophy. Such analogical moments produced the many neologisms for which the scholastic tradition is so justly famous, e.g., quasi-formal causality, substantial accident, supernatural habit. They are, in effect, modifications of the language of the ordinary to serve as an analogical language of the extraordinary. The effect was to link the cognitive potency of the ordinary (which neo-scholasticism claimed was exhaustively captured by the substance/accident metaphysic) to the often chimerical extraordinary. To the degree that neo-scholasticism succeeded, the theological achievement was remarkable. However, the logic of the substance/accident metaphysic stood in the way of any real and lasting success. Understanding this limitation is crucial if we are to grasp Rahner's relationship to his neo-scholastic inheritance.

The First Vatican Council expresses the basic form of this difficulty — the inability of the Aristotelian doctrine of substance to accommodate the similarities and partial relations implied in the use of analogy. In the Aristotelian framework, analogy has an inevitable tendency towards identity. Thus, the First Vatican Council took pains to drive a wedge between faith and reason. Harmonious association between faith and reason is not the only, or even the main, emphasis of the Council's teaching. Having fairly burst with enthusiasm for the positive value of modern science and affirmed the legitimacy of rational inquiry, the *Dei filius*, IV concludes with a crucial warning: "While, however, acknowledging this just freedom, [the Church] sternly warns lest [the sciences] fall into error by going contrary to the divine doctrine, or, stepping beyond their own limits, they enter into the sphere of faith and create confusion." In giving up terrain to independent reason, the condition has been carefully elaborated. Whatever might be discerned or experienced in this realm cannot have salvific significance. The sciences might grow into mighty systems of thought with explanatory powers greatly enhanced, but knowledge of our ultimate destinies is dependent upon the workings of another order altogether. This order, the supernatural, the realm of grace, must be theoretically and conceptually distinguished from nature, and knowledge of its inner workings and access to its benefits is possible only through the revelation preserved and promulgated by the Church. In this way, science is kept in its place.

Close association or sharp distinction — which shall it be? Church proclamations before and after the First Vatican Council have not hesitated to express quite different and contrary emphases in very nearly the same breath. However, a disciplined theology must make the effort to explain with clarity and consistency what the tradition affirms. The career of neo-scholasticism is largely the struggle between these two alternatives. Is grace intimately and even intrinsically bound up with nature? The desire to make grace relevant and real suggests that the answer must be "Yes." But this intimate and intrinsic relationship implies a partnership between the ordinary and extraordinary which threatens the sovereign gratuity of grace. How could the extraordinary be truly grace if it were already bound up with the ordinary, whether in the form of a natural need, a natural capacity, or a natural desire? To respond to this threat, the great difference between nature and grace must be emphasized, even if such an emphasis courts the dangers of divine unreality and irrelevance. Grace is extraordinary because it is unnecessary, unexpected, and in some respects, perhaps, even unwanted. Thus, the challenge for systematic theology is to find a way to express the real relationship between the ordinary and extraordinary — real in the sense of articulating an interpenetration of the two, but real also in the sense that this relation avoids conflation.

Any Christian theology would toil with this difficulty. However, for neo-scholasticism the tension between finding a role for grace in the natural world of human existence and protecting both the ordinary naturalness of human life and, more importantly, the extraordinary gratuity of grace became extreme, and in the end, overwhelming. A *real relationship* between nature and grace seemed impossible to express, because the substance/accident metaphysic which defined the neo-scholastic method forced the question of the relationship between nature and grace into a stark either/or. For the Aristotelian thinker, substance is the very stuff of reality; substance gives the "to be" to all that is, and to have a certain kind of substance entails *being* a certain kind of thing in the most fundamental sense. If it does not entail this fundamental kind of identity, then it is an accident rather than a substance. What is crucial for the Aristotelian is that substance is the exclusive and exhaustive identity of the thing, whether this is conceived of in terms of the individual thing in its concreteness (e.g., this chair, my dog, Pius IX) or the form that makes the thing what it is (e.g., chairness, doghood, manhood). Either the substance is what it is, or it is not; either things are identical (either in concreteness or in terms of their form), or they are different.[8] As a consequence, at every turn neo-scholasticism feared that the

---

8. For a treatment of the Aristotelian doctrine of substance see D. M. MacKinnon, "Aristotle's Conception of Substance," *New Essays on Plato and Aristotle,* ed. R. Marbrough (1965), pp. 97-119 and " 'Substance' in Christology — a cross-bench view," *Christ, Faith and History: Cambridge Studies in Christology,* ed. W. Sykes and J. P. Clayton (1972), pp. 276-300. The latter essay is especially helpful in sorting out the theological role of Aristotle's notion of substance. Of especial merit is MacKinnon's defense of the ongoing significance of "substance" in Christology. For MacKinnon, the unequivocal and clear identity generated by the use of substance as the defining feature of existence is indispensable. In a passage well worth citing at length, he writes, "It may be claimed for the *homoousion* that it makes it possible for us so to grasp the mystery of Christ's relation to the Father that we are measured by that mystery and not confused by the problems which we have set in its place. If we say that Christ's invitation to the heavy laden is not a *similacrum* of the divine invitation but is *in fact* the invitation made concrete, are we not involved in something very close to the *homoousion?* Again, when in the fourth gospel Jesus addressing his Father said, 'Father, the hour is come', does not the *homoousion* enable us to recognize that the

articulations of the close association between nature and grace were, finally, statements of identity. Thus, statements of difference and disjunction were inevitable. Our human identity is grounded in our natural substance. The life of grace is founded upon an altogether different "substance," that of divine rather than natural origin.

This feature of the Aristotelian philosophy of substance explains the nineteenth century rejection of the many non-Aristotelian "mediating" theologies. What neo-scholasticism called Rationalism and Semi-Rationalism was a wide variety of philosophical and theological programs which attempted to develop a link or continuity between the ordinary and the extraordinary, a link which is necessary if one is to give theological expression to the soteriological truth of Christianity, the *real relationship* of the ordinary and extraordinary. Typically, a claim was made that the human project contained some movement toward the supernatural, whether understood in terms of reason, feeling, culture, or history. In even the most subtle approaches, the neo-scholastic response was reductive. Continuities were interpreted as conflations.

This consequence of the Aristotelian doctrine of substance is fully evident in the first "error of our time" listed in The Syllabus of Condemned Errors (1864). The Syllabus imputes the following positions on the many attempts to link the truths of faith to the powers of reason:

---

hour is indeed the ultimate hour because the agent of the action which belongs to it is the ultimate agent of that which the Father has appointed shall be done on earth by the one who was with him before the foundations of the world were laid, who is 'one thing' with him, yet always his obedient executant? Again, does the *homoousion* enforce the radically paradoxical character of the great christological saying, "I am in the midst of you as he that doth serve'? Christ's *diakonia* is presented not as a parable of God's regnant service to his creatures, but as that service itself become concrete. Does not the conceptual apparatus of substance provide the means by which the truly revolutionary paradox of what is affirmed in terms of action, event, etc., may be approached for what it is, and not dismissed as a kind of likeness, *homoioma,* of the ultimate" (p. 290). We do well to keep these words in mind, for the failure of the doctrine of substance in neo-scholasticism by no means condemns that philosophical tool to the "dustbin of history." Indeed, a strong case has been made that Rahner's rejection of substance creates precisely the problems of *homoioma* in his Christology. See Bruce Marshall, *Christologies in Conflict* (Oxford: Basil Blackwell, 1987), for what might well be seen as an extended meditation on the virtues of an application of a form of the Aristotelian doctrine of substance (via P. F. Stawson) to Christology.

There exists no divine Power, Supreme Being, Wisdom and Providence distinct from the universe, and God is none other than nature and is therefore mutable. In effect, God is produced in man and the world, and all things are God, and have the very substance of God. God is, therefore, one and the same with the world, and thence mind is the same thing as matter, necessity with liberty, true with false, good with evil, justice with injustice.

As the final sentence's march through the horrors of reductive similarity indicates, the anathema in 1864 assumed that whatever is not absolutely distinct at the fundamental level of its substance is, in the end, identical.

A reductive assessment of the mediating theologies of the nineteenth century was by no means restricted to official Vatican documents. The great German theologian Matthias Scheeben identifies the basic thrust of the Rationalist and Semi-Rationalist approaches with Pelagianism. In each instance, Scheeben reduces the basic theological dynamic of mediating theologies to the view "that man's nature carried within itself at least the seed of all good which it could ever reach, including the Christian good."[9] More specifically, the natural is thought to share the prerogatives and fruits of the supernatual. This sharing is not possible in the Aristotelian framework unless the substance of humanity is, in fact, supernatural, or the supernatural is really just a remarkable form of the natural. Neither alternative is acceptable. Thus, Scheeben concludes his assessment of the threats posed by the new, epistemological form of the old, moral conflation entailed in Pelagianism: "The crisis has not yet been completely settled, and it will not be settled until the supernatural order is frankly, adequately, and radically distinguished from the natural order."[10] And this radical distinction is, of course, secured by the definition of nature and grace as two different *substances*.

In thinking along these lines, neo-scholastics in general, and Scheeben in particular, were not unaware of the problems raised by this complete separation of the natural life of the human person from the life of grace and glory. Feeling the force of something like Cleanthes' arguments against Demea, neo-scholasticism could not retreat behind the doctrine of divine incomprehensibility. Unlike Demea's approach, neo-scholasticism would not reduce faith to blind obedience. The clear distinction between nature

9. *Nature and Grace* (New York: B. Herder Book Co., 1954), p. 1.
10. *Nature and Grace*, p. 13.

and grace could not be the last word. Thus, just as Rationalism and Semi-Rationalism were rejected, so also the radical transcendence of Fideism in all its forms was attacked, though with less vigor, perhaps, than was directed against the conflating, immanent agendas.

For example, Scheeben repudiates Lutheranism, Jansenism and nineteenth century Traditionalism. In his eyes, each accentuates the difference between the natural and supernatural to an unacceptable degree. "They exalt grace by contending that it displaces and destroys nature." For Scheeben, "that amounts to praising God as giver of grace while insulting and disparaging Him as Creator." The insult has dire consequences. For Scheeben, where the Pelagians and their modern progeny absorb grace into nature, Luther and his followers radically dichotomize, and the result is a vision of humanity in which grace can never be really part of life. Thus, whatever difficulties the immanence of the Rationalist and Semi-Rationalist projects might present, "praise of God's grace does not require any depreciation of nature."[11]

Scheeben's interest in the integrity of nature extends beyond a desire to defend the dignity of God's role as Creator. At stake here is the real partnership of grace and natural existence. For Scheeben, the goal of theology "is to bring out the supernatural character of Christianity in its true genius . . . ,"[12] and truly committed to the Aristotelian framework, he assumes that the reality of everything, grace included, is "the ontological or metaphysical element." This assumption leads to the crucial positive role of the Aristotelian doctrine of substance in the nature/grace scheme. As Scheeben observes:

11. *Nature and Grace*, p. 49. This polemic against the Reformation is inevitable if one interprets human existence in terms of substance, because all Reformation talk of the "essential" or "fundamental" or "intrinsic" sinfulness of the human creature will be read as assaults upon human nature, and this assault separates nature from grace, making any commerce between the two seem impossible. Thus, even as late as the 1920s so wise an author as Jacques Maritain gave expression to the common Tridentine assessment of Luther. "Beware," he writes, "in Lutheran theology grace is always wholly extrinsic to ourselves (for Luther, grace is nothing else than the simple *exterior favour* of God), man is walled up in his nature and can never receive in himself the seeds of true participation in the divine life, nor (child of wrath as he is) can he produce a substantially supernatural act" (*Three Reformers: Luther — Descartes — Rousseau* [New York: Charles Schribner's Sons, 1929], p. 17). This criticism, as we shall see, has more to do with the neo-scholastic frame of reference than it does with the teachings of the Reformation.

12. *Nature and Grace*, p. 15.

In the natural order this [ontological or metaphysical] element is plain
enough; no one has ever philosophized about the natural order of life
in man without starting from, or at least reverting to, the nature of man
on which it rests and to which it conforms. But in the supernatural
order this point is often neglected; no foundation analogous to nature
is looked for, and that is the reason why a clear, sound idea of the
supernatural order is so rarely achieved.[13]

For Scheeben, then, the evident ordered reality of natural life, so essential
that even those of his contemporaries enraptured in Hegelian reveries were
forced to revert to it in spite of themselves, casts a penumbra of ordered
reality upon its all too often elusive partner, grace.[14]

Scheeben sends a clear signal to this effect when he privileges the term
"supernature," for the nominative suggests a substance directly parallel to
that of nature. He notes the obvious sense in which the neo-scholastic use
of substance lends itself to the development of this parallel structure. "[The
supernatural] consists in that dignity, those qualities, powers, activities and

13. *Nature and Grace,* p. 16.
14. Thomas F. O'Meara, O.P., insists that in spite of studying with neo-scholastic *pater*
Joseph Kleutgen in Rome, echoing standard neo-scholastic characterizations of non-
Thomistic theologies, and embodying in his own outlook on the late nineteenth century
a visceral anti-modernism, Scheeben "was not a papalist or neo-scholastic." Whether or
not Scheeben was a "papalist" is not relevant here, but his status as a neo-scholastic is
crucial. How are we to understand O'Meara's insistence?

Like so many contemporary Catholic theologians, O'Meara has a reductive view of
neo-scholastics. They are the "bad guys" who produced stultifying manuals when they were
not too busy suppressing creative thinkers. Sheeben did neither. O'Meara writes, "He
evaluated various positions, was not inclined to write a theology simply repeating Aquinas,
and found a model in the irenic theologian at Munich, Alois Schmid" (*Church and Culture:
German Catholic Theology, 1860-1918* [Notre Dame: The University of Notre Dame Press,
1991], p. 64). It would seem that because Scheeben was not a stupid, tyrannical drone,
he could not have been a neo-scholastic.

O'Meara's tendentious definition of neo-scholasticism misses, quite literally, the *substance* of neo-scholasticism. The single defining feature of the neo-scholastic method is not
Thomistic commentary. Recent decades have witnessed an outpouring of commentaries
on Thomas which are anything but neo-scholastic. Rather, what identifies neo-scholasticism
is the application of Aristotelian metaphysics to the question of nature and grace. From
that application emerges the notion of *natura pura,* the protected uniqueness of grace and,
as Scheeben so effectively illustrates, the possibility of a structured ontological symmetry
between nature and the supernatural. On this account, Scheeben is most definitely a
neo-scholastic.

relations which are found in nature but are so superior to anything within the province of nature, that is, anything grounded on and flowing from the essence and substance of a thing, that they pertain to a higher order." That which does not arise from the natural substance of an entity is, by definition, supernatural. Yet, Scheeben is unsatisfied with this use of the natural. He observes, "All this gives us no more than a negative idea."[15] Scheeben hopes to move beyond this apophatic moment in order to understand the supernatural as more than what it is not. We need to grasp what it *is*. We need to gain some sense of the essence or substance of the supernatural precisely as an analogue to nature. With the cataphatic in mind, he writes, "With respect to the rule for determining what belongs to nature or to supernature, the general norm is to observe which powers nature has, how far these powers extend, and what end must be appointed for them if nature is to reach its suitable development and achieve rest and perfection." Then, "whatever is outside this list — hence the powers that do not emanate from the [natural] essence, and in general all that is unattainable by the unelevated powers from the [natural] essence — is supernatural, and if it pertains to a symmetrically organized life, counts as supernature."[16] This parallelism is the key to Scheeben's highly regarded synthesis, for as ordered substances, nature and supernature can be analogous even as they are distinguished. The upshot is a positively defined, but ontologically distinct, realm of supernature.

This is neo-scholasticism at its best. The concept of *natura pura* has reached its fullest potential as a material principle. Grace is protected by the strategy of separation. It is fully and completely distinct from nature. However, the supernatural is not an irrelevant incomprehensibility. The life of grace is grounded in an identifiable, ordered, and structured substance, supernature, comprehensible precisely as a distinct, but symmetrical realm. Yet, in spite of this accomplishment, can Scheeben in particular and neo-scholasticism in general give any sense to the Christian claim that *we,* somehow, participate in both? How can we be essentially natural beings, creatures *naturae purae,* and at the same time, participate in the supernatural, have supernatures? Can any account be given of our amphibious status, or are we faced with two symmetrical realms, two parallel ontological orders, without any way in which to make the pilgrimage from one to the other?

15. *Nature and Grace*, p. 28.
16. *Nature and Grace*, pp. 42-43.

One either has one nature or the other, but to say that one has *both* is to violate the first principle of Aristotelian metaphysics. The substance of a thing is that which makes the thing what it is. Either we are truly and "substantially" natural beings — in which case grace may well influence us or affect us in some way, but can only do so by modifying the *accidents* of our existence (cf. substantial accidents!) — or grace really does transform the ground of our existence, in which case we are no longer natural beings at all, but are constituted by an altogether new substance. Both alternatives are theologically unattractive. Either we remain immanent and the extraordinary offer of grace speaks to the edges rather than the center of the ordinary, or we are radically transformed and grace transports us to an entirely new mode of existence entirely separate from the ordinary.[17] Here neo-scholasticism reaches the limits of substance metaphysics. Scheeben may succeed in evoking a recognizable supernature (though this is very much an open question[18]), but providing an account of how we *participate* in that supernature while still remaining the natural beings that we are is a conceptual trick which will tax his commitment to the primacy of substance.

Scheeben is determined to give an account of our amphibious participation in the supernatural, and in doing so, he moves outside the Aristotelian framework. At a crucial point in his treatment of the gift of grace, Scheeben backs away from the conceptual tools of the substance/accident metaphysic. Taking inspiration from biblical and patrisitic sources, Scheeben explains that effects of grace are the result of our adoption as children of God. Adoption, however, is a juridical rather than ontological or metaphysical concept. Indeed, adoption is a juridical act which overrides nature. A child who is not related to a parent *by nature* becomes related *by law*. Of course, Scheeben insists that divine adoption, unlike human adoption, involves real change as well as a legal change. "When we are adopted by God we are not

17. Notice how this either/or is reflected spiritually and practically in the kinds of choices facing Roman Catholics who were formed by the vision of neo-scholasticism. On the one hand, the fullness of grace was equated with the life lived far from the ordinary in either the monastery or convent — an entirely new mode of existence. On the other hand, for those who remained "behind," Christian identity devolved into scrupulously circumscribed moments of authorized sacramental participation — grace at the edges of life.

18. For a trenchant criticism of the concept of "supernature," and by implication, the ordered symmetry so dear to Scheeben, see Henri de Lubac, *A Brief Catechesis on Nature and Grace* (San Francisco: Ignatius Press, 1984), pp. 33-41.

only called but actually are His children."[19] Metaphysical and ontological factors are crucial, the change is "substantial," but, and this is counter to all his initial remarks about the importance of nature and supernature as "ordered substances," the juridical act precedes and creates the new substance or "new creation," the elevated human creature.

This eruption of a non-Aristotelian and non-metaphysical concept into Scheeben's treatise on nature and grace is striking.[20] From this point of view we can look backwards to the origins of the notion of *natura pura,* the Counter-Reformation. Catholic polemicists claimed that Reformation doctrine had rendered grace extrinsic. Dwelling on Luther's use of the term "alien righteousness" and making much of his juridical metaphors of atonement, Counter-Reformation theology developed an opposite emphasis on the real, that is to say *ontological,* ordered symmetry of nature and grace. Yet, here we find Scheeben, one of the finest exponents of that very theological tradition, falling back upon a juridical metaphor which, implicitly, entails a distinction between alien and proper righteousness — the declaration of adoption by God and the real transformation of the adopted child — with priority assigned to the former![21]

---

19. *Nature and Grace,* p. 126.

20. The presence of this juridical conceptuality is all the more remarkable because Scheeben is perfectly capable of returning to the Aristotelian framework in other accounts of the offer of grace. For example, in Scheeben's more popularly catechetical *The Mysteries of Christianity,* he develops a soteriology which accentuates the "thingness" of grace in (modified) Aristotelian terms. He writes, "By his satisfaction and merit the God-man is the moral cause of man's restoration to the sonship of God; that is, he moves God, he begs God to forgive us." At this point, the appeal to the concept of "moral cause" is not clearly invested in the Aristotelian metaphysics of substance. To the degree that the notion has any meaning at all, it is as personalistic as it is ontological. However, Scheeben hastens to give Christ's role a more precise sense. He continues, "The grounds on which Christ's unexampled moral causality rests demand that we admit a physical causality." The turn to physical causality is typical of neo-scholasticism. The effectiveness of Christ's act of sacrifice is real just as the billiard ball striking another ball is real. Indeed, what other kinds of fundamental relationships could obtain between the ontologically distinct substances of nature and supernature? Physical causality is not, however, the final word. Grace does not work exactly like a physical cause. The strict logic of the Aristotelian framework must be bent to the purposes of analogy. Thus, Scheeben concludes by reformulating the ground of Christ's saving grace. It is not physical, but "better a *hyperphysical* causality" (p. 456, my italics). Another neologism joins the neo-scholastic vocabulary as a mechanism for explicating what an unbaptized Aristotelianism cannot.

21. The following remarkable passage written by Scheeben could well be read as a gloss

Is this subordination of the ontological to the juridical a consequence of Scheeben's recognition of the limitations of Aristotelian metaphysics in a theological account of how God's extraordinary offer becomes *real* in the ordinary life of the believer?

Scheeben's momentary subordination of the ordered "substances" of nature and supernature to the particular act of divine love also anticipates Rahner's own reconceptualization of the relationship between nature and grace. For in large part, Rahner puts his finger on the conceptual problem against which Scheeben struggles — the Aristotelian doctrine of substance. However, in order to fully grasp the force of Rahner's position, we need to consider a more direct response to neo-scholasticism. For the failure of neo-scholasticism to express the "real partnership" of grace was most often diagnosed as a consequence of the strategy of separation. Thus, the separation of nature and grace was questioned and tentative points of convergence were suggested. Rahner's genius is his recognition that such a response misdiagnoses the problem. Overcoming neo-scholasticism will require something much more revolutionary than opposing it.

2. Extrinsicism and Intrinsicism

THE DIFFICULTIES embedded in neo-scholasticism became more and more evident throughout the first half of the twentieth century. For Rahner, as for many of his peers, the neo-scholastic framework forces the analysis of

---

on the Inner Man/Outer Man distinction in Luther's understanding of our new creation in Christ: "God's love is not like man's love, which presupposes lovableness in the object but cannot confer a new lovableness. God's love makes a thing good by embracing it. It is necessarily operative; and we can say that God loves a person only to the extent that He makes him good and communicates goodness to him. How could this high love of God, the love that is called simply and pre-eminently God's love, be an idle affection for created nature? How could it confer on men the new name, God's children, which even from the juridical point of view means so much even though it is empty, without at the same time imparting to them a new, higher goodness and perfection? No, God's love, with which He loves us in His only-begotten Son, gives us not only a new external dignity, but a new internal goodness and beauty. It is so powerful that it makes us conformable to the image of His Son, inaugurates in us a new, higher man, and, in a certain sense, establishes in us the beginning of a new substance" (*Nature and Grace,* pp. 126-27).

grace into a position in which our "ordination to the supernatural end can only consist in a divine decree still external to [us]."[22] This extrinsic conception of our destiny in God undermines the crucial sense in which God's redemptive offer addresses us at the center, not the periphery of our lives. On the periphery, the possibilities of grace are so tangential to the ordinary lives of believers that a vacuum develops which only strengthens the hand of purely natural worldviews. Meditating retrospectively on the theological milieu in which he was formed, Henri de Lubac observes, "While wishing to protect the supernatural from any contamination, people had in fact exiled it altogether — both from intellectual and from social life — leaving the field free to be taken over by secularism."[23]

By failing to do justice to the inner purpose of grace in a self-confident world, the strategy of separation can easily backfire. The "unattainable" world of grace may not necessarily heighten our thirst for the extraordinary. Rather, an extrinsic conception of grace may simply encourage a shrug of disregard as modern society increasingly accepts naturalistic and purely immanent self-understanding as sufficient. Does the peculiar alliance between Demea and Philo not begin to look all too familiar, though this time with Demea acquiescing to Philo's immanence rather than the other way around? Rahner seconds this suspicion: "Is it *totally* misguided to see modern naturalism as having *some* connexion with this theory? Is it quite wrong to suggest that the modern lack of interest in the supernatural can only have developed on the basis of such a view of grace ?"[24] Moreover, the commitment to immanence may well become very combative. Instead of disregarding grace as irrelevant, the extraordinary might well be taken as an enemy of ordinary life. As Renan writes:

> Belief in a revelation, in a supernatural order, is the negation of criticism, a relic of the old anthropomorphic conception of the world formed at a time when man had not yet acquired a clear idea of the laws of nature. . . . The task of modern thought will be completed only when belief in the supernatural, in whatever form, is destroyed.[25]

22. *TI* I, p. 302.
23. *The Mystery of the Supernatural*, p. xi.
24. *TI* IV, p. 169.
25. Quoted from de Lubac, *A Brief Catechesis Concerning the Relationship of Nature and Grace* (San Francisco: Ignatius Press, 1983), p. 67.

The denial of the supernatural becomes a moral imperative. We must defend nature against the extrinsic claims of grace, otherwise the ordinary beauties of human life dissolve into fantasies of deification.[26]

The twentieth century concern about the extrinsicism of neo-scholasticism directly parallels Cleanthes' response to the separation of the ordinary and extraordinary entailed in Demea's radical transcendence. The extraordinary is protected from the reductive pressures of the ordinary only to die the death of irrelevance, or worse, to invite the crusaders on behalf of immanence to step up their attacks upon the shadowy realm of the supernatural. To be sure, Demea's alliance with Philo at the outset of Hume's *Dialogues* indicates that he views ordinary reason as antithetical to extraordinary faith, while the neo-scholastics insisted upon a positive and mutually illuminating symmetry. Nonetheless, across that symmetry the neo-scholastics could establish no real connection. The supernatural is not incomprehensible, but it would seem to be fundamentally inaccessible. A substantive bridge, an intrinsic relationship between the two, seems impossible.

In the theological conflicts from the Modernist Crisis to the Second Vatican Council, the dangers of the irrelevance of grace motivated numerable attempts to move beyond the impasse created by neo-scholasticism. By and large, both the strategy of separation and the Aristotelian form it took were rejected. For example, Catholic philosopher Maurice Blondel combined the development of a personalist philosophy with a correlation between nature and grace. Commenting on the reification of nature and the supernatural into two distinct "orders," Blondel writes, "It is not

---

26. In his classic consideration of the challenges facing modern Christianity, *The Drama of Aetheistic Humanism* (New York: Sheed & Ward, 1965), de Lubac suggests that of all the challenges to theism, Comtean positivism poses the deepest threat. Most especially, positivism tempts theology into an unholy alliance. Comte shared with his Catholic counterparts an antipathy for the insensible abstractions which undergirded liberal politics, as well as ambitious rationalist and romantic philosophies. The "fiction" of individual rights, the anarchy of private judgment, the baleful effects of Protestantism — all of these features of modernity need, argued Comte, to be superceded. These features of positivism, especially its "campaign against the individual," tend to unify Catholics and positivists. In both cases, the "impure" elements of modernity are burned away in the fires of a critical system of thought which scrupulously restricts the scope of "the real" (pp. 156-58). Thus, Comte gives ample room for the institution of the church and a foundational justification for the exercise of authority, but, and this is crucial for de Lubac, he precludes any reference to grace.

enough to show their opposition to each other; we must bring them together, *in eodem dramate.* . . . Between the two gifts a dynamic unity exists, and an intelligible relationship."[27] Blondel has no desire to override the neo-scholastic commitment to protecting the gratuity of grace, and with it the decisive critical authority of the Church, but rather, he objects to the enslavement of grace to the thoroughgoing strategy of separation. Surely, thinks Blondel, our understanding of the interaction of the human and divine must be formed by the already accomplished interpenetration of grace into natural life, an interpenetration not only required in principle by the *datum optimum* of creation, and the *datum perfectum* of grace, but also warranted by the experience of this interpenetration in the life of the Church. In short, in any treatment of the basic question of nature and grace, an account must be given of their relation which accords proper place to "the 'admirable exchange' *(admirabile commercium)* established once and for all by the Incarnation of the Word of God."[28] God's extraordinary initiative on our behalf must have a relevance for our ordinary lives.

In an effort to provide just such an account of the "admirable exchange" of nature and grace, the French theological movement known as *la nouvelle théologie* proposed a rejection of the strategy of separation which defines neo-scholasticism. In its most characteristic form this revision proposes to conceive of human nature as possessing, in its created state, an inner and unconditional desire for grace and supernatural elevation.[29] The effect of this theoretical change, of course, is to restructure radically the relationship of nature and grace. No longer can one see them as two realms carefully separated. Extrinsicism is replaced by an "intrinsicism." Now nature

---

27. *Exigences philosophiques,* pp. 256-57. Quoted from de Lubac, *A Brief Catechesis.*

28. Lubac, *A Brief Catechesis,* p. 44. The use of the image of admirable exchange, also an important Lutheran image, highlights the link between Reformation Christology and the Roman Catholic issue of the relationship between nature and grace. These two loci interlock both historically at Trent and conceptually as the theological location of the logic of the divine/human relationship. With this connection in mind, it would be possible to trace the history of Protestant disputes over Christology and Justification as parallel forms of the Roman Catholic debates about nature and grace, unified by a common concern to express the intrinsic reality of God's action on our behalf without thereby compromising the quality of the act as a free gift.

29. Rahner identifies this position with the anonymously published article, "Ein Weg sur Bestimmung des Verhältnisses von Natur und Gnade," *Orientierung* XIV (1950), pp. 138-41. The author, apparently, was Pierre Delaye.

reaches out to grace by virtue of its own inner dynamism. The upshot of this dynamism is to bring matters divine into close proximity with the everyday life of the modern person, precisely, thought *les théologiennes nouveaux,* what an increasingly complacent secular world needs to hear. The world of grace, they argued, must be shown to be the intrinsic end and fulfillment of all that we cherish both culturally and personally. Otherwise, the critical and transformative powers of God's Word will never come into relation to the ordinariness of our lives.

Neo-scholasticism saw in the intrinsicism of *la nouvelle théologie* exactly what Demea saw in Cleanthes' Argument from Design — an absorption of the extraordinary into the ordinary — and with good reason. To the extent that the repudiation of the strategy of separation left the Aristotelian metaphysics of substance in place, affirmations of a "natural" orientation towards God could not be interpreted as anything other than a collapse of the distinction between nature and grace.[30] If we have a natural desire for God, then our created natures have an essential need for grace. To be fully natural requires us to enjoy the supernatural. Participation in the fullness of the ordered form of nature *entails* participation in the ordered form of supernature. The "admirable exchange" becomes a reductive con-

---

30. For the most part, *la nouvelle théologie* did not, in fact, accept the Aristotelian assumptions of neo-scholasticism. As we noted, Blondel's philosophical agenda was directly opposed to Aristotelian methods. Further, the decidedly unsystematic historical *ressourcement* which characterized much of *la nouvelle théologie* infused diverse patristic schemes and concepts into theological controversy, none of which could be directly translated into terms regnant in the official Roman theology of the period. However, in spite of both self-conscious and unself-conscious rejections of neo-scholastic assumptions about metaphysics, *la nouvelle théologie* never clarified the theological consequences, and gave the impression of carrying on in the grand tradition of scholastic theology. Three factors contributed to this impression. (1) The Leonine emphasis upon the pedagogical value of Thomism had been so effective that neo-scholastic terminology was ingrained as the "real" language of theological precision. Even opponents of neo-scholasticism resorted to Aristotelian concepts when they wanted to show the fine nub of their reformatory agenda. (2) The climate of anti-Protestantism was as strong in early twentieth century Catholicism as anti-Catholicism was in the Protestant world. Intuitively, perhaps, the "new theologians" recognized that some form of neo-scholasticism was necessary to maintain the sharp edge of the anathemas of Trent. This encouraged attempts to reformulate rather than reject characteristic neo-scholastic approaches. (3) *Ressourcement* sought to reform by overwhelming neo-scholasticism with the multifaceted weight of the Christian tradition. This encouraged a process of adding new material on top of the structure of neo-scholasticism rather than a systematic rethinking of the neo-scholastic framework.

flation — exactly what the Syllabus of Errors had feared. Not surprisingly, nearly one hundred years after the promulgation of the Syllabus, Roman authorities who were still invested in the Aristotelian assumptions of neo-scholasticism issued *Humani generis* (1950) which, in effect, condemned *la nouvelle théologie* as yet another form of Semi-Rationalism. In the intrinsicist rejection of the strategy of separation, the neo-scholastic point of reference would see nothing but conflation.[31]

It is at this point in the debate about the relationship between nature and grace that Rahner enters in 1950. On the surface, Rahner's writings prior to 1950 would indicate a deep sympathy with the intrinsicist agenda of *la nouvelle théologie*. As Rahner notes, in neo-scholasticism "the offer of inwardly elevating grace remains *ex supposito* outside or above real experience, and only becomes known in a faith which knows of its object *ex auditu* alone."[32] At every turn the inability of neo-scholasticism to make grace more than a reality extrinsic to the believer, a reality which is restricted to explicitly institutional moments of religious practice, exasperates Rahner. Here, he stands ready to join the intrinsicist agenda. As Rahner writes approvingly, "One strives to 'experience' the reality of grace precisely there where one lives one's own existence; and so one tries to see supernatural — and not just medicinal — grace as the activation and the force of concrete existence."[33] The concern for the concrete, the desire to place the Christian life at the center rather than the fringe of modern life, the need to move beyond the ghetto or fortress mentality in all its forms

---

31. This is not altogether unreasonable. At a crucial moment in his articulation of the position of *la nouvelle théologie,* Henri de Lubac laces his account with terminology which raises numerable red flags for the systematically scrupulous neo-scholastic reader. Lubac writes, "the 'desire to see God' cannot be permanently frustrated without essential suffering." So as not to equivocate in his use of the term "essential," de Lubac clearly evokes the essence or substance/accident scheme when he reiterates, "This desire is not some 'accident' in me." Then, in a cascade of affirmations, he concludes, "God's call is constitutive. My finality, which is expressed by this desire, is inscribed upon my very being as it has been put into this universe by God. And by God's will, I now have no other genuine end really assigned to my nature or presented for my free acceptance under any guise, except that of 'seeing God' " (*The Mystery of the Supernatural,* p. 70). Passages such as this are so laden with the language of "essence" and "nature" that the reader is easily tempted to think that de Lubac is simply countering neo-scholasticism on its own terms, when, in fact, he is fighting with neo-scholasticism for control over the vocabulary of the tradition.

32. *TI* I, p. 300.

33. *TI* IV, p. 173.

seem to lead directly to a rejection of the neo-scholastic strategy of separation. As Rahner observes, "*Must* not what God decrees for man be *eo ipso* an interior ontological constituent of his concrete quiddity?"[34] His first two books provided him with occasions to reforge the philosophical tools of transcendental philosophy for the purposes of conceptualizing theological issues in a directly personal and existential fashion. Both *Spirit in the World* and *Hearers of the Word* stand as prolegomenal studies which open out directly onto a theology of the *admirabile commercium* of nature and grace in our rational and historical actuality. The stage is set for a direct leap into the program of *la nouvelle théologie* and its effort to break down the neo-scholastic strategy of separation.

And yet, at the very point when Rahner confronts the particular technical form in which the "new theologians" chose to express their ambitious program, a program with which Rahner so obviously felt a deep affinity, at the point when Rahner was poised to pour forth upon the Catholic world a torrent of reflections upon all manner of topics in theology and spirituality, he stepped back from the brink and took exception to the liberties which *la nouvelle théologie* had taken with the concerns of neo-scholasticism. When considering the mid-century efforts to overcome the extrinsicist limitations of neo-scholasticism, his question echoes the concern which was at the heart of the neo-scholastic synthesis: "The problem is this: is it still possible to conceive of grace as unexacted, supposing that the existential consisting of the inner and unconditional reference to grace and beatific vision were a constituent of man's 'nature' in the sense that man as such could not be thought without it?"[35] The answer is no. The "giftedness" of grace requires a separation of nature from grace.

In the end, for Rahner, the only way to give adequate expression to the unexacted quality of divine grace is to preserve the distinction between nature and the supernatural. *La nouvelle théologie* was wrong, in Rahner's eyes, to build a dynamism toward grace into the structure of nature. However, in typical fashion, Rahner finds a way to make a harmony out of the two widely differing intuitions promoted by neo-scholasticism and *la nouvelle théologie*. Rahner is determined to preserve the distinction between nature and grace and, at the same time, he is equally determined to move beyond the "extrinsicism" which results from the neo-scholastic

34. *TI* I, p. 302.
35. *TI* I, p. 304.

approach. The solution is direct and to the point — Rahner redefines the status of our dynamism towards grace. Instead of trying to conquer the concept of nature on behalf of the intrinsicist agenda as did *la nouvelle théologie,* Rahner defuses it as a central category of theological analysis by relegating it to the status of "remainder concept." This relocates our desire for beatific vision to a universally constitutive, but not natural component of human life. In so doing, he prises apart the intuitive connection between human existence and human nature. The result: he affirms the distinction between nature and grace while discarding the neo-scholastic commitment to substance/accident metaphysics.

3. Rahner's Solution

RAHNER'S THOUGHTS on the question of nature and grace move in two directions. With respect to the standard views of neo-scholasticism, Rahner rejects the ontological separation of nature and grace as hopelessly extrinsicist. Since neo-scholasticism analyzes ordinary life as grounded in an essential human nature which is, by definition, distinct from the order of supernature, the ultimate purposes of God are inevitably discontinuous with concrete human existence. Some continuity is necessary if we are to give meaning to the notion that *my* life is transformed by grace. Some connection is required to make the extraordinary *relevant.* At the same time, Rahner sets aside the coordination of nature and grace suggested by *la nouvelle théologie* as too thoroughly intrinsicist. Such an approach so identifies the structure of the natural order with the purposes of the supernatural that the two realms cannot be imagined apart. This position then compromises the extraordinary status of grace. Some distinction is necessary in order to preserve the integrity of that which is to be relevant.

The two directions — against extrinsicism and in favor of a real relevance for grace, as well as against intrinsicism and in favor of a fully extraordinary view of grace — are unified in the positive point of departure which Rahner enjoins. To move beyond the impasse, he suggests that we reverse neo-scholastic assumptions about the ground of theological clarity. We have seen how Scheeben assumed that our reality as natural beings should be the clear and evident basis for a theological account of the mysterious order of supernature. The manual tradition is even more straightforward. When considering the actions of God on our behalf, one of the standard manuals begins with an inquiry into the status of man as a purely natural creature. The first task "is to determine the natural basis for the supernatural endowment of mankind in Adam. . . ."[36] This is crucial, for "to obtain a correct notion of the Supernatural, we must begin by analyzing the concept of Nature, because Nature precedes the Supernatural and is presupposed by it."[37] The shape and significance of grace is established by a prior consideration of our substantial existence as natural beings. The task of the theologian is to discern the teleology of nature by analyzing our condition using Aristotelian categories so that grace might be clearly understood as the various "elevations" of the faculties, talents, powers and potencies that constitute the essence of human nature. For Rahner, "there is no way of providing a justification for this tacit presupposition starting from man, nor is it really proved by any theological argument."[38]

First, on philosophical grounds, can we, in fact, be confident that human life is purely "natural," or could it be the case that the numerous seemingly "natural" moments we experience are already shot through with the possibilities of grace? As Rahner asks, "How am I to know that everything I in fact encounter in my existential experience of myself . . . does in fact fall within the realm of my 'nature'?"[39] The answer is that we cannot presuppose that our actual existence is simply natural. In *Spirit in the World*, Rahner attempts to show exactly how unjustified is a purely "naturalized" account of cognition. There, his account of Thomistic epistemology highlights the mixed status of the most human of all activities, thinking.

However, philosophical arguments against the neo-scholastic approach to the concept of nature are not as important as Rahner's second and theological objection. For not only does his theological account cut more deeply into the neo-scholastic strategy of separation, showing as it does that the view of nature as substance is not just philosophically untenable but theologically improper, but it also provides the basis for Rahner's objection to *la nouvelle théologie*'s tendency toward making nature depen-

36. Pohle-Preuss, *God the Author of Nature and the Supernatural* (St. Louis: B. Herder Book Co., 1940), p. 124.
37. *God the Author*, p. 181.
38. *TI* I, p. 300.
39. *TI* I, p. 300.

dent upon the supernatural. In direct contrast to the neo-scholastic method, Rahner insists that grace must be the point of departure for any theological account of nature. The only way to cut through the opacity of our experience of the ordinary is to begin with the clarity of the extraordinary.[40] In a concise methodological statement, Rahner writes:

> A *precise* delimitation of nature from grace . . . and so a really pure concept of pure nature could thus in every case only be pursued with the help of Revelation, which tells us what in us is grace and so provides us with the means of abstracting this grace from the body of our existential experience of man and thus, of acquiring pure nature (in its *totality*) as a 'remainder.'[41]

For Rahner, this methodological decision is crucial, yet at this point it is purely formal. The way forward requires that he say something about grace itself.

In his seminal essay in 1950, Rahner brings the material content of grace into focus with the classical dogmatic notion of grace as "unexacted" or "unowed" — *ungeschuldet*. Rahner's choice of the term follows directly from his neo-scholastic predecessors. We have already seen how Scheeben equated Rationalism and Semi-Rationalism with Pelagianism as systems

40. For all the formal parallels to be developed between Rahner's solution to the dilemma of extrinsicist irrelevance (radical transcendence) and intrinsicist conflation (pure immanence) and Cleathes' amphibious account of transcendence, this decision to begin with the clarity of the extraordinary in order to illuminate the ordinary points to a fundamental distinction between the analogy used in the Argument from Design and the analogy of grace at work in Rahner's theology. Rahner reasons from God's designs for us (grace) to our capacities and purposes, not the other way around, as does Cleanthes. This difference is crucial.

41. *TI* I, p. 302. At this level, Hans Urs von Balthasar outlines an identical approach. Rejecting the neo-scholastic method of illuminating the darkness of grace with the light of a philosophical concept of nature, he counters, "*The positive definition of grace can only be given through grace itself.* God himself must reveal what he is within himself. The creature cannot delimit itself in relation to the Unknown reality. Nor can the creature, as a theologically understood "pure" nature, ever know wherein it specifically is different from God. Only the light of revelation can draw this distinction and make this clear." Given the priority of revelation, von Balthasar continues, "So we must define the theological concept of nature primarily by working from grace" (*The Theology of Karl Barth* [San Francisco: Ignatius Press, 1992], p. 279). He concludes, then, with an exact reversal of Scheeben's method.

which construe the human condition in such a way as to make the divine offer of grace mandatory. The Pelagian may petition for entrance at the gates of the heavenly kingdom on the basis of his moral rectitude. The Rationalist may force his way through on the strength of his arguments. The case of Semi-Rationalism, a notoriously ill-defined category of suspect approaches, is less clear, but the charge is similar. Like the others, the Semi-Rationalist subordinates the sovereign freedom of God to the needs and achievements of the creature. At each turn, some act or aspect of the human person turns God into a debtor, *ein Schuldner.* This is clearly the worry which animates *Humani generis'* response to the intrinsicist agenda of *la nouvelle théologie.* A benevolent diety owes, *schuldet,* grace to a creature which He has created with a natural desire for the supernatural.

Here, Rahner begins where he ends — with a radical transformation of neo-scholastic assumptions. He uses the classical term "unexacted," but he places it into a new context. Instead of casting the debtor/creditor relationship as a threat to divine sovereignty *in se,* he treats the freedom of grace as a constituent element of the logic of the Triune Godhead, a logic which is rightfully named "love." As Rahner observes, "One can and should define the essence of supernatural grace on its own terms. . . . It is correct to say that its essence is God's self-communication in love."[42] Love, then, is the "nature" of grace, the "substance" of the supernatural. As such, the divine self-bestowal in love, and not the metaphysical principle of divine freedom, is the point of departure for our understanding of the free relationship between God and creature. As Rahner observes in a crucial formulation, this free or "unexacted" relationship "is significant from a religious point of view: as God's real partner I must be able to receive his love . . . as an unexpected miracle. . . ."[43] The logic of love, then, must govern our understanding of the relationship between nature and grace, not an ontological analysis of either nature or grace.

Love, for Rahner, is both intrinsicist and extrinsicist. On the one hand, love binds together with a force comparable to natural necessity. We feel ourselves "destined" for another who, once we discover our love, becomes the innermost object of our lives. Indeed, a test of love is precisely its confrontation with the drives and purposes of human nature, and the fact that love does sometimes triumph over natural instincts would seem to

42. *TI* I, p. 307.
43. *TI* I, p. 305.

demonstrate how deeply the orientation toward the "Thou" runs within our existence. In this sense, the "real partnership" of love can be a primary constituent of our "concrete quiddity." We cannot imagine ourselves otherwise than loving this spouse or that child. The love is intrinsic to who we are. Yet, on the other hand, love can never be taken as "natural." The father who loves his child *simply* because of the natural, biological connection of parenthood, does not, in fact, love the child. Love requires an affirmation of the particular person as such and not because of their biological or social role. Indeed, all "love because" troubles us, for in each case the love is not purely given, but is either calculated or coerced. In other words, in some sense, the relationship of love must be extrinsic to the natural or even social condition of the partners. It must be a love *regardless,* or even *in spite of,* the constellation of biological and social necessities which constitute our human "nature." Here, the "real partnership" must always remain an "unexpected miracle."[44]

44. Rahner's appeal to the analogy of earthly love as the device for explicating the logic of love raises difficulties. At first glance, it would appear that he is backsliding into the method of using nature (earthly love) to illumine grace (divine love) — the neo-scholastic approach which he claims to be repudiating. A closer and more charitable reading would, instead, recognize that the conclusion which he intends to deduce from the insight that love is the essence of grace — that grace is an ever present determinate within the "earthly" form of human life — allows Rahner to use an *analogia gatiae,* if you will, rather than an *analogia naturae* as it would seem at first reading. For Rahner, then, the appeal to the analogy of earthly love is *not* a turn to a merely natural phenomenon. It does not entail defining grace by nature. Instead, given what we know about the grace, that it is love, we can also know that earthly life, including earthly love, is always already suffused with the dynamism of grace. Hence, the analogy is *gratiae* rather than *naturae.*

This is not, then, a backsliding to neo-scholasticism, but it is circular. We know only that the analogy is *gratiae* and not *naturae* because of the analysis of the relationship between nature and grace based precisely on what the analogy has told us about the logic of love! In Rahner's argument this circularity is materially nonproblematic but formally troubling.

Materially, the scriptural witness provides a perspicuous illustration of the relation of intrinsic and extrinsic forces in God's love for humanity. As the gospel stories wind their way to the culminating drama at Golgotha, the narrative action becomes more and more "inevitable." Jesus increasingly becomes the patient of events, the vessel of divine action. The final evening and day unfold with a strict necessity, as if each moment were charted according to God's eternal plans. At this point, Jesus' fate seems superordinate and extrinsic, imposed not chosen, predetermined not controlled by human decision. And yet, the depiction of Jesus in those final hours is of a man most human. No longer are we reading of a miracle-worker and sage, whose teachings and healings are narrated in earlier chapters. Jesus does not dwell upon the significance in his healing of the paralytic, and he does not

The exigencies of love condemn exclusively intrinsicist and extrinsicist tendencies. For Rahner, *la nouvelle théologie* tends to diminish the "unexpected miracle" of the grace which is divine love. In spite of verbal efforts to preserve the gratuity of grace, the attempt to reverse the strategy of separation by linking nature to grace with the postulate of a natural desire for God raises insuperable difficulties. Once we presuppose that the human creature is created with an orientation towards union with God, then the creator cannot "refuse this communion without offending against the meaning of this creation and his very creative act . . ." and "if the ordination [toward the supernatural] cannot be detached from nature, the fulfillment of the ordination from God's point of view is exacted."[45] Yet, this obligatory or necessary fulfillment violates the logic of love. There can be no "must" of this sort in the relationship of self-giving. Hence, "it follows from the innermost essence of grace that a disposition for grace belonging to man's nature is impossible."[46]

The force of Rahner's criticism of this tendency in *la nouvelle théologie*

---

tarry to explain the cascade of enigmatic teachings. Instead he hurries up to Jerusalem where, as the gospels draw to a close, the events and actions become more and more intrinsic to his identity. Thus, just as on the Cross Jesus is most passive under the forces of necessity, the necessities of power, the necessities of state, the necessities of the cosmic drama of atonement, so it is on the Cross that Jesus of Nazareth is most truly and fully himself, the man of sorrows, the man for others. In the culminating scriptural witness to divine love, we find the fullest intensifications of the extrinsic and intrinsic moments. As a result, there can be no material reason to reject the circularity of Rahner's argument.

The formal difficulties are another matter. The fact that Rahner appeals to an earthly analogy to explicate the logic of love in an argument designed to show the "engraced" character of our earthly existence when an *analogia fidei* lay so close at hand may raise serious doubts about his purported method of pursuing a strictly theological definition of nature "with the help of Revelation." Is Rahner serious about reversing the methodological presuppositions of neo-scholasticism, or is he prone to disguising his only partial moves with appeals to "spiritual" dimensions of earthly life — "the ultimate yearning, the most profound inner dispersion, the radical experience of the universally human tragedy of concupiscence and death" — without testing these "limit experiences" in any sustained way in light of the object of faith? Is this circularity symptomatic of a tendency to substitute "transcendence" for revelation, a tendency which does no material harm here, but which runs throughout Rahner's work and has unfortunate consequences in other contexts? On this matter we do well to note that these are precisely the kinds of questions which caused von Balthasar's enthusiasm for Rahner's theological project as a whole to wane.

45. *TI* I, p. 306.
46. *TI* I, p. 308.

is devastating. In its effort to wrestle nature away from neo-scholasticism, *la nouvelle théologie* remains trapped within the limitations of the sub-stance/accident metaphysics. To emphasize the real partnership willed by God, Rahner reads *la nouvelle théologie* as proposing that human nature "objectively includes the supernatural as the end intrinsically necessary to its existence." This certainly achieves one of the goals appropriate to a theological account of grace, to drive home the real partnership of grace. Grace fulfills our very nature. However, this particular way of conceptual-izing the intrinsic significance of grace "is immediately to threaten the supernaturality and unexactedness of the end."[47] Such a result is inevitable, for the Aristotelian grounding of existence in "nature" will always reduce the intrinsicist program to a contradiction since it involves equating "cen-tral to existence" or "fundamental determinate of human life" with natural substance. As such, an intrinsic orientation towards God simply must take the precise form of a natural desire, but it is a natural desire for something which cannot, by virtue of its reality as God's self-giving in love, be the object of a natural desire.

This rejection of the exclusively intrinsicist tendency of *la nouvelle théologie* cannot lead to an affirmation of the more clearly extrinsicist consequences of neo-scholasticism. Some way must be found to do justice to the "real partnership" between God and creature, for in his decision to ground his thinking in the dynamism of love, Rahner has foresaken the purely defensive posture of the ontological strategy of separation. Intrinsi-cist emphases are crucial. Rahner assumes that all theological systems must begin with the presupposition that "God wishes to communicate himself, to pour forth the love which he himself is. That is the first and the last of his real plans and hence of his real world too. Everything else exists so that this one thing might be: the eternal miracle of infinite love."[48] This commitment to the ultimate teleology of creation in redemption and consummation is at the core of the intrincist program, the central theme of *la nouvelle théologie*'s resourcement of Thomas and the passionate focus of its poetic spokesman, Teilhard de Chardin. In every respect such a view of creation as an echo of God's love would seem to demand a reevaluation of the neo-scholastic treatment of nature as independent and separate. If grace is to be first and last in God's plans, then surely he has structured

47. Both quotes *TI* I, p. 309.
48. *TI* I, p. 310.

the entire created order, including humanity, toward its consummation in him. "God must so create man that love does not only pour forth free and unexacted, but also so that man as real partner, as one who can accept or reject it, can experience and accept it."[49] In some sense, grace must be part of our world, and we part of the world of grace. Clearly, then, a strict separation of our ordinary lives from God's extraordinary self-giving in love is impossible.

Rahner's solution involves a reformulation of the relationship between nature and grace. This relationship must be materially intrinsicist while formally extrinsicist. The intrinsicist moment conditions our assessment of actual human existence. The ontological separation of nature and grace cannot define the human condition. Real partnership in love requires a genuine capacity to recognize and receive grace. There must be some "connaturality" between God and the human creature if the divine offer of love is to be a real possibility. As Rahner states, "Man should be *able* to receive this Love which is God himself: he must have a congeniality for it. He must be able to accept it (and hence grace, the beatific vision) as one who has room and scope, understanding and desire for it."[50] Moreover, this "room and scope" cannot be at the periphery of human life; the partnership is between God in His loving fullness and man in his created (and fallen) fullness. Thus, concluding his affirmation of the intrinsicist insight with a line indistinguishable from the spirit of *la nouvelle théologie,* Rahner writes, "The capacity for the God of self-bestowing personal love is the central and abiding existential of man as he really is."[51] The extraordinary is a live possibility in the midst of ordinary life.

How, then, does Rahner avoid affirming the reductive momentum of *la nouvelle théologie*'s correlation of nature and grace which he so persuasively argues is inconsistent with the positive content of grace as love? If an orientation toward grace is at the core of our concrete existence, how does grace remain the unexacted and unexpected miracle of love? The solution is to repudiate the ontological assumptions which generate the antithesis of either separation or equation. To do so, Rahner directs our attention to the exact status of our intrinsic capacity for grace. The central "room and scope" for divine love *cannot* be natural, for if it were, then

49. *TI* I, p. 311.
50. *TI* I, p. 311.
51. *TI* I, p. 312.

we would fall back into the contradictions of a love which is necessary in the unequivocal, natural, sense. Yet, we also cannot deny this capacity, for if we were to do so, then we would fall back into the contradictions of a love which has no partner. Thus, since grace is, in fact, God's self-communication in love, Rahner observes that the only possibility is that our "room and scope" for the divine "is itself to be characterized as 'supernatural'."[52] The capacity to receive grace is itself a gift of grace; it is a real potency for divine love which, though at the center of our ordinary existence, is not "natural." It is, as Rahner describes, a "supernatural existential."[53]

Here we need to recognize that the supernatural existential of receptivity for grace does not replace our identities as natural beings. Rahner does not substitute a new "supernatural" substance for the natural substance presupposed by both neo-scholasticism and (with less clarity) *la nouvelle théologie*. Recalling the rightful neo-scholastic insight, Rahner observes, "Were [man] simply this existential, and were this his nature, then it would be unconditional in its essence, i.e, once it has been given, the Love which is God would 'have to' be offered by God."[54] Even as the logic of grace requires us to affirm an always already supernaturalized form of actual human life, it requires us to posit a separate human nature. This is so because love seeks real partnership, not dependency. As such, the human creature must be imaginable without divine love. Moreover, such a relationship cannot be, finally, explicable as part of the ordered purpose of the natural realm. The more we know about God's decision to be *pro nobis,* the more we should recognize it as an unexpected miracle. As such, we need to acknowledge that our destiny could have been purely natural. To preserve the commitment to grace as love, then,

---

52. *TI* I, p. 313.
53. Rahner provides the following explanation of his terminology. "If one understands by 'existential' an enduring, continuing condition of a finite spiritual person, that which enables and is the ontological predetermination of personal behavior (that which, therefore, is involved in the free acts of a person), then I think one can signify well what is meant here by 'supernatural existential.' This existential is supernatural not only because it directs men toward the supernatural goal, but also because it is unowed. It is existen*tial* because it does not (as does the existen*tielle*) stem from the free act of the person, but rather is its presupposition" ("Uber das Verhältnis des Naturgesetzes zur übernaturlichen Gnadenordnung," *Orienteirung* XX [1956], p. 9. Quoted from William Shepard, *Man's Condition* [New York: Herder and Herder, 1969], p. 87).
54. *TI* I, p. 313.

our status as natural beings must be affirmed. But what is crucial for Rahner is that the affirmation is purely *theological,* and has no relation to the Aristotelian doctrine of substance. From this purely theological affirmation, a new definition emerges, " 'Nature' in the theological sense (as opposed to nature as the substantial content of an entity always to be encountered in contingent fact), i.e., as the concept contraposed to the supernatural, is consequently a remainder concept *(Restbegriff)."*[55] The strategy of separation remains, but Rahner has transformed it from an ontological to a *begrifflich* or, better, a "grammatical" distinction.

The upshot of this shift is that nature cannot serve as a privileged category for an analysis of the human condition. Rahner observes:

> When one undertakes to state with precision what exact content is intended by a concept of pure nature . . . the difficulties, indeed the impossibility, of a neat horizontal once again become apparent for us. . . . But these difficulties lie precisely in the nature of things: man can experiment with himself only in the region of God's supernatural loving will, he can never find the nature he wants in a "chemically pure" state, separated from its supernatural existential.[56]

55. *TI* I, p. 313. The idea that nature should be seen as a theologically derived concept rather than a point of departure is not Rahner's innovation. This approach has its roots in the very beginning of the career of *natura pura.* Counter-Reformation theologian Dominic Soto contributed to the emergence of nature as a decisive category in the polemics against the perceived pessimism of the Protestant view of original sin and the extrinsicism of the idea of imputed alien righteousness. Yet in that development, Soto scrupulously described nature as a theoretical construct. Soto hoped to treat man *in puris naturalibis mente concepto.* Rather quickly in the history of theology, however, the thought-experiment of pure nature became a material principle at the heart of revived Scholastic theology.

56. *TI* I, p. 315. In this way, Rahner meets Eastern Orthodoxy's particularly powerful complaint against scholastic theology by, in effect, embracing the criticism. As Vladimir Lossky writes, "The Eastern tradition knows nothing of 'pure nature' to which grace is added as a supernatural gift. For it, there is no natural or 'normal' state, since grace is implied in the act of creation itself." For Lossky, reality is already taken up into the drama of God's relation to the created order which culminates in Christ. " 'Pure nature', for Eastern theology, would thus be a philosophical fiction corresponding neither to the original state of creation, nor to its present condition which is 'against nature', nor to the state of deification which belongs to the age to come" (both quotes from *The Mystical Theology of the Eastern Church* [Crestwood, N.Y.: St. Vladimir's Seminary Press, 1976], p. 101). This is exactly Rahner's conclusion — pure nature is a remainder concept, a "fiction" which emerges out of the logic of grace as love, but which has no independent reality in a world

One must make clear distinctions *in mente* between the natural self and
the self addressed by grace — the distinction is required by the unexacted
quality of grace — but one cannot follow through with this distinction *in
re*. The elimination of the empirical application of this distinction cuts to
the quick of the neo-scholastic way of thinking.[57] The strategy of separation has no ontological significance. In this way, Rahner has formulated
a view of the relationship between nature and grace which though formally
extrinsicist — nature is always distinct from grace — is materially intrinsicist. Divine love addresses us at the center of our existence by virture of

---

which is under the Lordship of Christ from the very outset. However, the question which
Lossky must address is whether "pure nature" is a theologically *necessary* fiction, necessary
especially in a world which is so eager to control the gift of grace and put it to its own
"spiritual" purposes. Many inheritors of the Augustinian theological tradition, Rahner
included, have been so eager to overcome the extrinsicism of Latin theology that this
question has not been pressed as vigorously as it should.

57. The effect of Rahner's reconceptualization of the relationship between nature and
grace is best seen with respect to the neo-scholastic defense of the reality of grace by recourse
to the parallel structure of substances. Rahner is careful not to eliminate the distinction
between nature and grace. However, since nature is a remainder concept, it cannot function
as a point of departure for our analysis of grace. Grace, Rahner writes, "cannot be sufficiently
described by formal ontological categories alone (created 'quality,' accident, *habitus*, etc.)"
(*TI* I, p. 316). Since "nature" has no role as the substance undergirding the actuality of
ordinary life, the neo-scholastic form of Aristotelianism cannot function as the definitive
resource for structuring a theological account of our relationship with God. Instead, what
Rahner calls "personal categories (love, personal intimacy, self-communication)" become
indispensable. We might question Rahner's assumptions about the alternatives to the
neo-scholastic categories. However, his formulation of the relationship between nature and
grace clearly removes the substance/accident metaphysic as the privileged form of theological analysis.

Loss of privilege is less severe than elimination. Rahner is uncertain about the full
consequence of his turn to *Restbegriff.* He insists that his position does not conflict with
the encyclical *Humani generis,* and offers an interpretation of his position which indicates
that the idea of a supernatural existential does not so much dismiss neo-scholastic analysis
as deepen it. He claims that his solution to the extrinsicism/intrinsicism debate allows us
to "see more clearly how the Catholic theology of grace . . . can go beyond the notion of
a *merely* entitative, created state and the merely 'ontic' and non-existential element of a
physical accident" (*TI* IV, p. 177). The problem here is that the solution of shifting the
strategy of separation from an ontological to a grammatical role would seem to forbid *any*
analysis of nature (and by implication, grace) in terms of the Aristotelian doctrine of
substance. As such, Rahner's account would seem to eliminate this characteristic form of
neo-scholastic thought from the question of the relationship between nature and grace.

the supernatural existential, and at the same time, grace remains an unexpected miracle because in our reception of grace we recognize the way in which both the gift and the capacity to receive the gift are completely distinct from our capacities as purely natural beings.

4. Consequences and the Way Forward

UP TO THIS POINT I have narrated a short episode of the career of the Christian ideal of transcendence. This has been a story of extremes. The singular immanence of revolutionary society (or perhaps the radical transcendence of revolutionary rhetoric) was opposed by the institutional and theological counterweight of Roman Catholicism. This Christian movement, in turn, could be viewed as either an anti-modern society engaged in a corporate form of radical transcendence (the other-worldly sacramental Church) or a profoundly modern mirror of modernity (the political, totalitarian ecclesiastical machine). Without proposing any definitive assessment of the true shape and purpose of the modern Catholic Church, I did suggest that the *kulturkampf* between Catholicism and modernity had the effect of creating the "interminable divisions" of modern life which so distressed Rousseau, and which gave rise to the practical conditions for the mixed form of amphibious aspiration suggested by Cleanthes in Hume's *Dialogues*.

Within neo-scholasticism, this mixed possibility became a theological ideal as well as a practical reality. The notion of *natura pura* sought to explain and regularize the many overlays of worldly and heavenly imperatives in the lives of modern believers. However, this project was invested in a philosophical method that made "mixture" deeply problematic, and attempts to formulate the theological ideal of an ordinary life transformed by extraordinary grace inevitably fell in one of two directions: either toward the strict separation of extrinsicism or the familiar unity of intrinsicism. Both failed to express genuine amphibious existence. Rahner's theological achievement lies in his recognition of the priority of the theological ideal of mixed existence over the inherited conceptual apparatus and systematic strategies of neo-scholasticism, most particularly, the *ontology* of nature and grace. As we saw in his treatment of the issue, Rahner (1) shows that mixed or amphibious existence is entailed in the fundamental proposition that God is love, (2) insists that this ideal should control the technical articulation of the relationship between nature and grace, and (3) posits in that control the supernatural existential and redefines nature as a "remainder concept" and thus rejects the prevailing presupposition that the distinction between nature and grace can be read off metaphysical or ontological distinctions common to philosophical accounts of the ordinary and extraordinary in human life.

We need to recognize that Rahner's "solution" is purely theological. In no way does he eliminate or even reduce the real tension between extrinsicism and intrinsicism. Instead, his achievement is to show that this tension is *the* defining feature of the transcendence made possible by the offer of divine love. The pressures of intrinsicism and extrinsicism drive the Christian life as a pilgrimage in which the miracle of divine love (extrinsicism) is the most ordinary of events (intrinsicism), in which the Lord of all eternity is a particular historical person, in which the very God whose name we cannot utter is so intimately part of our world that we may rest our heads on his bosom. For Rahner, this mixture of the ordinary and extraordinary (e.g., particularity and universality) is not a problem for theology to solve by either separating the elements ontologically or by showing their deeper, essential unity. Instead, this combination of the ordinary and extraordinary is part of the logic of the divine offer of self-giving in love. The mixture is dictated by the divine transcendence which makes possible our transcendence.

In view of the importance of understanding how Rahner's "solution" functions with respect to the basic question of our amphibious participation in both nature and grace, we must consider the tension between extrinsicism and intrinsicism in a purely formal way. To do so, we need to define the two possible dispositions toward relations, external and internal, which characterize the more broadly theological agendas of extrinsicism and intrinsicism. This will have the benefit of clarifying the sense in which Rahner's solution is a purely theological construct, and will indicate the way forward to consideration of cognate areas of Rahner's thought relevant to the question of the mixed structure of the Christian vision of transcendence.[58]

---

58. The following account of relations represents a gloss on the rather complex analysis of the logic of relations in G. E. Moore's "External and Internal Relations," found in *Philosophical Studies* (London: Routledge & Kegan Paul, 1922), pp. 276-309. There, Moore is interested in refuting F. H. Bradley's claim that *all* relations are internal relations. The

External relations are defined in the following way. A relation is external if P is related to Q in such a way that if P were not related to Q, then P would still be P. For example, I am related to my pencil in such a way that if I were to set aside this pencil, or if I were never to have picked it up in the first place, I would still be who I am. The pencil has no essential or internal relation to my identity. The relation does not constitute me in any important way. Internal relations are quite opposite. A relation is internal if P is related to Q in such a way that if P were not related to Q, then P would no longer be P. For example, I am related to my mother in such a way that, if she were not my mother, then I would not be who I am. At least at the genetic level, my relation to my mother is intrinsic to my identity. The relation constitutes me in crucial and fundamental ways.

The conflict between neo-scholasticism and (a certain interpretation of) *la nouvelle théologie* involves divergent assessments of our relation to God's self-giving in love (grace). Let us consider idealized forms of the opposing arguments. For the extrinsicist, our relation to God's consummating love is external. P (the human creature) is related to Q (grace) in such a way that if P were not related to Q, then P would still be P. This relation must obtain because God has a special interest in (love for) us. In this love, reasons neo-scholasticism, God has conferred existence upon us. Yet, if the existence is *real*, that is to say, if we really have our own being, then we must be able to exist and still be ourselves outside of a continuing relation to God's ultimate purposes in love. Love creates for the sake of the beloved, absolute love creates absolutely for the sake of the beloved.

---

problems associated with this claim do not, strictly speaking, bear upon the question before Rahner. Rahner is concerned with the status of *one* particular relation, our relation to God. However, Moore's polemic against Bradley highlights an important connection between the theological question of our relation to God and the philosophical question of how all things stand in relation. For at root, two intuitions operate in the history of western philosophy. For Heraclitus, all is flux. The "to be" of a thing is found in the stream of relations which constitutes the cosmos. The nexus of relations grounds the thing. In contrast, for Parmenides, all is or is nothing. The givenness of the thing is basic and constitutes the possibility of relations. From these two positions — Heraclitus's affirmation that all relations are internal and Parmenides' conviction that all relations are external — flow two quite different philosophical traditions, one of which gives a relational account of being and the other of which gives a substantial account. Knowing how philosophical vocabularies function with respect to this basic distinction is crucial for their theological application.

A Being who governs by absolute love and has the power to create *ex nihilo* will confer being absolutely upon the beloved. Therefore, returning to the vocabulary of neo-scholasticism, who we are is essentially defined by our human *nature,* not our status in relation to God by *grace* — the strategy of separation.

The intrinsicist assumes otherwise. Here, the relationship between God's love and the creature is internal. Without a relation to grace we would not still be who we are. P (the human creature) is related to Q (God's self-communication in love) in such a way that if P were not related to Q then P would no longer be P. In some sense, this is even true of the neo-scholastic position, for when God confers being upon us in creation, this is rightly understood as an act of love. In other words, without *that* particular relation in creative love, P would not still be P; P would not be at all. However, for the neo-scholastic position, the loving interest of God in that original relation creates an independent being for whom all other relations to God are external. Hence, though we are quite obviously internally related to God as creator, for the extrinsicist, we are externally related to God as redeemer and consummator. For the intrinsicist, this makes no sense. Love has a purpose, the well-being or perfection of the beloved. Therefore, God's special interest in humanity is not to confer existence *simpliciter,* but to confer a special kind of existence, that is, existence *coram deo.* As such, the original relation of God to humanity in creation constitutes our being as always oriented toward relation with God in redemption and consummation. For the intrinsicist, then, we are internally related to God's love in every aspect. Echoing the language of *la nouvelle théologie,* we are created with a natural desire for the vision of God. Without that desire, and the relation implied, I would not be the human person that I am.

It should be clear why Rahner prefers the logic of external relations while, at the same time, affirms the role of internal relations. For Rahner, our existence cannot be internally related to God's grace. For ultimately our relation to God is governed by the pure love of God's self-giving, and love cannot be the "unexpected miracle," nor can it presuppose a "real partnership" if it is already constitutive of our human nature. Our relation to God's grace must be external; the creature must remain a creature even if unrelated to God's self-giving in love. However, for Rahner, the same love which vindicates neo-scholastic extrinsicism dictates a commitment to grace as internally related to the human creature. Divine love is surely the most powerful and dynamic reality encountered by the human person.

Love is purposeful, absolute love is absolutely purposeful. Hearing the promise of divine love, to say nothing of receiving the gift itself, must be transformative. Moreover, this love is at the center of God's being, and as such, creation, just as much as redemption and consummation, is an expression of divine love. It is difficult to see, then, how P can still be P without a relation to God's love in all its fullness. Our relation to God must, in some sense, be internal. Thus, Rahner posits the supernatural existential as a constitutive, but not natural aspect of our identities.

On the face of it, Rahner appears to be saying that our relation to grace is both external *and* internal. This is a logically suspect position to hold, for it is difficult to interpret the meaning of a claim that P is related to Q in such a way that if P were not related to Q, then P would both be and not be P. Rahner moderates the potential contradiction implied here by qualifying the consequent. In one sense, P would still be P. Without a relation to grace, we would still be the *natural beings* that we already are. The relation is external, hence the theologumenon, *natura pura*. However, in another sense, P would not still be P. As *personal beings,* without a relation to grace, we would not be the individuals that we already are. At this level of existence, then, the relation is internal, hence the theologumenon, supernatural existential. The relation does not consititute us *qua* natural beings, but it does constitute us *qua* personal beings.[59] This, then,

---

59. Rahner's approach echoes the Chalcedonian use of both nature and person. In both the anthropological and Christological contexts, the concepts are used to insure salvific relationship between God and humanity which does not collapse into a form of identity. Thus, the Council of Chalcedon revised the earlier notion of the unity of Christ as of one nature. Such an expression allows for the suggestion that the divine and human are fused together in Christ, and this fusion risks absorbing the humanity of Christ into a *tertium quid* between the divine and human. This absorption either renders Christ's person and work extrinsic to ordinary and purely human affairs or, in an inevitable intrinsicist echo, suggests that human nature has a divine teleology toward the divine-human fusion. Similarly, the anthropological career of *natura* has been a protracted struggle with the twin dangers of extrinsicism and intrinsicism. In both cases, something like Rahner's grammatical solution appears. The crux of Chalcedonian Christology is the distinction between nature and person which allows the divine and human to be both externally (as nature) and internally (as person) related in Christ. As we see here, Rahner constructs his account of human existence with the same dual relation in mind.

A striking feature of Rahner's work is that he has an ear for the Christological coda in theological anthropology. Yet, the parallel is unmentioned and even, perhaps, unnoticed. Any genuinely comprehensive theological assessment of Rahner must consider both his remarkable ear and his equally remarkable silence.

would seem to be the way in which Rahner handles the logical dilemma of affirming both an external and an internal relation to grace.

Some observations need to be made about this solution. We need to be clear about the operation of Rahner's escape from the potential contradiction implied in affirming both external and internal relations — "P would be both P and not P" Through an understanding of the role of this distinction between natural and personal existence, I intend to argue that (1) logically, Rahner's theology as a whole must be grounded in the particularity of Christian revelation, and (2) conceptually, this grounding redefines that Christian understanding of metaphysics, and (3) materially, the resultant vision of our amphibious situation must govern reflection on the logic of human transcendence.

(1) The status of Rahner's appeal to the distinction between natural and personal existence is decisive. This distinction is, admits Rahner, purely notional. Natural existence, as we will recall, is a *"Restbegriff,"* and the distinction between it and the constitutive feature of personal existence, the supernatural existential, does not map onto actual existence in any clear way. The two are always intermixed in actual experience. The fact that this distinction is not, then, empirically identifiable evokes one of two responses. First, we may respond by rejecting the distinction as specious. After all, we cannot find conclusive evidence for it in everyday experience. In this case, we return to the potential contradiction implied in affirming both an internal and external relation to grace, and either try to find another way to moderate the logical difficulties or repudiate the dual affirmation. Our second alternative is to accept the distinction as a way forward through the potential contradiction. However, in this case, accepting the distinction must be on grounds other than experience.

As Rahner suggests, these other grounds are notional, or grammatical. Our acceptance of the distinction between natural and personal existence is intelligible in light of accepting a nexus of notions, or some grammar, as a whole. The beginning point in Rahner's treatment of the question is the proposition that God is love (plus some, perhaps problematic, assumptions about the logic of love). And how do we know that God is love? Rahner does not explicitly designate the source of this proposition in his essay on nature and grace, but he does say, generally, that Revelation will govern. The suggestion, then, is that the proposition that God is love is embedded in the notional structure or grammar of Christianity itself. Thus, if we are to accept the distinction between *natura pura* and the supernatural existential neces-

sary to handle the apparent contradiction between affirming both intrinsicism (an internal relation to grace) and extrinsicism (an external relation to
grace), then we can do so only for purely theological reasons.[60]

This might strike the reader as a rather tedious digression. It is, however,
very important for any systematic reading of Rahner's work as a whole.
For if I am correct in my analysis of the logical implications of Rahner's
position on the question of intrinsicism and extrinsicism, then there can
be *no* philosophical reasons sufficient to affirm the distinction between
natural and personal existence. At the most basic level, this means that
there can be *no* philosophically adequate account of whether or how God
is love, or *pro nobis*. More specifically, there can be *no* philosophical reasons
sufficient to affirm the technical apparatus Rahner deploys to develop and
explicate that distinction, e.g., the supernatural existential. In which case,
when reading Rahner, we must either say that his basic categories of
analysis (the personalist-transcendental terminology) are only warranted
theologically (because they presuppose the distinction between natural and
personal existence), or Rahner is systematically inconsistent because he
assumes that the distinction between natural and personal existence is
empirical (and is therefore philosophically warranted) rather than notional.

This kind of systematic inconsistency would be devastating, for a shift
from a notional to an empirical distinction between natural existence and
personal existence, between *natura pura* and the supernatural existential,
would vitiate the very solution to the problems associated with neo-
scholasticism and *la nouvelle théologie* which Rahner claims to solve. This
is the case because an experimentally identifiable distinction between the
two would return us to the either/or of separation or conflation. If we
could, in fact, pick out the "natural" moment over and against the "personal" moments, then we would be faced once again with a *de facto*
separation of existence into two ontologically separate realms. This is

60. I need to alert the reader that the connotatively laden terms "Revelation," "Christianity itself" and "theological," as well as seemingly technical terms such as "notional
structure" and "grammar," are intended in the most neutral possible sense. The texture
and subtlety of Rahner's theological agenda depends upon the content assumed in each
case (is Revelation an event or a thing? Is Christianity a kind of experience or a set of
propositions? Is the term "notional structure" to be given a Hegelian or Wittgensteinian
spin?). However, these specific directions in Rahner's thought are not my immediate
concern. Instead, I am trying to push Rahner's position to the point at which it has the
minimum of recognizably "Rahnerian" aspects and is, therefore, more simply Christian.

precisely the structure of neo-scholastic extrinsicism and would, quite likely, produce a new "ghetto mentality." Much of what passes for modern spirituality presupposed such a separation in its efforts to seek a realm of "transcendence" or "the sacred." This psycho-spiritual project has the inevitable consequence of separating "spirituality" from life, since the "transcendent" is not the stuff of everyday life. Further, the unsatisfactory separation, in turn, motivates new intrinsicist efforts to show how the natural is entailed in the personal, or the personal in the natural. The consequent conflations and reductions inevitably follow. Indeed, "systematic" attempts to use Rahner's supernatural existential as a foundational category have produced conflations and reductions characteristic of intrinsicism. To avoid these consequences, the distinction must remain grammatical, and the use of the anthropological categories *natura pura* and supernatural existential must be governed theologically.

There are some reasons to think that Rahner is inconsistent, not the least of which is a widespread opinion of Rahnerians that Rahner is a "fundamental" or "foundational" theologian in the sense that he provides philosophically compelling reasons for affirming traditional Christian claims. I do not think that this is the case. Although I will take up Rahner's use of the term "foundational" in Chapter Six, I will provide no full scale assessment of Rahner's work as a whole. I will instead simply assume that Rahner is consistent and will read him accordingly.[61] I may not be right

---

61. Reading Rahner in this way is buttressed by an interesting parallel with Karl Barth, who formulates his position with vigorous and polemical affirmations of the priority of revelation. Like Rahner, Barth seeks to bring all features of human existence into the light of divine love. No part of life is merely "natural" or independent of God's purposes in Christ. As Barth declares, "What God created when He created the world and man was not just any place, but that which was foreordained for the establishment and history of the covenant, nor just any subject, but that which was to become God's partner in this history" (*Church Dogmatics*, III/1, p. 231). As such, Barth describes the covenant as the inner basis of creation. In words which are interchangeable with characteristic Rahnerian assertions, Barth writes, "Because God loves the creature, its creation and continuance and preservation point beyond themselves to an exercise and fulfillment of His love" [p. 95]). Though Barth eagerly and aggressively defines God's love in Trinitarian and Christological terms ("the free love of God" is that "which God has declared in Himself in the covenant of the Father with His Son," p. 97), while Rahner characteristically floats in abstractions such as "God's self-communication," and though not enough can be said about this difference, both agree that human existence is internally related to grace. Further, like Rahner, for Barth the internal relation alone does not adequately describe our condi-

about Rahner's work as a whole, but at least it will be more interesting to proceed in this way. For such an approach will, in principle, allow the proposition that God is love to saturate some of the seemingly far-flung outposts of Rahner's thought.[62]

(2) The proposition that God is love shapes not only the structure of theological reflection, but also redefines the meaning of its central concepts, most importantly, the concept of "essence" or "substance." As we saw in the neo-scholastic approach, a thing is what it is because of the substance which constitutes it. This assumption is not so much rejected by Rahner as reinterpreted. In his consideration of the relation between nature and grace, he explicitly sets aside the neo-scholastic explanation of the fundamental "to be" of human existence. There is no "human nature" which might be identified and analyzed. No metaphysical (or physical) accounts of human existence fully explain or establish the inner origin and purpose of ordinary human existence. This way is barred because we (and by implication, all other beings) must *be* according to the "necessity" found in the logic of divine love. In this respect, our identities are constituted by the proposition that God is love. This proposition is, then, the real "essence." We are "grounded" in a "substance" and this substance is defined

tion. For Barth, "creation is not itself the covenant. The existence and being of the one loved are not identical with the fact that it is loved" (p. 97). In other words, creation is externally related to grace. Hence, like Rahner, Barth affirms *both* an internal and external relation of human existence to divine love. Of course, Barth need not tarry to show how such an affirmation is logically possible, because he has already committed himself to a Chalcedonian framework. Recognizing that Rahner works toward the position which Barth establishes at the outset is crucial for any attempt to read Rahner consistently.

62. Though I intend to provide a reading of Rahner in which God's self-communication governs, this does not indicate wholesale affirmations of this theological project. Rahner's account of the relationship between nature and grace indicates a direct dependence upon God's revelation. Yet, Rahner does have a tendency to either mishandle or neglect the particular identity which vindicates his grammatical solution. For example, when Rahner turns to Jesus Christ in *The Foundations of the Christian Faith,* he expends a great deal of energy showing how God's self-communication in Christ *fits* rather than *governs* the shape of our transcendence. There, as in many other places in his work, he preserves the logic of amphibious transcendence, but inverts the solution provided in his account of nature and grace. As a consequence, though he sustains the architecture of the Christian vision of transcendence across diverse theological loci, he does not adequately treat the Architect. The result is a nearly inevitable slide away from the grammatical solution and toward a position in which the logic of amphibious transcendence is taken for granted.

as that form of existence shaped by the offer of divine love, and as we have seen, that form of existence is both natural *(natura pura)* and personal (the supernatural existential).

This redefinition of "essence" precludes the independent ontological analysis which is central to the neo-scholastic method. Consider one of the standard manuals, the Pohle-Preuss *Dogmatic Textbook.* This multi-volume work begins with epistemological questions, proceeds to consider the nature of God, and then takes up the analysis of God's actions on our behalf. The transition from the treatment of God *in se* to His actions *ad extra* begins with a metaphysical account of human nature.[63] The shape and significance of grace is discerned by a prior consideration of our substantial existence as natural beings. From this basis, the account of grace becomes an exercise in enumerating the various "unexacted" modifications of human faculties, talents and powers — the parallel structure envisioned by Scheeben. However, since the proposition that God is love entails the mixed conclusion that human existence is always both "natural" and "supernatural," this approach is no longer viable. At no moment can the theologian speak accurately about the purely natural aspects of human life.

This theological definition of essence does more than set aside the characteristic neo-scholastic theology of grace. Such an account of the "to be" of human existence also prohibits theology from ascribing foundational significance to independent metaphysical analysis of any sort.[64]

63. This use of human anthropology in the manual tradition shows how closely extrinsicism is linked to its mirror, intrinsicism. For the intrinsicist, the crucial role of human nature in the move from God's nature to God's grace shows the natural teleology of our created condition toward consummation in God's love. (Karl Barth recognized this linkage in his many attacks upon the "copulative 'and' " in the neo-scholastic method. E.g., *Church Dogmatics* II/2, pp. 528-34.) This close link has the perverse effect of both heightening the need to separate nature from grace to prevent any slide toward conflation, and inviting by its very structure the conflation it so vigorously condemns.

64. An interesting illustration of the depth of Rahner's subordination of metaphysics to the logic of divine love is Mark Lloyd Taylor's detailed and probing attempt to interpret Rahner's position within the framework of classical metaphysics. For Taylor, this framework shows that Rahner's "solution" to the tension between extrinsicism and intrinsicism does not work. For Taylor, "If one decides [as Rahner does] to defend the freedom of the divine love by arguing that God could create a world and yet not love that world in the full personal sense implied in the notion of divine self-communication, then one must also accept a necessary consequence of this view, namely, that God is only acciden-

This means that however we are to interpret Rahner's affirmations of modern philosophy, they cannot be "foundational." Instead, philosophical concepts such as "transcendental experience" must be understood as tools for elaborating the real essence of human existence, that is, the proposition that God is love. In this way, Rahner's solution to the nature/grace question shifts the terminology of theology away from a "substantial" metaphysic, as well as a "transcendental" metaphysic, and towards a "grammatical" metaphysic.[65] The basic concepts for the analysis of existence are shaped by the notional structure of Christian belief, e.g., *natura pura* and the supernatural existential, two "non-actual" constituents of human existence,

---

tally, and not essentially, love for others" (*God is Love: A Study in the Theology of Karl Rahner* [Atlanta: Scholar's Press, 1986], p. 280). Taylor's claim is that Rahner simply shifts the intractable extrinsicism/intrinsicism tension from the question of the relation of nature and grace and into the Godhead where, Taylor argues, Rahner cannot move beyond a "merely verbal solution" to the problem (an accusation Taylor makes throughout Part II of *God is Love*). Either love is extrinsic to God's essence or freedom is extrinsic. My argument is that Rahner's response parallels his account of human existence. The "essence" of God, like the essence of humanity, is constituted by the logic of divine love. The "fact" of love grounds the essence of the divine, and this "fact" (which, like all "facts," must take the "merely verbal" form of a sentence in order to be manipulated logically) entails both an internal and external relation to creation. All beings have both an independence from and an affinity for the divine self-offer. In this sense, Taylor is right that Rahner does not "solve" the metaphysical contradiction. However, since Rahner redefines the status of metaphysics, classical concerns about divine freedom and impassability can no longer shape the kind of "necessity" which governs a logically consistent Doctrine of God. Instead, the "necessities" of love, which Taylor rightly sees are "contingent" in the sense that they depend upon the man Jesus, establish the conditions of consistency. As we have seen, under such conditions, it would be *inconsistent* to say that God is not both externally related ("free from") and internally related ("essentially committed to") the world. In this respect, consistency is "grammatical" rather than metaphysical, and all of Taylor's quite detailed and illuminating charges of logical incoherence are transformed into helpful guides towards the wider implications of Rahner's solution to the nature/grace question.

65. Rahner's move away from independent metaphysical analysis is evident elsewhere in his work. When considering the nesting conceptual dilemmas of Christology — time and eternity, immanence and transcendence, change and impassability, difference and identity — Rahner foresakes a general metaphysical solution. He writes, "The proper *topos* for achieving an understanding of the immanence of God in the world in theology is not a treatise on God worked out in abstract metaphysical terms, but rather the treatise on grace" (*TI* XI, p. 225). The particular form of God's self-offer of love is the point of departure for speculative questions.

rather than the notional structure of Christian belief being shaped by an analysis of existence.[66]

(3) In this grammatical metaphysics, anthropological considerations must account for our dual relation to God. Our internal and external relation to God's offer of love has already redefined the concept of nature and created a new concept, the supernatural existential. So also, when Rahner turns to a more detailed consideration of aspects of human existence, we should expect him to preserve both the extrinsicist and intrinsicist insights by distinguishing between natural and personal existence without identifying that distinction with any actual states of affairs in human life.[67] This will allow for a real dynamism in human life, a dy-

66. Rahner's close argument regarding the relationship between nature and grace shows how Christian theology cannot identify "the real" with substance or essence. This insight is not alien to the theological tradition. For example, in his polemics against Pelagius, Augustine draws similar conclusions. Augustine observes that Pelagius proposes a powerful argument against our interpretation of sin as a serious and debilitating wound. Pelagius recognizes that sin cannot be a substance, for God creates all things and sin is evil, thus God would not have created it. Pelagius continues, "How could that which lacks substance have weakened or changed human nature?" This speculation leaves Augustine exasperated. Augustine quotes the Psalmist's plea, "Heal my soul, for I have sinned against thee (Ps. 40:5)." For Augustine, this petition indicates that sin is a reality which, though *not* a substance, cuts deeply into who we are, so deeply that, barring divine intervention, it will utterly determine and pervert our destiny. The logic of the Scriptures dictates shifting attention away from substance and toward other forms of understanding our being. Using the metaphor of food, Augustine buttresses this shift. He reminds us that abstinence from food is not itself a substance, but this abstinence certainly shapes us by depriving us of nourishment. And this food analogy is a happy one, for Augustine observes the Psalmist echoing the same theme: "My heart is withered and beaten like grass, because I forgot to eat my bread (Ps. 101:5)." (All quotations from *Natura et gratia, Fathers of the Church,* vol. 86, p. 36). Thus, on the question of sin, Augustine pushes the notion of substance or essence into the background and draws the particular grammar of Christian revelation into the foreground. This shift away from substance or essence as the determinate ground of "the real" is, I would argue, characteristic of the Christian theological tradition as a whole. Rahner simply gives the issue rigorous form in his consideration of the relationship between nature and grace.

67. This caveat is crucial. The important point is that the natural/personal distinction does not entail an equation of "natural" with scientific data and "personal" with existentialist or phenomenological conditions of human existence. In fact, to the extent that such philosophical assumptions begin to acquire "substantial" weight as a new science of the human condition which merely replaces the scholastic approach, the characteristic vocabulary of Rahner and Rahnerian must be discarded, for such a "new science" merely inverts

namism toward God, without risking conflation. Recalling the terminology developed in our consideration of Hume's *Dialogues,* the dual relation to God will affirm relevance without the danger of pure immanence, and genuine otherness or mystery without the extremes of radical transcendence. The upshot will be a more refined and conceptually clear articulation of Cleanthes' vision of amphibious or mixed transcendence.

Two aspects of Rahner's thought bear out this consequence, his account of human knowing in general and his observations about the intellectual dimension of Christian identity. There is a natural overlap. Rahner is well aware of the fact that our epistemic commitments are deeply embedded in our social identities. Nonetheless, a rough and ready distinction can be made between Rahner's philosophy of mind, or perhaps more accurately, his metaphysics of knowledge, and his less sustained and less systematic observations about the Christian form of life and theological method. In both areas Rahner takes up the basic concerns animating Hume's *Dialogues.* For Cleanthes, the key to the vision of amphibious transcendence is the Argument from Design, and the fulcrum of that argument is the use of analogy. Analogy, in turn, was at the center of both Demea's and Philo's objections. These challenges assumed, shall we now say, that our relation to the extraordinary must either be purely external or purely internal. Both Demea and Philo draw reductive conclusions from Cleanthes' attempt to balance both through the use of analogy. Demea turns the possibility of analogy into rank identity. To have the empathy sufficient to recognize the purposes of an author is to *be* the author. Similarly, Philo exploits the intrinsicism implicit in Cleanthes' position and ignores the "common sense" observation that we have some interest in keeping God different and in some sense extrinsic to the human condition. In his attempt to preserve both moments, Cleanthes foreshadows Rahner's interest in am-

---

the extrinsicism of neo-scholasticism. Just as the neo-scholastic method cut off grace from the ordinary physicality and sociality of life, so also an existentialist or phenomenological attempt to "define" the personal — systematic use of typical Rahnerian gestures toward the "abyss of existence" or any number of assumptions about "immediate self-consciousness" — severs the relationship between our destiny in God's love and ordinary forms of life. In the end, our destiny in God, i.e., our *personhood,* is not defined by any philosophical account of "personal existence," but rather by the particular form of God's offer of love. In what follows, I shall assume that Rahner's grammatical formulation of our internal and external relation to grace is controlling, and I shall downplay his tendency to subsume the personal into transcendental philosophy.

phibious transcendence. We might do well, then, to read Rahner's meta-physics of knowledge as an attempt to defend Cleanthes' amphibious vision (Chapter Five).[68]

Not only were Demea and Philo united in their assault upon Cleanthes' amphibious use of analogy, but they also agreed that an unquestioning immersion in the Christian form of life is the only way to secure faith. Both defended a form of Christian indoctrination where a pedagogy of doubt about human rational capacities prepared the way for a credulous affirmation of traditional doctrine. This vision presupposes a certain view of the nature of the Christian form of life which Cleanthes implicitly calls

68. Not only can we look forward toward Rahner's metaphysics of knowledge, but now that the necessity of theological governance over the question of transcendence has been stated in clear, logical terms, we can look back to the enigmatic final scene in Hume's *Dialogues* and explain why Cleanthes, while unable to sustain his position philosophically, continues to exert a charm over the debate as a whole. At root, this is because the focus of the debate, *analogy,* is implicated in precisely the dilemma of internal and external relations which characterizes the question of nature and grace. To recall Balthasar's formu-lation, "Grace is something *for* a nature and *in* a nature. And thus it *presupposes* a nature, logically if not necessarily chronologically. Indeed, insofar as grace is flowing out and nature is receiving, it is also already a graced and transformed nature. And so nature exists concretely in the transformed, exalted "mode" of being graced. But the subject that has been so transformed is none other *(non alter)* than that of nature, even if it has become something different *(aliter)*. In this *aliter, non alter* we encounter the ontological *funda-mentum in re* of the noetic analogy . . ." (*The Theology of Karl Barth,* p. 281). When we apply Balthasar's observations to the *Dialogues,* we see that Cleathes insists upon the *non alter* in his rejection of Demea's radical transcendence, yet at the same time he requires the *aliter* when he sets aside Philo's pure immanence. And Cleanthes cannot do otherwise, for both are required if analogy is to function as a principle of the Argument from Design. Yet, by what deeper principle might Cleanthes defend analogy itself? How can he justify the *aliter, non alter* of his use of analogy? Is this dual commitment to both internal and external relation in analogy an equivocation if not an outright contradiction?

The answer, here, must be theological. The principle of truth is the one in whom the divine and human are *non alter* (internally related) as the single *person* Jesus Christ, and *aliter* (externally related) as the two *natures,* divine and human. This principle of truth allows us to think back to Philo's attempts to push analogy toward identity and acknowledge that Philo is quite right. A proposition is true if and only if it *is (non alter)* true. The logic of identity must govern our use of analogy. However Philo does not recognize that the truth is Christ, and that the logic of his identity is both *aliter* and *non alter.* Thus, if we confess that the truth *is* Jesus Christ, then we can recognize that Philo is formally quite right but materially incorrect, and on the basis of that revealed identity of truth in Christ, Cleanthes' use of analogy is vindicated.

into question with his use of analogy and Rahner quite explicitly rejects in his occasional observations about Christian existence and in his more extended meditations on the purposes and methods of theological reflection. In both cases, Rahner develops in some detail a view of Christian existence which cannot be statically credulous. In the mixed form of transcendence, where the ordinary and extraordinary cut across the actual distinctions which characterize human life, becoming faithful overtakes being faithful as the model of ecclesial identity (Chapter Six).

CHAPTER FOUR

❧   ❧

Recovering the World at
Our Fingertips

*The idea that it is by leaving the world that one finds oneself is
an ancient and very alluring one, but is it the most productive
way of regarding ourselves, particularly from a Christian theological perspective?*

Theology after Wittgenstein, p. 14

THE CHRISTIAN LIFE moves towards God. However, as Rahner's treatment of nature and grace has made evident, moving toward God
does not necessarily mean moving away from ordinary life. The problems
facing the Christian pilgrim are not embodiment, sociality, or economic
and political life *simpliciter*. The world is not a troubling impediment to
be overcome. Indeed, if anything, Christianity intensifies the role of the
ordinary as constitutive of human destiny. The Church is the visible body
of Christ. The bread and wine stand as the eternal feast of the Lamb. The
man Jesus is "of one substance" with the Father. In each instance, a real,
tangible and ordinary part of the world — an institution, food and drink,
a man's life — is decisively important, and not as a representative or
temporary symbol of the "real thing," but as an integral part of the
extraordinary offer of grace itself. A fullness of life is implied in the logic
of divine love. Worldliness, then, and not the world, is the impediment
to be overcome. The direction of life, not its location, is the focus of
struggle and fulfillment.

For Fergus Kerr, the western philosophical and theological tradition has failed to perceive and sustain this decisive insight into the ordinariness of the Christian vision. Inevitably, the brute facts of human physicality and sociality have been viewed as the problems to be overcome in our spiritual pilgrimage. Indeed, the very term "spiritual" has come to be equated with a state beyond the merely physical, and as a result, the peculiar combinations of the extraordinary and the ordinary found in the Christian ideal of transcendence have been distorted. A thinly disguised (if not openly proclaimed) version of radical transcendence is substituted. The Christian life ignores (if it does not actually repudiate) the ordinary conditions of existence.

How has this come to pass? For Kerr, the dominant western modes of thought, typified by but not limited to Enlightenment epistemologies, push theological discourse towards an otherworldly vision. The concepts and thought patterns, not just of modernity, but the entire "metaphysical way of thinking," lead to an "antipathy to the body" and an "indifference to community." The upshot is the same separation which marked neo-scholasticism. Our ordinary situation, the present context of everyday life, is divorced from the extraordinary aspirations of the mind, the will, the spirit. Not surprisingly, then, in the passage from Wittgenstein which sets the theme for Kerr's inquiry into the philosopher's writings, the problem of extrinsicism is central:

> It is very *remarkable* that we should be inclined to think of civilization — houses, streets, cars, etc. — as distancing man from his source, from what is sublime, infinite and so on. Our civilized environment, along with the trees and plants in it, then seems as though it were cheaply wrapped in cellophane and isolated from everything great, from God, as it were. That is a remarkable picture that forces itself on us.[1]

We have already seen this reasoning. Since the ultimate end of human life is something other than the ordinary conditions of existence, our aspirations become fundamentally discontinuous with the kind of people we really are. As Cleanthes has taught us, this discontinuity leads to a profound religious irrelevance regardless of the pious illusions which we might entertain about the significance of our beliefs.

---

1. *Theology After Wittgenstein* (Oxford: Basil Blackwell, 1986), p. 3. The passage is from *Culture and Value* (Oxford: Basil Blackwell, 1958), p. 50.

In light of this failure, Kerr looks to Wittgenstein as a guide for a diagnosis of the appeal of radical transcendence and the path through the thickets of the metaphysical way of thinking toward the recovery of the world.[2] Like Rahner, he wants to make the ultimate purposes of human life intrinsic to our concrete identities as worldlings. He hopes to reaffirm the ordinary in all its bodily, linguistic, and social dimensions. However, unlike Rahner, Kerr is not confident that a delicate balance may be struck between the ordinary and extraordinary. More than a sophisticated re-formulation of the technical theological question of nature and grace is necessary. The depth of the western infatuation with the extraordinary needs to be plumbed and its charm understood. And this infatuation is not purely "philosophical." Theologians are not innocent victims of metaphysical terms that they do not fully understand. Kerr observes that "many theologians regard this [otherworldliness] as inevitable and even desirable."[3] Disdain for the ordinary is not alien to theology. "If certain metaphysical options have swayed theology, they themselves have a theo-logical matrix," writes Kerr. In a Wittgensteinian mode, Kerr observes, "The eggshell clings to the thinking."[4] As a result, the theologian who is serious about the ordinary needs to be more than careful with the philo-sophical tools of the metaphysical tradition. Theology needs to question the very air which it breathes, the air of a culture which erodes the integrity and significance of the ordinary in all its forms: as language, social role,

---

2. This chapter, indeed this entire study of the Christian idea of transcendence, falls under the long shadow of Wittgenstein. Nonetheless, we will prescind from the question of what Wittgenstein himself thought and said about matters discussed throughout. His work and the vast jungle of secondary literature which has grown up around his work and "influence" since his death requires major exegetical effort. The aporetic quality of his later writings and the bitter struggles among Wittgensteinians over his legacy have forced this writer to abjure from judgment about what Wittgenstein did or did not mean to say. The desire is to engage and understand the position put forward by Kerr, a theologically motivated commentator, rather than to question his fidelity to the Master. Moreover, as we develop Kerr's account of the fate of transcendence we shall push rather hard in directions suggested by the logic of his Wittgensteinian polemic against transcendence, rather than attending to the specific shape of his own positive proposal. This reading of Kerr may violate a basic principle of theological charity (presume orthodoxy!), but such a vice may be necessary in order to flush out certain tendencies in the Wittgensteinian agenda, tendencies which theologians need to understand and avoid.

3. *Theology After Wittgenstein*, p. 10.

4. *Theology After Wittgenstein*, p. 24.

customs, and tradition. In this self-examination, Kerr concludes that nearly all the western tradition, Rahner's theology included, needs to be "taken to the cleaners."

1. The Metaphysical Aspiration

FOR KERR, the otherworldliness of the metaphysical way of thinking is best understood as centered around issues in epistemology. Descartes is the crucial modern figure. As Kerr summarizes, Descartes confronts the problem of certainty by turning inwards. I might be deceived about my beliefs, but, reasons Descartes, about one thing I may be certain. I am, at the very least and without a doubt, a thinking thing. Such a proposition I cannot doubt. From this certainty Descartes is able to build outwards to resecure the existence of God and the external world, all of which he has entertained as, in principle, dubitable. Kerr's point, a position which he shares with a whole range of critics of Descartes and the tradition of modern philosophy which makes epistemology foundational, is that the outward building movement of Descartes is hollow. The inward turning project of doubt is and remains decisive. The reflective capacity to identify thinking is the locus of certainty. Thus, a privileged feature of the self, *res cogitans,* provides the foundation for all that endures.

Regardless of how much of the external world Descartes hopes to revitalize afterwards, since the *cogito* is the lynchpin of his project, his entire philosophy is colored by the reduction of certainty to the fact that I am essentially a thinking thing, or worse, that I am essentially conscious of myself as a thinking thing. Concentration on thinking saves Descartes from the solipsism of the evil demon. Without this move our world crumbles into the labyrinths of possible deception. Thinking, then, is something separate from the world, prior and more secure, foundational and more certain. In this way, Descartes's philosophy instills in his readers' minds the ideal of an "epistemological subject who can view everything from a standpoint outside history and community."[5] As a result, the momentum of Descartes's project creates a view of the ultimate purpose of the self — thinking — as distinct and distant from the ordinary world. This ideal constitutes a pure expression of what Kerr calls our "metaphysi-

---

5. *Theology After Wittgenstein,* p. 24.

cal aspiration"; it is a retelling at the threshold of modernity of "the myth of the worldless (and often wordless) ego."[6]

Kerr's analysis of the logic of Descartes's philosophy is in large part convincing. We may find his characterizations of Descartes's "turn to the subject" at times tendentious. Descartes certainly believes that clear and distinct ideas are independent of what *I* want to believe. In that sense, the Cartesian method is neither purely subjective nor solipsistic. But Descartes's unhappiness with common knowledge and his quest for certainty do communicate a desire to overcome the ordinary ambiguities of life in order to reach a higher level of epistemic existence. And this desire devalues received wisdom and traditional authority, as well as the reports of our senses. In both these respects, then, the method developed in Descartes's *Meditations* creates a distance between the individual as *res cogitans* and the fact of embodiment and membership in a historical community. A clear separation emerges between the ordinary ways in which we know — language, tradition, authority, the senses — and the extraordinary form of certainty attained in the *Meditations*.

The specific form of Descartes's escape from the ordinary is unique, but the general aspiration to move beyond the ordinary is widespread. Bertrand Russell bears witness to the fundamental appeal of the turn to some special or extraordinary epistemic state in modern philosophy. Given its empirical point of departure, Russell's thought runs in different channels than Descartes's philosophy. In his discussion of truth, Russell is emphatic in denying the introspective moment which is so central to the *Meditations*. As Russell claims, "If I believe that Charles I died on the scaffold, I believe truly, not because of any intrinsic quality of my belief, which could be discovered by merely examining the belief, but because of an historical event which happened two and a half centuries ago."[7] The world has a priority and certainty which is independent of our cognitive states. In this way, Russell separates the question of the nature of truth from the question of criteria for judging beliefs as true.[8] Yet, even when considering the latter

6. *Theology After Wittgenstein*, p. 23.

7. *Theology After Wittgenstein*, p. 121.

8. Russell is very much alive to distinctions between theories of truth and theories of knowledge. With reference to the example of Charles I, he writes, "We are not asking how we can know whether a belief is true or false: we are asking what is meant by the question of whether a belief is true or false. It is to be hoped that a clear answer to this question

he swerves away from the Cartesian approach. The point of philosophy, for Russell, is to increase our capacity for knowledge and diminish our tendency towards error. And though he shares this goal with Descartes, in practice he does not engage in the Cartesian project of systematically "peeling off" everything except the brute fact of thinking. Philosophy cannot eliminate or overcome doubt. It is an impossible goal. "All our knowledge of truths," Russell observes, "is infected with some degree of doubt, and a theory which ignores this fact would be plainly wrong."[9] The Cartesian quest for pure certainty is wrongheaded. As Russell writes, "To reject the beliefs which do not appear open to any objections, however closely we examine them, is not reasonable, and is not what philosophy advocates."[10] Descartes's hypothetical evil demon is just the sort of unreasonable occasion for doubt which Russell would reject. Descartes' doubt is global, and his ideal of indubitable knowledge rests upon a subjective inward experience of certainty. In contrast, Russell advocates a doubt which is particularized rather than universal, and a certainty which is outward and empirical. We doubt only when we have reason to doubt, and we formulate judgments in light of the evidence.

In spite of the fact that Russell's radical empiricism opposes the Cartesian project by restricting doubt and defining certainty in outward and empirical terms, Russell also alienates the subject from the world. With an interesting twist on his rejection of the Cartesian project, Russell argues that the deepest value in philosophy is its uncertainty:

> The man who has no tincture of philosophy goes through life imprisoned in the prejudices derived from common sense, from the habitual beliefs of his age or his nation, and from convictions which have grown up in his mind without the co-operation or consent of his deliberate reason. To such a man the world tends to become definite, finite, obvious; common objects rouse no questions, and unfamiliar possibili-

---

may help us to obtain an answer to the question what beliefs are true, but for the present we ask only 'What is truth?' and 'What is falsehood?' not 'What beliefs are true?' and 'What beliefs are false?' It is very important to keep these different questions entirely separate, since any confusion between them is surely to produce an answer which is not really applicable to either" (*The Problems of Philosophy* [Oxford: Oxford University Press, 1959], p. 120).

9. *Problems of Philosophy*, p. 135.

10. *Problems of Philosophy*, p. 151.

ties are contemptuously rejected. As soon as we begin to philosophize, on the contrary, we find . . . that even the most everyday things lead to problems to which only very incomplete answers can be given. Philosophy, though unable to tell us with certainty what is the true answer to the doubts which it raises, is able to suggest many possibilities which enlarge our thoughts and free them from the tyranny of custom. Thus, while diminishing our feeling of certainty as to what things are, it greatly increases our knowledge as to what they may be; it removes the somewhat arrogant dogmatism of those who have never travelled into the region of liberating doubt, and it keeps alive our sense of wonder by showing familiar things in an unfamiliar aspect.[11]

Russell's ideal is painted in bold strokes. The driving force behind the critical passion of philosophy is the vision in which "the free intellect will see as God sees, without a here and now, without hopes and fears, without the trammels of customary beliefs and traditional prejudices, calmly, dispassionately, in the sole and exclusive desire for knowledge."[12] So, in spite of important differences, the detached ego which Kerr finds at the center of the logic of Descartes's philosophy remains signal. Russell joins Descartes in promoting a vision of radical transcendence. The true fulfillment of human life is "beyond." Ordinary epistemic practices — the "tyranny of custom" — are "cheaply wrapped in cellophane."

Russell's empiricism parallels the rationalism of Descartes in a shared central commitment to this epistemic form of radical transcendence. This pattern of thought runs through the western tradition and cuts across any number of important philosophical differences. How could this thought be so powerful? For Kerr, the root is deep. Basic urges and desires condition us as philosophers. These impulses are variously "the longing for unrestricted uncorporeal freedom . . . , the craving to burst out of the bounds of the body and of time . . . , an inability ever to be satisfied with *anything* . . . , a certain notion of the body as weighing down and trammelling [the transcendent spirit] . . . , [a] dream of being wordlessly transparent to each other . . . , a longing to communicate in some more direct way than by using symbols."[13] These urges and sentiments are not something

11. *Problems of Philosophy*, p. 157.
12. *Problems of Philosophy*, p. 160.
13. *Theology After Wittgenstein*, pp. 44-45.

we can control. They are quite often unconscious. Typically, Kerr describes their power as part of the "bewitchment of language," temptations that arise out of the first person pronoun. Whatever the ultimate cause, in each instance the normal state of affairs for human life — bodiliness, finitude, limitation, and most importantly, language — is felt as an impediment. The true purpose and destiny of human existence radically transcends this ordinary form of life.

The basic problem with these urges is that they set up a metaphysical contrast between the ordinary world around us and our "true" and eternal selves. Because of our frustration with (what we imagine to be) the limitations placed upon human existence, "we are easily tempted into contrasting human ways of knowing with putative divine ways."[14] Who we are is separated from who we would like to be. The real is separated from the ideal. Russell's ideal of transcendence — "to see as God sees" — expresses this contrast. For Kerr, this strategy of separation defines the western philosophical tradition. He observes, "Whether it is Plato's forms or the colour patches of Russell's atomism, there is a powerful inclination to get up or down to something simple and ultimate: that which defies all further analysis, something self-sufficient and elemental."[15] In every case, the consequences of this powerful inclination are debilitating for the project of living a necessarily *human* life, and thinks Kerr, are at odds with the true content of the Christian Gospel.

2. The World Lost

THE NEGATIVE CONSEQUENCES of the metaphysical way of thinking fall under two broad heads: antipathy to the body and indifference to community. Kerr's interpretation of these consequences is both problematic and important. With difficulty do we discern a direct and necessary relationship between deep philosophical views and practical attitudes. However, exactly such a connection is at issue in the debate about intrinsicism and extrinsicism. A certain form of life is bound up with a certain way of thinking. Extrinsicism pushes grace out of life, or perhaps more accurately, onto the margins of life. Intrinsicism absorbs grace into the

14. *Theology After Wittgenstein*, p. 44.
15. *Theology After Wittgenstein*, p. 62.

givenness of life. The shape and direction of our pilgrimage is governed accordingly. Dispositions, character, and behavior are, somehow, linked to these theoretical patterns of thought. Understanding Kerr's assessment of the practical upshot of the metaphysical way of thinking is crucial, because he sees something like the neo-scholastic strategy of separation and resultant extrinsicism as characteristic of western philosophy and theology as a whole, and, I shall argue, he proposed an essentially intrinsicist remedy.

We have already surveyed Russell's commitment to an intellectual ideal beyond the worldly. A clear desire to transcend bodily and temporal conditions seems to follow. As Russell explains, "The free intellect will value more the abstract and universal knowledge into which accidents of private history do not enter, than the knowledge brought by the senses, and dependent, as such knowledge must be, upon an exclusive and personal point of view and a body whose sense organs distort as much as they reveal."[16] The body distorts, our personal commitments are distracting accidents — one could hardly hope for a clearer expression of the picture of the epistemological ideal for the self as a "worldless ego." Yet, Bertrand Russell the philosopher is the very same Bertrand Russell the social activist who, in one of his phases, founded a school which scandalized England by its advocacy of open nudity. Russell is hardly a person who might be accused of antipathy to the body![17] In his case, the logic of his philosophy does not seem to influence his character and behavior in any clear or direct way.

There is a tighter fit between Kant the philosopher and Kant the

16. *Problems of Philosophy,* p. 160.

17. Beyond Russell's efforts at educational reform there is the matter of his trenchant iconoclasm. One of the twentieth century's most famous atheists, he denied personal immortality. He claims, "Mental life ceases when bodily life ceases" (*What I Believe* [New York: E. P. Dutton & Co., 1925], p. 7). Commenting on the traditional strategies for getting around the evidence against immortality, Russell writes, "Believers in immortality will object to physiological arguments, such as I have been using, on the ground that soul and body are totally disparate, and that the soul is something quite other than its empirical manifestations through our bodily organs. I believe this to be a metaphysical superstition" (p. 9). Russell would like to opt out of the "metaphysical way of thinking" in order to affirm our fundamental bodiliness. He writes, "I think that in all descriptions of the good life here on earth we must assume a certain basis of animal vitality and animal instinct; without this life becomes tame and uninteresting" (p. 27). Taking a shot at Kerr's own target, Russell concludes, "The ascetic saint and the detached ego fail in this respect to be complete human beings" (p. 28).

moralist. For Kant, freedom from heteronomous desire is central to his moral philosophy. His continual polemic against eudaemonistic ethics demonstrates the fact that, at best, he wishes to keep bodily needs at arm's length when considering moral obligations. When reading the *Groundwork* or second *Critique* we certainly find a picture of the self as morally alone. Rectitude is something which we must choose out of our inner being for its own sake. The moral life is a commerce between my will and the universal law — no mediating structures or realities may intervene. Yet, in his elaboration of the actual shape of the moral life in *The Doctrine of Virtue,* Kant knits the body back into the moral life.[18] Thus, though Kant does elaborate a moral philosophy for rational beings independent of their bodiliness, it does not seem to lead him toward any actual expressions of antipathy to the body. Kant is not Russell embracing the body against the repressive mores of Victorian England, but then neither is he a gnostic eager to deny the body.

Both Russell and Kant provide evidence that the metaphysical way of thinking underdetermines our attitudes toward the body. Kerr, however, seems uninterested in this level of connection between our global vision of transcendence and our more local attitudes and behavior. The actual normative positions held by figures such as Kant and Russell are not at issue. Antipathy to the body is not necessarily present in explicit beliefs and practices. It has to do with where one locates the center of gravity of one's thought. Kant clearly expresses a "longing for unrestricted incor-

---

18. Reiterating his commitment to moral principles which hold simply by virtue of their status as universal laws for rational beings, Kant introduces his metaphysics of morals by observing that a full moral theory must consider the application of such principles to human beings. "Just as a metaphysics of nature must also contain principles for applying those universal first principles of nature to objects of experience, so a metaphysics of morals cannot dispense with principles of application; and we shall often have to take as our object the particular *nature* of man, which is known only by experience, to show in it the implications of the universal moral principles" (*The Doctrine of Virtue,* trans. Mary J. Gregor [Philadelphia: University of Pennsylvania Press, 1964], p. 14). Angels and humans are obliged by the very same universal moral law, but unlike angels, humans have bodies, and Kant is quite willing to consider this particular feature of human nature in the elaboration of duties and obligations. To this end, Kant allows that we have an indirect duty to promote our own happiness, since unhappiness is a great temptation to vice. And more importantly, he insists that we have a direct duty to promote the happiness of others. Thus, concerns of the body — food, clothing, shelter, medical care — find indirect self-regarding and direct other-regarding significance.

poreal freedom," or more accurately, he urges us to assume the capacity for rational freedom which we already possess though distorted by corporeal desires. Throughout his lifelong modification of the particular elements of his epistemology Russell painted a picture of our mental lives as motivated by "the craving to burst out of the bonds of body and of time." These two positions, the unrestricted will and the limitless mind, are two forms of the same commitment to radical transcendence, and Kerr insists that regardless of particular moral and social beliefs, this commitment has a dramatic effect upon our psychological lives. As he puts the matter, "We never learn to own our finitude."[19] Thus, we do not so much hate our body as find it difficult to affirm physicality as in any way relevant to what really "counts" for us.[20]

For Kerr, our inability to own our finitude in its physical, bodily sense is closely linked to our indifference to community. And just as our attitudes toward the body are not directly determined by the metaphysical way of thinking, this indifference to community is often in spite of pronouncements to the contrary. For example, a positive appraisal of community is found in Kant. Consistent with the ideal of rational freedom are at least two different levels of community. In the first place, Kant takes as his point of departure the shared moral world of ordinary life. Describing the *Groundwork*, Kant writes, "I have adopted in this work the method which I think most suitable, proceeding analytically from common knowledge to the determination of its ultimate principle, and again descending synthetically from the examination of this principle and its sources to the common knowledge in which we find it employed."[21] In spite of the presumption that reflection will lead well beyond ordinary understanding, homage is paid to "common knowledge" both coming and going. More

---

19. *Theology After Wittgenstein*, p. 45.

20. We can return to Russell's anti-Victorian approach to the body and see that he would seem not so much to affirm the body as relegate it to the status of a "merely natural" fact. Nudity is neither moral nor immoral, it is amoral — "why cover it, it is just a body!" What we do with our bodies is not relevant to our moral or intellectual status, and so, for Russell, the Victorian anxieties about matters sexual stand as foolish confusions about what *really* matters in life. This anti-Victorianism entails a neglect of the body which is just as otherworldy as the most radical asceticism. Indeed, Russell's "openmindedness" about sexual matters may betoken a greater otherworldliness, since even the most extreme denials of the body still regard our physicality as *relevant* to our transcendent aspirations.

21. *Foundations of the Metaphysics of Morals* (New York: Bobbs-Merrill, 1959), p. 8.

pointedly, as Kant articulates the first principle of morality he dwells upon its intersubjective form as the kingdom of ends. Kant is clear that we can attain moral rectitude in isolation. A pure will is a sufficient condition for moral integrity. Yet, in fact, we do not exist in isolation; therefore, Kant argues, we must then take a properly moral interest in developing "the union of different rational beings in a system by common laws."[22] Needless to say, this kingdom of ends is a far cry from the social world which we now inhabit. But to deny that Kant takes an interest in community would only betray some deeper assumptions about what counts as a community.

Kerr harbors deeper assumptions. The ideal community is no substitute for the actual community in which we find ourselves. He observes, "Nothing is more foundational to the whole human enterprise than the community that we create in our natural reactions to one another as they have been cultivated and elaborated in a very contingent historical tradition."[23] Concern for community cannot, then, take the abstract form of Kant's kingdom of ends. Moreover, this sense of community comes to function as the warrant for resisting any attempt to drive a wedge between the extraordinary and the ordinary features of physicality and sociality which constitute our social world. The fact that nothing is more foundational than my own contingent historical tradition flows from the observation that *meaning* is equivalent to the longstanding custom of the community. To stand apart from the community as Kant most certainly urges with his *"sapere aude!"* is to risk meaninglessness, isolation, alienation. For Kerr, "Our very existence as rational beings . . . depends upon our being bound together as participants in innumerable vital activities, in that *Sprachspiel* which is 'the whole, consisting of the language and the activities with which it is interwoven' (*PI* 7)."[24] Kerr, then, is insisting that regardless of ameliorating convictions and attempts to moderate the chasm which separates our moral and epistemological ideals from ordinary life, the metaphysical way of thinking yields an extrinsicism in which the self is separated from its true home. Human flourishing involves enmeshing oneself *in* the cultural, social and linguistic givenness of one's life. The metaphysical way of thinking tries to lift us *out* of the ordinariness of life. Faced with these contrasting directions, Kerr assumes that anything less

22. *Groundwork*, p. 50.
23. *Theology After Wittgenstein*, p. 76.
24. *Theology After Wittgenstein*, p. 135.

than a *foundational* commitment to this particular community yields a *de facto* "antipathy to the body" and "indifference to community."

The key illustration of the consequences of the metaphysical way of thinking is language. For Kerr, our frustration with physical finitude carries over to a frustration with the materiality of language. Just as Russell contrasts abstract knowledge with particular, sensate knowledge, and Kant distinguishes between moral principles *in se* and their application to bodily human beings, Kerr detects a distinction in the regnant patterns of thought between language and meaning. We assume a dualism between what we want to say and the mechanics of how we say it, privileging the former and ignoring, if not denigrating, the latter. This attitude towards language conditions our disposition towards community. If we assume that the content of our communication is independent from the actual forms in which we communicate, then we can distance ourselves from the context in which we use language. There is a separation between what we want to say and how and when we say it. In a series of programmatic rhetorical questions, Kerr drives home what he regards as the inevitable consequence of this separation:

> What if the exclusion of the materiality of signs from the constitution of meaning is one more version of the myth of the mind as a ghostly presence hidden inside the body? What if we find it hard to learn what we are able to say from our signs simply because we do not want to do so? What if despising signs for their inert and inorganic materiality is to collude, however unwittingly, in centuries of discrimination against the mundane realities of how human beings live in community with one another?[25]

A dualism between meaning and use expresses our antipathy towards the physical cause of linguistic signs — the body — and shapes our discomfort with the forum of language use — community.

In view of these interconnections, the fact that Kerr's discussions of the body trail off into the question of intersubjectivity ought not surprise us. At issue are not normative beliefs in isolation. "Owning" our finitude is not really a matter of overcoming a kind of anti-body asceticism. Indeed, unlike the metaphysician, the practical ascetic takes the body with deadly

---

25. *Theology After Wittgenstein*, p. 49.

seriousness. The body is the origin of dangers to be overcome. In this sense, one never encounters indifference in ascetical literature. At issue, then, in the metaphysical way of thinking is not so much the specific negative attitudes (or, as in the case of Russell, the particular positive attitudes he had), but the structure of thought. The metaphysical way of thinking consistently privileges the extraordinary, and does so by separating the goals and purpose of human existence from the everyday "stuff" of life. In so doing, the ordinary is not so much rejected in the mode of ascetical denial as rendered irrelevant.

In the modern era, the extraordinary is exalted by ascribing powers and capacities to the self which are independent of ordinary life in general, and the materiality of signs in particular. For Descartes, the introspective turn yields a certainty which is independent of, and in fact, grounds, the certainties of ordinary life. Our worldliness, for Descartes, contains the possibility of deception. Only the capacity for thought, or more enigmatically, the capacity to see oneself as a thinking thing, can secure worldly certainties. Kant makes parallel claims in his moral philosophy. The self, Kant says, is vested with the power and responsibility for right action. Moral rectitude, however, can never flow from the structures of society, the organization of community. The social world may provide positive or negative influences, but only the self as such can act in accordance with the moral law in rational freedom, thus securing actions and states of affairs as truly moral. Our capacity for moral freedom secures worldly instances of rectitude. What is decisive for Kerr is not the actual powers or capacities of the self which Descartes and Kant favor. He tends to emphasize the Cartesian use of introspection because it dovetails nicely with Wittgenstein's concentration on consciousness. But Kant could just as well be the focus of the polemic. For the very fact that Kant and Descartes try to drive a wedge between the self and the ordinary practices and language of the world is sufficient to range them among those who promote an indifference, even an antipathy by virtue of culpable neglect, toward the ordinary. Kerr suggests that in *any* case where the metaphysical tradition reaches for something more than the ordinary, our worldliness — culture, language, traditions, community, the body, conversation — becomes irrelevant to our extraordinary destiny.

3. The World Regained

FOR KERR, the value of Wittgenstein's philosophy is that it sets out "to design a set of practical exercises to curb the reader's inclination to frame the familiar in an alienating picture and lose his place in the world."[26] This involves an "exorcising of certain self-images" and the development of new forms of self-understanding. We need to be brought back from the dualisms of metaphysics which contrast our extraordinary destiny "to [our] home in everyday conversation (*PI* 116)."[27] Against this aspiration away from the ordinary, Kerr insists, "What constitutes us as human beings is the regular and patterned reactions that we have to one another. It is in our dealings with each other — in how we *act* — that human life is founded."[28] Community, tradition, the practices of everyday life are the true location of human flourishing. We are deeply immersed in the practices of concrete traditions. Recognizing the foundational significance of the ordinary will eliminate the transcendental ideal which motivates the strategy of separation and the resultant extrinsicism.

In pursuit of this goal, Kerr concentrates his energies upon the problem of naming. He points out, "Wittgenstein plays with the prejudice in favour of the natural priority of naming in order to get at the roots of the metaphysically generated conception of meaning as an internal mental activity."[29] For a radical empiricist such as Russell, one of the simple and ultimate forms of intellection is naming — e.g., "Red patch now." By correlating sense impressions with certain descriptive words and sentences which stand as representations in language, a system of knowledge can be developed which corresponds with reality. Sensory limitations intervene, a certain fallibilism obtains, but in some small way the idea of direct description allows us to see as God sees. Against this view that language takes its meaning from correlations to special sense impressions, Kerr joins Wittgenstein in arguing that "there is nothing to say what words designate except the kinds of use to which people put them (*PI* 10)." A word's reference is not established by naming sense impressions; instead, reference grows out of use. Kerr reports, "It is impossible to isolate naming, or any

26. *Theology After Wittgenstein*, p. 51.
27. *Theology After Wittgenstein*, p. 43.
28. *Theology After Wittgenstein*, p. 65.
29. *Theology After Wittgenstein*, p. 71.

of its surrogates, from a cluster of other activities, at least so as to hold it up as what alone makes other activities possible (*PI* 23)."[30] The putatively foundational activity of empiricism is, then, a social process.

If naming is a social phenomenon, then as Russell digs down for the atomic experiences necessary to transcend custom, tradition, and prejudice, he grasps a practice which is itself fundamentally social, customary, and traditional. Naming *seems* to be a foundational mental act that *I* perform independently of any social practice. When I introspect in the manner of Descartes, for example, "it seems possible for the mind to conduct its most important business without being beset by custom and technique, community and surroundings." But questions as to the source of the intelligibility of certainty intervene. How do I come to recognize a sentence such as *cogito ergo sum* as certain? How can I associate the word "certainty" with the experience of being above all a thinking thing? Wittgenstein observes that recognition and association are social practices. In Descartes's case, we can say that his use of certainty does not arise out of introspection, but rather it derives from a very sophisticated training in the practices of logic and mathematics, the disciplines of certainty. As Kerr notes, "The designation of objects, whether in the private seclusion of one's consciousness or by pointing out into the external world, far from being the privileged and foundational experience which the narcissistic metaphysics of subjectivity inclines to suppose, comes very late in the course of one's education."[31] For Kerr, rationalism and empiricism, two strategies for identifying the grounds of transcendence, are both based upon the sophisticated practices which constitute the educational process.

The conclusions which Kerr draws from Wittgenstein's observations about naming are decisive and thorough in their opposition to any form of separation characteristic of the metaphysical way of thinking. On Kerr's reading:

> What [Wittgenstein] seeks to show is that, however intuitively appealing the thought may be, I do not have some natural way of being in touch with external reality (say by pointing or meaning), or any equally natural way of being directly in touch with my inner life (by introspection), as

30. Both quotes from *Theology After Wittgenstein*, p. 70.
31. Both quotes from *Theology After Wittgenstein*, p. 73.

if such possibilities were independent of my membership of a lifelong *conversation*.[32]

The metaphysical position which generates a dichotomy between our current condition and a deeper or more real form of existence is ruled out, because the "deeper" and "more real" is simply part of the texture of the social context of our present condition, part of our "forms of life." For example, the project of introspection is inner-directed only in a narrow, psychological sense. At bottom, "I discover myself, not in some pre-linguistic inner space of self-presence, but in the network of multifarious social and historical relationships in which I am willy-nilly involved." The steady rock of personal identity rests upon social factors. "Wittgenstein wants us to acknowledge that the stability there is, such as it is," reports Kerr, "is already given in the customs and practices of everyday human discourse."[33] The claim on behalf of *Lebensformen* is even expressed in the rhetoric of the metaphysical way of thinking:

> The "foundations" upon which I exist as a self-conscious and autonomous being are the innumerable practices that collectively establish the tradition which is my native element. There is nothing deeper — there need be nothing deeper — than the unending "game" which is "the whole that consists of the language and the activities with which it is interwoven" (*PI* 7).[34]

In this way, Kerr folds all the aspects of our lives which have traditionally been privileged as extraordinary — experience, introspection, autonomy — into the unending games of our ordinary forms of life.

With this exclusive affirmation of the ordinary, Kerr would seem to be rejecting the tendencies toward radical transcendence by counterposing a form of pure immanence. This may not be Kerr's intention. For example, he writes, "Certainly everybody needs to have the courage to be critical of the decrees of any authority, political or religious, that demands unthinking loyalty and mindless obedience."[35] However, Kerr does not sustain this claim. His goal of overcoming the metaphysical way of thinking

32. *Theology After Wittgenstein*, p. 74.
33. Both quotes from *Theology After Wittgenstein*, p. 69.
34. *Theology After Wittgenstein*, p. 74.
35. *Theology After Wittgenstein*, p. 17.

is at odds with this recognition of legitimate critical transcendence over prevailing customs and practices. When Kerr makes the claim that "nothing is more foundational to the whole human enterprise than the community that we create in our natural reactions to one another as they have been elaborated in a very contingent historical tradition,"[36] he cannot sustain any gulf between our ideal of critical courage and our "very contingent historical tradition." Just as Descartes cannot discover the meaning of "certainty" except by virtue of its use in the practical exchanges which constitute his social world, so also Kerr himself cannot privilege courage and critical thought as aspirations which we can recognize independent of the very tradition which forms them and gives them meaning. The point of Wittgenstein's philosophy (and Kerr's recapitulation aimed at theologians) is to make us *own* our finitude, make us *at home* in our world, *enmesh* us in community; therefore, what counts as courageous and critical is itself established by social practice and use. Yet, in that case, how can we be courageously critical? How can we recognize unthinking loyalty and mindless obedience if our "very contingent historical tradition" is so foundational that it is the sole source of meaning for notions such as "unthinking" and "loyal," or "mindless" and "obedient"? Kerr's energetic efforts to uproot all forms of separation characteristic of our metaphysical aspiration make such questions difficult to answer, and concerns about critical autonomy begin to drop out of the picture.

Kerr's complete rejection of the strategy of separation is felt in other places as well. When Kerr meditates on Wittgenstein's enigmatic remarks about describing the aroma of coffee, his desire to enmesh the self fully into the world of language use leads to some counter-intuitive conclusions. Wittgenstein asks whether we have ever tried to describe the aroma of coffee and not succeeded. The desire to surpress any critical transcendence over prevailing linguistic practices leads Kerr to respond, "The voice of common sense assures us that we describe things as well as we need to."[37] When providing descriptions there is no reason, he thinks, to doubt that we have succeeded. The fact that common sense tells us that we fail all the time in our descriptions, and social practices presuppose the fact that others may be mistaken (e.g., the courtroom), does not deter Kerr. Allowing that we may be mistaken about anything opens the door to the

---

36. *Theology After Wittgenstein*, p. 76.
37. *Theology After Wittgenstein*, pp. 164-65.

philosophical value of doubt, which Russell trumpets as the driving force of our intellectual quest to move beyond the ordinary. The questioning impulse propels us away from a first-order relationship to custom, tradition and prejudice. Doubt opens up a gulf between our paradigms of truth and accuracy and our *Lebenformen.* The strategy of separation returns. Against this Kerr is implacably opposed, and as a result, preoccupations with truthfulness must be set aside.

This rejection of the possibility of descriptive error follows from Kerr's larger solution to the extrinsicism of the metaphysical way of thinking. Traditional ideals of intellectual completeness and exactitude tempt us to draw unfavorable comparisons between our current thoughts and forms of expression and some more perfect intellectual state. Against such comparisons Kerr urges, "We do better to awaken to the possibility that our way of life is the incomparable thing that it is, without compulsively contrasting it all the time with alien alternatives."[38] To think otherwise entails allowing a gulf to develop between our capacities for description, reflection, and intro-spection and the prevailing linguistic practices. In short, a failure immedi-ately to affirm our forms of life opens the door to traditional strategies of separation in which *my* experiences, *my* thought, *my* autonomy, are privi-leged over *die Lebenformen.* To prevent such a possibility, Kerr insists that the ordinary must be the beginning, middle, and end of all that "counts" for us. In his words, "*Das Leben* is 'the given.'"[39]

4. Theology and the Ordinary

KERR'S EXCLUSIVE EMPHASIS on the ordinary runs against the grain of much of the western theological tradition. At root this is because his attempts to overcome the alienating distinctions between the ideal and the actual, the infinite and the finite, the way a thing "really" is and our "inadequate"

---

38. *Theology After Wittgenstein,* p. 166. Here, Kerr echoes Richard Rorty's strident manifesto for a post-modern pragmatism. Of pragmatists Rorty writes, "When they suggest that we not ask questions about the nature of Truth and Goodness, they do not invoke a theory about the nature of reality or knowledge or man which says that 'there is no such thing' as Truth or Goodness. Nor do they have a 'relativistic' or 'subjectivistic' theory of Truth or Goodness. They would simply like to change the subject" (*Consequences of Pragmatism* [Minneapolis: University of Minnesota Press, 1982], p. xiv).

39. *Theology After Wittgenstein,* p. 133.

descriptions also lead Kerr to suppress the distinction between God and humanity. Since the metaphysical aspiration so often works itself out in the form of metaphysical dualism, if Kerr is to follow through on his "cleansing" of our language, then he must also take great care with this most central of dualisms. This by no means leaves Kerr with nothing to say about God. Kerr is quite eager to revitalize theology, not eliminate it. However, the theological framework that emerges is ordinary through and through, and as such, it poses a direct challenge to Rahner's mixed view.

The defining move for Kerr involves our understanding of the meaning of the word "God." He assumes, rightly or wrongly, that the theological tradition has tended to define God over and against the human as extrinsic or externally related. We are finite, God is infinite. We are bodily, God is immaterial. We are temporal, God is eternal. We are an amalgam of constraining impulses and desires, God is pure freedom, and so on. In every contrast, the emphasis falls upon the radical difference between God and humanity. Over and against this strategy, Kerr argues that "it is only by listening to what we say about God (what has been said for many generations) . . . that we have any chance of understanding what we mean when we speak of God."[40] For Kerr, the theologian needs to recognize that the seemingly exalted character of the discipline does not excuse theology from the "obvious fact" that "we have nothing else to turn to but the whole complex system of signs which is our human world."[41] Driving home the point, Kerr writes, "Theological concepts, like all concepts, are rooted in certain habitual ways of acting, responding, relating, to our natural-historical setting."[42] Our theological discourse, like all our reflection and communication, has a perfectly ordinary point of origin — our form of life. Although the term "God" and the traditions of talking about God called "theology" connote other-worldly origins and purposes, *this* linguistic behavior, like all linguistic behavior, is grounded in the most ordinary and worldly of realities, *das Leben*. Thus, for Kerr, "Religions are an expression of human nature long before they give rise to reflections about the divine."[43] God is intrinsic or internally related to the givenness of human life.

40. *Theology After Wittgenstein,* pp. 147-48.
41. *Theology After Wittgenstein,* p. 147.
42. *Theology After Wittgenstein,* p. 183.
43. *Theology After Wittgenstein,* p. 162.

Religion in general and Christianity in particular are expressions of human nature. With this formulation, Kerr's desire to reform theology threatens to take the same form as Feuerbach's. To be sure, along with the metaphysical tradition, Kerr rejects Feuerbach's emphasis on consciousness and "species being," for which he substitutes behavior and *Lebensformen*. In order to extirpate all the idealist aspects which cling to even the most thorough Feuerbachian, Kerr hints at the instinctual basis of tradition and community. Christianity, he suggests, grows out of something "deep and sinister in *us*,"[44] such as the inescapable need for us to execute scapegoats.[45] Far more than Feuerbach's idealized assumptions about the basic impulse of love within the human species, Kerr's approach keeps theology as close as possible to the brute, and often brutal, "facts" of human nature. Yet, in spite of these modifications, Feuerbach's basic insight that theology is anthropology carries forward. For Kerr, theological concepts are "rooted in" our "natural reactions" to ordinary human life.

Aligning Kerr with Feuerbach does more than uncover a similar explanation of religious meaning. This convergence also helps us to see the depth of the challenge which Kerr poses to traditional western theology. For Feuerbach, the ultimate warrant for affirming the anthropological basis of religion is "theological." Only his approach, he argued, could make the true essence of Christianity real and efficacious. Stripped of the alienating distance of God from humanity, theology could preach the value of love directly and from its true source within the human breast rather than speaking of love only indirectly in the language of a God separated from humans. In much the same way, Kerr hopes to free theology from a way of thinking which hides in a distant extraordinary ideal rather than revealing the Christian message of salvation in the foundational ordinariness of life.

And what is that message? Kerr (like Feuerbach) speaks far more clearly about the distorting old view than the perspicuous new view. Some indications of Kerr's positive theological agenda do emerge, however, in his attempts to think with Wittgenstein about the font of much of the western tradition, Augustine. The crucial text is the *Confessions,* where Augustine gives an account of his own quest for transcendence, that is to say, his pilgrimage toward God. As Wittgenstein, and Kerr with him, rightly

44. *Theology After Wittgenstein,* p. 162.
45. Cf. *Theology After Wittgenstein,* pp. 180-82.

realize, a great deal hangs on our understanding of our present situation and the direction of our travel.

The feature of Augustine's *Confessions* which captures Wittgenstein's attention is the story of how Augustine learned to speak. The basic picture is that of the infant as a self-conscious being who enters into the world with mature ideas and intentions, lacking only the skills necessary to externalize them in communication. As Wittgenstein put the matter, "The infant arrives like an immigrant in a strange land, already able to speak but completely ignorant of the alien language."[46] Eventually the infant Augustine learns to speak and the barriers to communication are reduced, but they are never fully overcome. Kerr takes this account as decisive evidence that Augustine supports a theory of language in which meaning is viewed "as some essentially occult state or act inside one's consciousness, radically inaccessible to anyone else."[47]

For Kerr, such a view of meaning underwrites an anthropology which has the basic characteristics of the metaphysical way of thinking. It involves a distinction between the true "inner self" and the troublesome "outer world." In the larger scope of the narrative, Kerr uses this contrast to interpret Augustine's pilgrimage. Kerr writes, "Augustine repeatedly cast himself as a prodigal son in the parable . . ." wherein " . . .the far country in which he has squandered his property in loose living is identified with the temporality of the human condition."[48] In other words, Augustine views his life as the struggle of his true and pure inner self against the weighty, inherently sinful external world. This simplisitic dualism, thinks Kerr, determines the logic of Augustine's thought.

To a large extent, Kerr's (and Wittgenstein's) concentration on the passages describing Augustine's infancy overdetermines his reading of the text as a whole. The dualism between our true selves and our present situations is not, in fact, the simplistic inner/outer dualism. Foisting this dualism on Augustine allows Kerr to mount purely philosophical criticisms. The notion of meaning as a private phenomenon is deeply problematic, and Wittgenstein's so-called private language argument provides powerful criticisms of such a view. As we shall see, Kerr attempts a similar strategy with Rahner. In

---

46. *Theology After Wittgenstein*, p. 32. Kerr is paraphrasing *Philosophical Investigations*, paragraph 32.
47. *Theology After Wittgenstein*, p. 42.
48. *Theology After Wittgenstein*, p. 40.

both cases, the deeper, theological agenda remains hidden. In order to uncover this agenda, we need to consider Augustine more closely.

For Augustine, our life is very much a *problem*. The far country in which we now find ourselves is characterized by sin, darkness, self-love. In our present state, we persist in self-deception, thinking that all is well. In a perspicuous illustration, Augustine observes that in ordinary practice we are much more likely to be censured by our peers for mispronouncing "human being" than for mistreating a human being. The ways in which this far country can distort us is further developed in a passage in which Augustine foreshadows Wittgenstein's notion of "language games":

> I doubt whether any good judge of things would say that it was a good thing for me, as a boy, to be beaten for playing some ball game simply on the grounds that by playing this game I was impeded in my studies, the point of which was that I should be able to perform, when I grew older, in some game more unbecoming still. For this was the behavior of the teacher who beat me. If he was defeated on some trifling point of argument by another schoolmaster, he was far more bitter and more tortured by envy than I was if I was defeated in a game of ball by one of my playfellows.[49]

Augustine is not in the bondage of the privacy of language, the interiority of intentions struggling against the heavy weight of embodiment. Kerr's inner/outer distinction has no purchase on this story. Here, his far country is not "finitude" viewed as some kind of abstraction, but rather it is a language, a very definite "form of life" which is very powerful indeed. Here, the point is not that language, the body, eternality or community burden us. Rather, as sinful beings we misuse these realities. Recalling the pagan stories he learned as a child, Augustine writes, "Not that I blame the words themselves; they are like choice and valuable vessels. What I blame is the wine of error which is put into them."[50] The problem facing the self is both without and within. We are both tempted and we succumb. We are formed by destructive practices, yet we cherish those practices. Thus, though Augustine certainly makes heavy use of distinctions so characteristic of proponents of radical transcendence, his pilgrimage out of the far country cuts across such dualisms as the inner/outer distinction.

49. *Confessions*, Book I, 9.
50. *Confessions*, Book I, 16.

Would such a reading of Augustine satisfy Kerr? Probably not, for the transcendence implied in the notion of pilgrimage itself, not the particular metaphysical devices used to characterize the journey, is the real issue for Kerr. Although Augustine may not be beholden to an inner/outer dualism, he certainly promotes a dualism between the true and false self, and this dualism dominates the *Confessions*. As such, Kerr is quite right to view Augustine as refusing to accept his own life as the "incomparable thing that it is." After all, for Augustine, righteousness is a strenuous path. God and our life in His love is a very strange, extraordinary and, finally, threatening new possibility. This new possibility meets with forms of resistance, not the least of which are the "games" of human life. As Augustine questions, "The river of human custom, who can stand firm against it?"[51] Only those who surrender to God are able.

The contrast is instructive. For Kerr, no one may stand against the river of custom. *Das Leben* is foundational. The inner/outer dualism is merely a symptom of the impulse to swim against the stream, the disease which motivates the metaphysical way of thinking. Against this impulse, Kerr reads Wittgenstein as providing a "reality" therapy. At the most basic level, Wittgenstein tries to reduce our alienation from ordinary life, and nothing could be more alienating than the thought that much of the nexus of beliefs and practices into which we have been socialized might be wrong or even perverse. Yet this is precisely the thought which Augustine urges us to entertain! Losing our place in this world, like his loss of position and rank in Roman society (a loss he resisted for quite a while), is the intended result of reading the *Confessions*. But is losing our place in the world the same as leaving the world behind? In his vision at Ostia, Augustine rises up into the heavens, shedding the very categories of createdness, bodiliness, language, temporality. Leaving the far country seems to entail leaving the world as a whole. Kerr takes such a vision as prototypical of the metaphysical aspiration.[52] Yet, the bulk of the *Confessions* describes Augustine's journey out of

51. *Confessions*, Book I, 16.

52. Though a common reading of Augustine's dramatic ascent in Book IX of the *Confessions*, the details of his vision strike a different, more subtle note. Augustine does echo the neo-platonic theme of return to the One. However, at the culmination of his ascent, as Augustine transcends his own soul and passes on to a realm of unending comfort, he characterizes his destination as the place where God feeds Israel forever with the food of truth — a figural expression of the heavenly eucharistic celebration which is very much at odds with the neo-platonic metaphysical aspiration to leave behind all historical partic-

the far country in terms of changed relationships to practices, language games, and forms of life. In the end, becoming a new person in Christ does not send Augustine above or beyond the world. Instead, that extraordinary new possibility sends him down a new and in many respects still very ordinary path *through* the world. However, this possibility does not diminish Kerr's polemical fervor. For Augustine's pilgrimage still entails a separation between the old and the new in the Christian life, a separation which prevents us from being at home in the world.

Kerr's criticisms of the Augustinian legacy in the West, a legacy very much at the center of Rahner's theological system, presuppose the same logic of transcendence which Hume identifies as so prone to either radical transcendence or pure immanence. Kerr seems convinced that Christian attempts to express the delicate balance (or violent tension) of the ordinary and extraordinary in the life of pilgrimage always fall by the weight of their concepts and the inner desire for escape into Demea's camp of radical transcendence. As Kerr puts the matter, the eggshell clings to the thinking. Kerr might well admit the subtlety of Augustine's treatment of language and social custom, as well, perhaps, as Augustine's personal refusal to leave the world behind in lifelong retreat at Cassiciacum. However, just as the stated beliefs of Russell or Kant do not save their thought from the "inevitable" consequences of the metaphysical way of thinking, Kerr is convinced that Augustine's thought also decays into the simple dualism of the ideal and the actual. Augustine's movement "through" the world always drifts toward a gnostic movement "beyond" or "above" the world.

In light of this "inevitability," Kerr is suggesting (implicitly, for he

---

ularity. Immediately following Augustine's insertion of Israel and the eucharist into the life of the Eternal, he describes the pinnacle of his vision: "The life is that Wisdom by which all these things that we know are made, all things that ever have been and all that are yet to be." And he continues, "That Wisdom is not made: it is as it has always been and as it will be forever" (all quotes from *Confessions,* Book IX, 10). Is this account of Wisdom a rather typical description of a timeless, immaterial realm which is antithetical to ordinary life? Perhaps, but Augustine and his readers might hear such formulations as a distinctive echo of liturgical doxology. In this way, Augustine seems to make neo-platonic themes dance to the liturgical tunes familiar to his audience. Thus, rather than reading Augustine's vision at Ostia as a metaphysical escape from the world, perhaps we ought to read it portraying our destiny in God as a fulfillment of His purposes in history — feeding Israel with the unending bounty of Christ, which takes the form of perpetual doxology according to the eucharistic forms already familiar to us in our ecclesial practice.

mounts no arguments) that contrary to received wisdom, Philo — and not Demea — is the true friend of Christianity. The amphibious vision of existence so readily decomposes that the clear-minded and honest thinker must make a choice: either radical transcendence in pursuit of an extraordinary goal untethered from (if not antithetical to) ordinary life, or a pure immanence which forsakes the alienating allure of the extraordinary. For Kerr, the choice is clear. The dangers of extrinsicism which follow from radical transcendence are evident. Moreover, in a religion based upon the stories of a wandering Jewish teacher and miracle worker, a man all too human in the end, and in a religion based upon the practice of sacrifice, a ritual all too visceral and instinctual, we cannot lose the ordinary and still call ourselves Christian. Quite the opposite of what most suppose, his meditations on Wittgenstein lead Kerr to conclude that Christianity may survive the loss of the extraordinary, but it cannot survive in a framework which devalues the ordinariness of human life.[53] As a consequence, Kerr

53. Here, Kerr's parallels with Feuerbach are again clear and helpful. For Feuerbach, the true threat to Christianity is not an atheistic denial of the supernatural. Such a disposition, he explains, is but an echo of the alienation caused by theological dogma which has severed ordinary life from religious truth. Characteristic of dogmatic theology, thinks Feuerbach, are speculative dualisms which devalue human life and exalt the unknowable, or to use one of Feuerbach's characteristically earthy metaphors, the indigestible. For Feuerbach, what does not nourish has no *reality* for humans. As he observes, "That which has no predicates or qualities [i.e., ordinary existence], has no effect upon me; that which has no effect upon me has no existence for me" (*The Essence of Christianity* [New York: Harper Torchbooks, 1957], p. 14). To formulate a typically Feuerbachian inference: metaphysical concepts do not nourish; therefore, they do not exist, except in the minds of believers and the speculations of theologians as a debilitating distraction from the task and purpose of human existence. Thus, the metaphysical or supra-ordinary which so preoccupies theology and religious philosophy is, finally, anti-human, and the atheist is merely raising a legitimate voice of protest by rejecting the radical transcendence implicit in traditional theological accounts of the deity.

Such a conclusion bears family resemblances to Kerr's polemic against the metaphysical tradition in philosophy and theology. But further, Feuerbach, like Kerr, is not a purely critical voice. Because Feuerbach views his criticism as a necessary condition for revitalizing Christianity, he does not exhibit the destructive pleasure which characterizes many nineteenth century anti-religious authors. For Feuerbach, the singular message of Christian dogma is the triumph of love. This is the inner meaning of the Incarnation. There, Feuerbach never tires of trumpeting, God renounces his divinity out of love for humanity, a love which is more powerful than divinity. What, then, ought to be the focus and goal of the Christian life — God or love? Clearly love, reasons Feuerbach, since love is higher

will reject *any* notion of pilgrimage which alienates us from the ordinary. Echoing Wittgenstein, life simply *is* the incomparable thing that it is. All that really and finally matters is already "at our fingertips." Our destiny in God is fully intrinsic to our current form of life. The only pilgrimage to be made is therapeutic — we must cure ourselves of the "bewitchment of language" which tempts us to say that there is something more. We must overcome our thirst for the extraordinary so that we can stop contrasting ourselves with "alien alternatives." In the language of the Christian tradition, being saved entails learning to "own our finitude." Life *coram deo* is identified with life *coram mundo*.

This judgment poses a direct challenge to Rahner. Kerr is convinced that widely various philosophical systems, often articulated as antithetical, boil down to a single "metaphysical way of thinking." The extraordinary is always exalted over the ordinary, the ideal surpresses the actual. Whether this is true of the history of philosophy or not is something we cannot decide here. Instead, Kerr's extension of this conviction to theology draws our attention. He assumes that the theological systems which invest themselves in the western tradition of philosophy also reduce to the metaphysical way of thinking. The philosophical thought-forms cannot help but

---

than divinity. The conclusion Feuerbach draws is direct: "We, out of love, should renounce God" (p. 53). This would be nothing more than imitating Christ! If Feuerbach is correct, then a theology which emphasizes theism cannot be Christian, for such an emphasis fails to correspond to the dogma of the Incarnation. A metaphysical aspiration to move beyond the human has a logic exactly opposite that of the Incarnation. Here, Feuerbach foreshadows Kerr's Wittgensteinian approach; Christianity requires us to reach into our humanity, not beyond it.

That Kerr can be thus allied with Feuerbach is by no means a condemnation. However inconsistent and awkward his analysis, Feuerbach is prophetic in his criticisms of the "metaphysical way of thinking." More importantly, in a way strikingly uncharacteristic of his age, Feuerbach pursues the radical consequences of Christ's identity as the Son of God rather than trying to find moral or psychological ways to moderate the creedal vision. Whatever his failures — his Christ is never the man Jesus found in the gospels, but rather is "God made man," a formulation as indigestibly metaphysical as that which he repudiates — or his excesses — always leaping to the conclusion that because Christian dogma is focused on love, it cannot be about God — Feuerbach's repudiation of radical transcendence and affirmation of the ordinary rings so true to the logic of the Incarnation that he must be a benchmark for all theologies which seek to come to terms with the claim that Jesus of Nazareth is the Son of God. We ought never to say less than Feuerbach about the triumph of love. The task is to say more.

carry other-worldly valences which control theological expression, regardless of the stated intentions of the theologian. For example, the question of religious belief inevitably becomes an epistemological concern revolving around a transcendent ideal of truth or certainty. Or the interplay of moral action and grace in notions of sanctification decays into conundrums of divine power and human freedom driven by the abstract logic of autonomy. In other contexts, the rich texture of the Christian form of life is translated into either the simple verities of dogmatic propositions or the thin subjectivity of religious experience. In each instance, the metaphysical aspiration gains control over theology, extirpating the ordinary language and practice of Christian faith and thereby distorting its content and undermining its integrity.

My presentation of the Christian ideal of transcendence largely agrees with Kerr's assessment of the dangers of distortion. Although his emphasis on the predominance of the inner/outer distinction may not catch the complexities of the philosophical tradition, the philosophical tools of theology certainly have a weight of their own which constantly exerts pressure on the Christian vision of transcendence. As we saw, the Aristotelian doctrine of substance continually subverted efforts by neo-scholasticism and *la nouvelle théologie* to express the extrinsic and intrinsic relation of grace to the human person. In this and so many other ways the Christian vision of transcendence is unstable and is easily drawn into the various dualisms which motivate the metaphysical schemes which have prevailed in the West. What begins as a pilgrimage through the world ends as a yearning to escape the world. This observation does not vitiate Rahner's own investment in transcendental philosophy. However, if Kerr is correct in the most general sense to warn that philosophical commitments exert a powerful "bewitchment" over theological reflection, then Rahner's solution to the nature/grace question is all the more important. For unless Rahner is able to exert strict theological control over his philosophical formulations, we should have little hope that he avoids the temptations of the "metaphysical way of thinking" and its consequent flight from the ordinary. In this respect, his success in sustaining the Christian view of transcendence depends upon his ability to articulate a genuinely "grammatical" metaphysic in which the logic of divine love rather than the other-worldly metaphysical aspiration controls the direction of pilgrimage. The next chapter invites the reader to assess Rahner's success in this effort.

Although Kerr's conceptual worries about the dangers of philosophical distortion are well founded (even if he is wrong to think that they reduce to an inner/outer dualism), his escape from these dangers is unacceptable. If Rahner's analysis of the relationship between nature and grace is correct in tracing the implications of the proposition that God is love, then Kerr's turn to pure immanence is theologically unsound. The foundational affirmation of *das Leben* cannot do justice to the "unexpected miracle" of divine love. Kerr's insistence that the meaning of life is to be found in an immersion in the ordinary cannot account for the ways in which grace is an extraordinary new possibility. Kerr is right to recognize that Christianity cannot survive the loss of the ordinary. What he fails to see is that Christianity also cannot do without the extraordinary. Whatever might be the distortions of the metaphysical way of thinking, the theologian may not escape. The task of articulating the mixed form of the Christian ideal of transcendence — a new life which is both truly and fully new even while remaining unequivocally the same human life — is a necessary constituent of a theology governed by the Christian revelation that God is love. In the final chapter, Rahner tries to suggest some of the senses in which this strange combination of the ordinary and extraordinary is a Christian "necessity."

CHAPTER FIVE

ᕷ   ᕷ

The Transcendental Mode

In the reform of ecclesiastical studies, the first object must be a better integration of philosophy and theology. These subjects should work together harmoniously to unfold ever more deeply the mystery of Christ.

Optatum totius, art. 14.

Metaphysics cannot possibly die so long as man has not degenerated into a clever animal or finally destroyed his own nature.

TI XIII, p. 75.

I s THE TENDENCY towards radical transcendence and the consequent loss of the world so deeply embedded within the metaphysical language of western philosophy that it must be completely repudiated by contemporary theologians who wish to do justice to the affirmation of the ordinary in the Christian vision of transcendence? In raising this question Kerr places the problem of philosophy exactly where it belongs. How do philosophical concepts serve or subvert the theological vision? For Kerr, by the very logic of their movement away from the given and ordinary, the many philosophical approaches which orbit around the metaphysical aspiration to be anything or anywhere that we are not already *must* subvert the Christian vision. No matter how nuanced, the language of transcendence will always lead to radical transcendence, and as we have seen, radical transcendence gives rise to a spiritual extrinsicism in which ordinary life becomes separated from the goal and aspirations of God's extraordinary offer of love.

In one sense, Rahner is sympathetic to Kerr's polemic against the western metaphysical tradition. Rahner's solution to the clash between extrinsicism and intrinsicism depends upon a rejection of the standard interpretation of nature and grace as two ontologically separate realities. As a result, nature can no longer function in the context of the substance/accident metaphysic. In a certain respect, this conclusion is deeply anti-metaphysical. The mixed form of existence — natural and supernatural — which Rahner stipulates as the actual state of human life, will resist *all* foundational forms of analysis, not just neo-scholastic metaphysics. The supernatural existential is part of the givennness of the human condition. However, it is a fundamental determinate, the shape and purpose of which is grounded not in human nature, but in the proposition that God is love. Thus the supernatural existential must always be included — otherwise the metaphysical account of the human condition would be incomplete — but it cannot be explained or fully integrated into a consistent metaphysical scheme since the "substance" or "form" of the supernatural existential is only discoverable in our grasp of God as love.

In spite of this shared "anti-metaphysical" stance, Rahner does not draw the same conclusions about the *language* of the metaphysical tradition as does Kerr. In fact, Rahner seems to take a stance opposite Kerr's. We need not fear the other-worldly weight of the metaphysical tradition. Instead, under the guidance of the revelation that God is love, we might indeed be very bold in our conscription of the metaphysical way of thinking into the service of a properly Christian vision of transcendence. For example, although the neo-scholastic foundational dependence upon Aristotelian metaphysics is rejected, typically Aristotelian concepts may well have useful "notional" roles to play in a grammatical metaphysics. Moreover, Rahner does not assume, as does Kerr, that the metaphysical tradition reduces to a single way of thinking. Rahner identifies a well-developed break with Aristotelian thought-forms, the so-called transcendental philosophy found in Kant and his successors. This break in the philosophical tradition provides the resources for counteracting the "entitive analysis," the "thing-oriented analysis," which characterizes the neo-scholastic dependence upon the substance/accident metaphysic. For Rahner, then, transcendental philosophy has a special (though not foundational) role to play in the theological task of articulating the consequences of his account of the relationship between nature and grace.

1. Philosophy and Theology

WHEN KERR PROVIDES his account of the "fall" of Christianity beginning with Augustine, the myth of the soul and the "metaphysical way of thinking," it is primarily a philosophical story. Our self-understanding as human beings is, thinks Kerr, distorted by the ideal of radical transcendence which generates an alienation of the ordinary from the extraordinary. In a more irenic fashion, Rahner's occasional comments about neo-scholastic theology and ecclesiastical culture express a similar concern about unexamined commitments: the logic of our philosophical approaches can distort our material commitments. As we have seen, for Rahner, the Aristotelian structure of neo-scholasticism can lead theology into a false disjunction between nature and grace. In other contexts, Rahner also observes that the philosophical culture of neo-scholasticism tends toward false and distorting standards of "scientific" precision which suppress the legitimate pluralism in theology and obscure the mystery of the object of faith. In this respect, both Kerr and Rahner agree that philosophy is a potential source of trouble for theologians.

The theological status of philosophy in general is, then, a matter of some concern for Rahner. How, he asks, ought we to understand the relationship between the two different sciences of philosophy and theology? So far, we have relied on a rather simple-minded duality. Theology has denoted the disciplined explication of the material commitments of the Christian faith, the "kerygma." In this respect, theology is a positive and historical science. In contrast, philosophy represents the body of systematic thought which, as Rahner puts it, "is simply there" populating our intellectual world.[1] Rahner accepts this distinction at the most general level. However, he sees the need to probe more deeply. As he does so, a number of questions emerge. Of the two sciences, which sets the standard for justified true belief? Is philosophy "simply there" for the theologian as a resource to be mined and exploited, or is it a form of reflection which ought to be nurtured by theologians for its own sake, or even for the sake

1. *TI* VI, p. 72.

of future theological reflection? Is philosophy properly independent of theology, or is there something like a Christian philosophy which believers are obliged to promote? Finally, concerning the difficult question of historical interrelationship, can we really take up an attitude towards philosophy as "simply there," or must we come to terms with the fact that the western philosophical tradition is awash with crypto-theological concerns and influences?

Rahner turns to the First Vatican Council to explicate the basic structure of the relationship between philosophy and theology which will help answer such questions. From the outset, like the account of reason and faith canvassed in Chapter Three, the Council's teaching clearly subordinates philosophy to theology. As Rahner explains,

> One stresses with the Vatican Council the duality of knowledge by natural reason and by revelation supported by grace; it is said that these two cannot contradict each other because they both have their ultimate source in God, the One Truth; it is denied that philosophy and the philosophers can emancipate themselves completely from the higher norm of revelation and of the Church's magisterium.[2]

In spite of this strong affirmation of the priority of the norm of revelation, the Council does not envision a direct control of the content and methods of philosophy by theology. Philosophy has its own proper independence, and theology's dominance is understood in the limited fashion of a *norma negativa*. In this respect we must recognize that the papal commendation of Thomism in *Aeterni patris* did not privilege neo-scholasticism for strictly theological reasons. Thomist Aristotelianism was assumed to be philosophically compelling as well as theologically indispensable.

On the face of it, the priority of theology is difficult to sustain. Theology, unlike philosophy, is a positive science, which Rahner envisions according to its proper object which takes three forms: God in Christ, the faith of the Church, and the act of faith itself.[3] These three forms are *de facto* correlated with Scripture, tradition and, for lack of a better term, the experience of the Spirit. Of course, as Rahner attends to these forms in detail he rules out exclusive and unequivocal links. Nonetheless, the practical role of these three forms, especially Scripture and tradition, gives

2. *TI* VI, p. 72.
3. *TI* XIII, p. 61.

theology a determinant historical center of gravity which sets it apart from philosophy. The contrast is evident. Philosophy is defined by its very lack of a determinant, positive point of departure. The scope of philosophical thought is universal. To be sure, no philosophy is in fact universal, but reflection which claims the pedigree of philosophy "enquires into *all* and each within the totality."[4] Thus, philosophy abjures the positive and determinate orientation which is at the heart of theology. Its concern is not with the significance of any one particular moment in human existence, but rather with human existence as such. As Rahner states, "Philosophy can *never* exclude *anything* from the outset as a subject which is *a priori* alien to it."[5]

The universal ambition of philosophy gives rise to an objection to the role Rahner proposes for it. The generally accessible point of departure and the high degree of generality sought by philosophy dictate that it should be dominant over theology. This is not to deny that theology has its own legitimate concerns. The claim is simply that the universal scope of philosophy subordinates the particularity of theology as one moment among many others. For example, in a court of law the lawyer is in charge of the case. We do not rely on philosophers of law to navigate the shoals of particular legal codes. So also within the Church the theologian has a decisive normative role. Yet we turn to philosophers of law, not practicing lawyers, for a theory of the universal significance of law. In the same way, the theologian must rely on the philosopher in order to achieve the most comprehensive understanding of himself as a believer. According to this line of reasoning, then, theology is subordinate to the philosophical enterprise.

Just as the threat of intrinsicism engenders a reactive extrinsicism, the capacity of philosophy to assume dominance inspires an anti-philosophical reaction. Vatican I's restriction of natural knowledge to the existence of God, barring knowledge of his nature, is designed to stem the ambitions of philosophy. However, for those who fear the ambitions of philosophy, restrictions are insufficient. The logic of philosophical inquiry prevents it from ever being restricted or controlled. It will always rise up to seek domination in the self-understanding of the Church and the individual believer. In order to prevent this possibility, the Vatican I defense of the

4. *TI* XIII, p. 63.
5. *TI* XIII, p. 63.

legitimate role of philosophy is ignored and the integrity of philosophy is denied. The anti-philosophical reaction reasons that philosophy must be understood as a moment, if not the paradigmatic moment, of sinful self-assertion. The universalizing imperative of philosophy, the desire to inquire into *all,* is an instance of Promethean desire. The quest for comprehensive understanding represents a form of notional self-justification, salvation by intellectual works. A strategy of separation ensues. Intellectuals may think systematically and formulate all sorts of claims that resemble the truth, but this intellectual work is valid only if it is directly controlled by theology. Theology, then, is a *norma positiva,* keeping a close eye on every step of internally unfruitful "philosophical" reflection.

Like the strategy of separation in the nature/grace relation, the anti-philosophical position too often bears the fruit of spiritual isolation and potential irrelevance. Theology requires a vibrant philosophy as both a medium and a challenge. Without philosophy, theology sinks too deeply into the particularity which is its identifying core. This yields the perversions of dogmatic and biblical positivism. Biblical positivism is all too familiar to Protestants. Dogmatic positivism is the distinctively Roman Catholic danger — Denzinger Theology, as Rahner calls it. Rahner describes the essence of dogmatic positivism:

> It *confines* dogmatics to the ordering and structuring of official doctrinal statements and — ultimately — to rendering the latter intelligible by means of the retrospective history of dogma. It does all this *only* within the terms, conceptual modes and horizon of understanding provided by these official pronouncements.[6]

Denzinger is shot through with many philosophical terms and concepts, but Rahner observes that for the dogmatic positivist these terms and concepts do not add up to anything on their own; they are dead. They neither constitute a medium for reflection, nor do they challenge official interpretations of the dogmatic content of Christianity. Without a living philosophy as the medium for theology, there is nothing to goad the believer toward new perspectives, insights and formulations with respect to the dogma. Without the comprehensive vision of philosophy, the intellectual work of grace is impeded. If we stand in the post-modern world

6. *TI* IX, p. 49.

without, or even actively denying, the desirability of a "philosophy" in Rahner's sense of a universal form of reflection, then revelation itself can be all too easily restricted to the "religious" or "spiritual" realm. We may find the Christian faith one hermetic epistemic compartment among others. To avoid this subdivision of the self, philosophy must be affirmed as an important component of the Christian form of life. Like a potent dye, revelation needs the water of philosophy in order to spread its distinctive coloring into our lives. The theologian needs to seek truth in a philosophy, or at least be motivated by the universalizing passion of a philosophy or philosophies, in order to function effectively as a theologian. Theology cannot, then, exist in an anti-philosophical mode. It cannot even remain agnostic with respect to philosophy. For Rahner, theology thrives to the degree that theologians take an interest in, and develop, philosophical insight for its own sake.[7]

The crux of the issue, for Rahner, is to avoid the extremes of either an absorptive philosophy (intrinsicism) or a jealous theology (extrinsicism) and show how the universal ambitions of philosophy can, as Vatican I teaches, be subordinated to the particular purposes of theology without subverting the integrity of either. Will the universal scope of philosophy not tempt theological discourse away from its particular point of departure? Will not the practical purposes of theology impose an alien, localized agenda on the properly expansive scope of philosophy? Rahner observes:

> The difficulty in all this lies in the fact that the indispensable *ancilla theologiae* can be such only if it is at the same time *domina* in its own

---

7. Kerr himself takes an ambiguous stance with respect to philosophy. On the one hand, he is clear that the "spiritual exercises" designed by Wittgenstein have a "universal" validity. He mentions no person or culture for whom the anti-transcendent goal of Wittgenstein would not be applicable. In fact, philosophy enjoys a striking priority in relation to traditional Christian claims. It would appear that Wittgenstein's remarks about Frazier are sufficient condition for overriding traditional claims that Christ's death was unique and unrepeatable (cf. *Theology after Wittgenstein*, pp. 180-82). Yet, on the other hand, the anti-transcendent goal is pursued with such rigor that Kerr often attacks reflection in general as destructive. Religion is interpreted as a non-intellectual phenomenon. It "has to do with something deep and sinister in *us*" (p. 162). He denies that prayer is primarily a mental act — faith is not in our minds, but "under the left nipple" (cf. pp. 148-50). In each of these cases, the Wittgensteinian position is valuable not because it presents good arguments for a different view of the world, but because it clears away any reflective alienation which might distract from the immediacy of *das Leben*.

house without the role of *ancilla* being simply a part-time job alongside the principal job of being master, and that this mastery is possible only through the service it renders to theology as *ancilla*.[8]

Philosophy is useful to theology if and only if it has integrity as its own form of universal inquiry, but at the same time, this universal inquiry must, of its own internal logic, lead towards the very particularized concerns of theology.

Here, Rahner is making the argumentative move which is, I think, characteristic and crucial. He recapitulates the "kerygmatic" norm which dictated the technical solution to the problems concerning the relationship between nature and grace. In both contexts, Rahner wants to affirm conflicting pressures. Grace must be both intrinsic to the human condition and yet also extrinsic. As Rahner states with respect to the question of grace, "Grace, understood as the absolute self-communication of God himself, must always presuppose as a condition for its own possibility (in order to be itself) someone to whom it can address itself and someone to whom it is not owed; which therefore means also someone who can be thought of without contradiction even apart from this communication."[9] When considering the relation of philosophy and theology, Rahner brokers the conflicting needs of *domina* and *ancilla* in the same way.

Strictly speaking, philosophy is fully independent. Just as grace requires as the condition for the possibility of its being grace, i.e., a free gift, the independent integrity of its recipient, so also "theology must, of its own nature, will that man shall freely, independently, and on his own responsibility, achieve an understanding of himself."[10] Yet, just as is the case with *natura pura,* the nature of philosophy as a form of reflection independent of revelation is a "remainder concept." It is necessary *de jure,* because it accounts for that very real possibility that serious and strenuous philosophical reflection could be accomplished without revelation. But, claims Rahner, *de facto* all reflective activity stands under God's will toward self-communication. Rahner notes, "Grace is not a *thing,* but a particular condition of a spiritual person."[11] Moreover, "grace exists by affecting a spiritual, personal substantiality, by being the divinizing condition *of the*

8. *TI* VI, p. 75.
9. *TI* VI, p. 75.
10. *TI* VI, p. 77.
11. *TI* VI, p. 72.

latter, and hence presupposes and incorporates into itself the whole reality of the person."[12] This means that the noetic component of grace does not remain a patina of revealed propositions laid over human knowledge. Instead, the inner purpose of revelation is to penetrate and transform our understanding of the whole of reality. As such, just as the human person is conditioned by the supernatural existential, so also philosophy is always conducted in the light of revelation.

This application of the nature/grace solution explains the sense in which an independent philosophy pursued with integrity is *ancilla theologiae* even as it is *domina* in its own house; i.e., philosophy serves the particular purposes of theological discourse while it pursues its universal agenda. Since philosophy is the inquiry into all as such, and since the human "all" is shaped by its openness to grace (an existential though not natural condition), philosophy must account for this basic openness. This means, concretely, that a philosophy which is true and honest will recognize that it cannot fill the deepest longings of the human condition. Philosophy's greatest integrity is Socratic: knowing what it cannot know. In light of such a self-understanding, philosophy will, of its own accord, seek to function as a propaedeutic to *some* kind of theology. However, for Rahner the relation of philosophy to theology is more than Socratic. The point of contact between the two sciences is substantive as well. This is so because God, in Rahner's eyes, has made a universal offer of divine adoption. Each individual stands not only conditioned by an ability to respond to grace — the openness of the supernatural existential — but also by the very offer of grace itself.

The "kerygmatic" claim — that God's salvific will is universal, serious, and efficacious — is, of course, at the heart of the controversial notion of anonymous Christianity. Its significance for our issue is plain. To the degree that philosophy reflects upon the human condition and to the degree that the human condition is fundamentally shaped by the divine offer of grace, the results of philosophy are, at least in part, crypto-theological. Rahner tries to evoke this substantive overlap when he writes, "The depth of the human abyss, which in a thousand ways is *the* theme of philosophy, is already the abyss which has been opened by God's grace and which stretches into the depths of God himself."[13] As the philosopher honestly

---

12. *TI* VI, p. 73.

13. *TI* VI, p. 78. We should not be led astray by the restriction of the language of the "abyss" to continental existentialism. Kerr himself seems determined to bring theology into

and independently seeks to discern the truth about the way things are, she finds what the theologian knows by virtue of the revelation of God as love — that human existence is always already conditioned by God's offer of self-revelation. As Rahner states the matter:

> [The] self-clarification of man's existence which we call philosophy can certainly be "pure" philosophy in a particular sense; namely in the sense that it does not take any of its material contents and norms from the official, socially constituted and hence ecclesiatically special and thematized revelation; it is not true in the sense that the unthematic illumination of human existence, out of which it draws life and which it never adequately catches up on or can replace, *only* contains elements arising out of the *natural* being of man.[14]

Thus, Rahner is able to conclude, "There can be no philosophy which could be simply a-Christian."[15] In fact, according to Rahner's principles, the truer a philosophy, the more clearly and directly Christian will be its content (although its practitioners may be quite unaware of this versimil-

---

the realm of the Wittgensteinian spiritual exercises precisely by looking into the abyss of human existence. With reference to Frazer's attempt at explaining human sacrifice of the King of the Wood at Nemi, Kerr approvingly quotes Wittgenstein to the effect that the fact that it is terrible is sufficient explanation for the ritual practice. This, thinks Kerr, is the most important insight about Jesus' Crucifixion. The fact that it is at the heart of our religious tradition "reveals something deep and sinister in our ways of thinking and behaving: something that . . . unites us with those who slew the priest-king" and this "surely also offers the possibility of uniting us with the adversaries of the Jewish wandering prophets" (*Theology After Wittgenstein,* p. 181). Having seen the sinister reality of who we are, "irascible and concupiscent animals" in Kerr's words, having looked, in so many words, into the abyss, we can then understand the importance of Christ's death. "To survive," writes Kerr, "every tribe needs a supply of scapegoats. . . . Purely ritual sacrifices . . . absorb the essential social-psychological need for victimizations" (pp. 181-82). The importance of Christ is that he is willingly scapegoated, and thus "the cycle was apparently broken. . . . His execution effected something that, granted the place of scapegoating in any human group, could not have been achieved in any other way" (p. 182). Unlike the King of the Wood, Christ can lift us out of the abyss of victimization, and carry us forward to the point at which we do not need to destroy others in order to hide from our own sinfulness. Whatever one might think of Kerr's use of Rene Girard as the guide for a doctrine of the Atonement, it is clear that the point of departure is a confrontation with the "abyss."

14. *TI* VI, p. 78.
15. *TI* VI, p. 81.

itude), and the closer it will come to the classical role of perennial philosophy as a *praeambelum fidei*.

Rahner has some strong convictions about the particular form which philosophy should take. Although he never expresses an absolute and unequivocal support, he finds transcendental philosophy most persuasive, both in its role of *ancilla* and *domina*. With reference to the "turn to the subject" which so distresses critics such as Kerr, Rahner writes, "One could say quite rightly that the turning from a cosmocentric objective philosophy of the Greeks to the anthropomorphic transcendental philosophy of the modern is perfectly Christian in principle."[16] The affirmation is manifold. Transcendental philosophy is, *de facto,* the structure of modern self-understanding. As such, it is the challenge which theology must face in the interpretation of revelation. Further, transcendental philosophy is a particularly effective "medium" for dogmatic constructions. We have already seen how its emphasis on human *existence* as opposed to the Aristotelian emphasis on human *nature* was the key to Rahner's ability to broker the conflicting imperatives in the debate about nature and grace. He also demonstrates its strengths in his treatments of the development of dogma and the Trinity. These points of affirmation should be understood as *ad hoc* evidence in favor of transcendental philosophy. But he goes much further in his affirmation of such a philosophy. Transcendental philosophy is his preferred approach because he is convinced that it is, in fact, the truest philosophy; and because it is most true, it already contains the light of revelation. Rahner hinted at this when he spoke of the abyss which is the central and overriding theme of his interpretation of transcendental philosophy. For him, then, the transcendental approach to philosophy enjoys an *analogia formalis* with what he identifies as *the* theme of all theology — the dynamic possibilities of a life lived under the offer of divine love. Given these important marks in its favor, we must turn away, for a moment, from the "kerygmatic" and take some time to see what Rahner means by "transcendental philosophy."

16. *TI* VI, p. 79.

2. Knowledge and Transcendence

How OUGHT WE to characterize Rahner's transcendental philosophy? His use of terminology is not always consistent. His relationship to prior philosophical figures is eclectic and opaque. Heidegger, the philosopher who bequeaths to Rahner the bulk of his technical apparatus, is explicitly set aside as a major influence. Maréchal, the Jesuit philosopher whom Rahner does acknowledge as a major influence, is rarely mentioned. And Thomas, the focus of Rahner's first work, *Spirit in the World,* and putative source of Rahner's philosophical reflections, is separated from Rahner's thought-world by a chasm far too deep to fathom by the standard techniques of historical study. Kant, whose shift from metaphysics to critique is privileged by Rahner as a decisive development in western philosophy, is explicitly opposed at the most basic level.[17] The difficulty which we confront when attempting to explain Rahner in terms of his relationship to various historical figures in philosophy points up the strength of Fergus Kerr's approach. At issue for Kerr is not Rahner's status as Thomist, Kantian, or Heideggerian. The sweep of Kerr's concern is much broader. His interest rests with the basic tendencies of the metaphysical way of thinking and the seemingly intractable conflict between the worldliness of

---

17. In his introductory remarks to *Spirit in the World* (New York: Herder and Herder, 1968) Rahner observes that the Kantian-Heideggerian philosophical expressions which he deploys do not control the philosophical analysis. Against the misinterpretations likely to arise from the neo-scholastic tendency to read linguistic differences as material, philosophical differences, Rahner writes, "Let it be said here explicitly that the concern of the book is not the critique of knowledge, but the metaphysics of knowledge, and that, therefore, as opposed to Kant, there is always the question of noetic hylomorphism, to which there corresponds an *ontological* hylomorphism in the objects, in the sense of a thoroughgoing determination of knowing by being" (p. liii). Here, Rahner rejects what is commonly taken to be the Kantian shift, radicalized by his idealist successors, in which being is determined by knowing.

This affirmation is central to Rahner's philosophical explorations, and not surprisingly, it involves the rejection of a philosophical tendency to reify a necessary difference. Just as nature and grace are not the same, knowing and being are not the same, but like nature and grace, they are also not different in any sense which could serve as the point of departure for a philosophical account of either knowing or being. For Rahner, the "hylomorphism" means that even as we struggle to know the way things are — there really is a difference which must be overcome — our epistemic identities are always already embedded in the world.

the commitment to immanence and the other-worldliness of radical transcendence. The basic picture of life, not the patrimony of the ideas, guides Kerr's inquiry.

Kerr's focus on the deepest structure of our thought points up his suitability as a conversation partner with Rahner. He not only helps us avoid tortured questions of philosophical influence, but also prevents us from foundering over the transcendental form of argument which provides the "method" for Rahner's distinctive philosophical explorations. Inquiry into "conditions for the possibility" such as Rahner enjoins is not the same as inductive or deductive argument. Rahner does not try to marshal instances of experience as would a psychologist or sociologist, nor does he deduce his philosophy from first principles by strict syllogism. Instead, the goal is less rigorous. In spite of some loose talk of "necessary conditions" and "transcendental deductions," the approach relies on what Thomas calls "fittingness." At issue is the way in which principles and concepts fit into and illuminate the sorts of things we take for granted.[18] Philosophizing is more than logical deduction and less than fanciful speculation. Kerr characterizes the interpretation of philosophy which he shares with Rahner in spite of their material differences:

> Despite what is often supposed, even by themselves, philosophers are, at their best, no more interested in knockdown logical refutations of this or that thesis than they are in spinning airy speculations. They try, rather, to search out the obscure motivations in the recurrence of fresh guises of certain metaphysical prejudices which, although often "refuted," retain their vitality and charm.[19]

18. Cf. Kathryn Tanner, *God and Creation in Christian Theology* (Oxford: Basil Blackwell and Co., 1988), pp. 21-23. The transcendental form of argument is the key to Rahner's interest in Kant. Though he carries forward none of Kant's material conclusions, Rahner employs the method used in the *Critique of Pure Reason* to free himself from the ontological naivete of the Thomistic approach. Just as Kant presents the categories of understanding as "synthetic *a priori*" results of "transcendental deductions," Rahner can use terms such as "agent intellect," "possible intellect" and "conversion to phantasms" independent of the empirical connotations of Thomas' Aristotelian framework. In this way, Kant's transcendental method allows Rahner to distinguish philosophical anthropology from scientific inquiry into the human conditon. In *Spirit in the World*, this opens the way for Rahner to reinterpret characteristic expressions of Thomas' treatment of knowledge as "metaphysical" in the Kantian sense — synthetic *a priori* — rather than as outdated cognitive science.

19. *Theology After Wittgenstein*, p. 26.

Setting aside Kerr's appeal to images of the therapeutic world, Rahner accepts this description of the intellectual task of philosophy. Of course, when confronted by the vitality and charm of certain metaphysical prejudices, especially the prejudice that supposes us to be subjects who seek, in some decisive way, more than our physical, social, and historical conditions, i.e., seek transcendence, they part ways. While Kerr seeks to undermine this metaphysical prejudice and clear the ground for a "non-metaphysical way of thinking," Rahner wants to affirm the usefulness of the otherworldly valences of metaphysics within the Christian framework.

The crux of the differences between Rahner and Kerr over the role of the metaphysical aspiration involves a conflict over the nature of the human person. As we have seen, Kerr argues that there exists in the Western tradition, especially since Descartes, a way of thinking called "metaphysical," and it revolves around the ascription of powers and capacities to the self which reach beyond the limitations of physical and cultural factors, i.e., it describes a subject who is in some important respect different than the rest of created order. Allowing that the human person has such powers and capacities, insists Kerr, leads us to interpret this difference in pejorative terms. We know ourselves to be other than the vast network of "facts," some social, some biological, that consititute our lives, and we therefore assume that these constitutive details are irrelevant to the "more" which we possess. The psychological dynamic is quite simple. If we have some qualities which are not strictly dependent upon the particularity of our social condition, then we will not be fully devoted to such particularity. More strongly, if the most important aspects of human life — knowledge, moral rectitude, salvation — are not strictly dependent upon our immediate social and historical identities, then we may be led to ignore or resent these immediacies. To do this, assumes Kerr, is both to descend into a self-destructive fantasy world and to tempt Christian faith with crypto-gnostic heresy.

Rahner's position is that the human person is capable of the "more" of transcendence without coming untethered from ordinary life. We are more than particular participants in the natural order; we are not simply "at home" in our part of the world. We also have a sense of the whole, a momentum toward the perspective which Russell has called seeing as God sees. Yet, unlike Russell's way of thinking, which Kerr identifies broadly as the metaphysical tradition, Rahner does not regard the extraordinary "more" of human existence as a derogation of our particular place in the world. Instead, for Rahner, the "more" is built into the particularity of our lives. The more we are ourselves, the more we attend to the particular "facts" of our ordinary lives, the greater our sense of the whole. The extraordinary is to be found in and through the ordinary. In short, our sense of ourselves is shaped in the form of the Christian view of transcendence.[20]

For Rahner, one decisive location of our "more" is the capacity for knowledge. Across the diversity of our particular identities, we are unified by a common interest in affirming truth and avoiding falsity. In view of this common interest, Rahner joins Kant in asking the critical question: How are we and the world structured so as to make this interest a real possibility? The answer which Rahner gives (and here he departs from Kant from the very beginning) depends upon the principle of dynamism. The condition for the possibility of knowledge is a threefold dynamism: the dynamism of the self toward the world, the dynamism of the world toward the intellect, and dynamic relationship between self and world, a relationship which Rahner characterizes as "questionability."

Attention to the third aspect, questionability, is a fruitful way to enter into Rahner's position. This questionability places a stumbling block before Kerr's commitment to *das Leben* at the very outset. When considering our epistemic relationship to the world, Rahner joins the metaphysical tradition by observing that our capacity for knowledge is exercised in a medium threatened by error and falsehood. Knowledge is not delivered up to us

---

20. In this formulation I deliberately beg the question of priority. In Chapter Three I argued that for Rahner (and for anyone else who asserts that humans are both internally and externally related to God's love) the particular offer of grace must be *logically* prior to an accurate grasp of the structure of human existence as both ordinary and extraordinary. However, Rahner is not at all clear about temporal or "existential" priority. Does the order of discovery follow the logic of the matter, or is it the case that we can recognize the Christian view of transcendence only if we have already grasped the outlines of the amphibious view in our own self-understanding? Rahner is unclear. At the outset of *Spirit in the World,* he observes that the "question of man" falls under the umbrella of the question of grace. In the language of that text, "The essential ground of man is considered ultimately only insofar as it is the place for a *theological* event, insofar as it can be addressed by revelation" (p. 15). Such a remark would suggest that knowing who we are as human creatures entails first knowing the structure of the theological event of revelation. However, this is not the approach of the text. Instead, Rahner begins with our consciousness of ourselves as creatures capable of knowledge in order to build up to the Christian view of transcendence.

fait accompli, nor is it, to turn the Wittgensteinian phrase a bit, at our fingertips. Instead, knowledge is an accomplishment for which we must work, a triumph over the forces of temptation which reside in the self and the barriers thrown up by the opacity of the world itself. For Rahner, the questionability of things as they are would seem a necessary condition for a human *interest* in truth, for if we were to possess truth *simpliciter,* then it could not be a project for us. The strength of the question drives the passion for an answer.

This vision of the relationship of the self to the world in terms of questionability runs against the strictly participatory or contextualized view of life advocated by Kerr. Integration into the world of culture, tradition, community, and nature stand as the decisive feature of human existence for Kerr. At his most extreme, we are enmeshed in the world to such an extent that we cannot be descriptively mistaken. We describe the aroma of coffee as well as we need to. Kerr claims that if we do not acknowledge this worldliness, then we would have difficulty seeing why knowledge ought to be a matter of our concern. For if the worldliness of our lives does not define us, then our attempts to discern truth from error would be of no note. Instead, we would seek to bend our intellects toward some ecstatic movement beyond the world. In such a situation, we would be hard put to explain the worldly *relevance* of knowledge. In short, the problems of extrinsicism emerge. For Rahner, just as the dangers of extrinsicism in neo-scholasticism cannot be overcome by an equal and opposite intrinsicism, the other-worldly tendencies of the metaphysical way of thinking cannot be appropriately handled with an opposite this-worldly monism. Instead, he seeks to analyze questionableness in the same fashion as he analyzes the gratuity of grace, as requiring a relation both internal and external.

The fact that knowledge is a project motivated by the questionableness of our human situation illuminates two features of the relation of the self to the world. The first is alienation. The pursuit of knowledge clearly arises out of an epistemic dissatisfaction with the current form of our relation to the world. Questions emerge when we have a sense that all is not right, that our "knowing" is out of step with "being." In other words, to a certain degree, the world is extrinsic or external to our cognitive lives. We see this alienation in, for example, the aroma of coffee. Like wine, coffee seems to provide a smell and taste which encourages connoisseurship. Moreover, this interest in smell and taste is not pursued in solitude. Certainly in wine tasting circles, and to a lesser extent among those who are taken by the aroma of coffee, conversations and debates develop about how to describe the sensations associated with the drink. These conversations and debates seem inextricably bound up with the practices of those who take a deep interest in wine or coffee. Part of the passion for coffee or wine is a passion to extend and refine the vocabulary for *describing* the aroma. And this extending and refining reveals one of two possibilities about the practices of wine and coffee afficionados. Either they are deceived by the metaphysical tradition and need to be awakened to the fact that they already describe the aroma of coffee as well as they need to (or can), or their cognitive states are in some sense "alienated from" the fullness of the aroma of coffee and their efforts to reach for a fuller descriptive power, for something "more," are an inevitable upshot of an interest in truth, an interest in making the mind (here the description) more adequate to the thing (the aroma of coffee).

Alienation cannot, however, be the full and final word. Were we utterly unhinged from the world, then knowledge would appear an impossible goal, for we would have nowhere to begin our search, no clues, no leads, no base of operations in our inquiry and reflection. For the wine taster or coffee afficionado, there would be no basis upon which to assume that the debate about accurate description makes sense. If the world is simply a strange place, then we can have no confidence that our conversation partners are talking about the same thing. We would be utterly separated from the "facts" of life, and in that separation, the world would be totally extrinsic to our identities as rational creatures. And if this were the case, then it is difficult to see how knowledge is in any way relevant to the task of being a human *creature*. Our descriptions of the aroma of coffee would float above the world in which we smell and drink the beverage. Thus, reflects Rahner, just as much as questionability entails alienation, so also does it imply that we are already in proper relationship to the world. The questionability which motivates our epistemic lives grows out of a genuine participation in the world. We can debate about the aroma of coffee because we can assume that such an aroma is part of the world that we share in conversation. In some important and intrinsic or internal respect, then, we are at home in the world.

The dynamic questionability of human life is not only a consequence of alienation and participation of the self from and in the world. The dual aspect of our relation to the world is matched by a parallel duality in the relation of the world to us. For Rahner, I bother to use my mind because driving the existential dialectic of alienation and participation is a world which is both luminous and hidden. In its first aspect, the world is knowable. There is nothing intrinsically indescribable about the aroma of coffee. Indeed, the fact that one can go to specialty coffee shops and select among dozens of beans and roasts is a clear indication that the aroma of coffee is a powerful reality which evokes our descriptive responses. We may not use the vocabulary of the connoisseur, but we pick out the kind of coffee we like. The aroma of coffee positively invites subtle distinctions and decisions of taste. In this sense, all beings contain an internal dynamic towards intelligibility, a luminosity which grasps our intellects and demands our attention. I bother with the task of knowing because I cannot help myself. I am not master of my intellect. In this fundamental respect, the world, what Rahner often calls Being, calls forth my epistemic energies.

Of course, were the world pure luminosity, the experience of the world as questionable would transform itself into pure intelligibility. The aroma of coffee would be "self-interpreting," and the deliberative and argumentative practices of connoisseurs would make little sense since all one would need to do is smell the coffee and all would be revealed. As a consequence, the hiddenness of being stands as a countervailing force. As intellectual beings we must penetrate the world, we must abstract, reflect, judge. Reality invites us by its luminosity, but impedes us with its hiddenness. Our epistemic lives are dynamic projects of seeking truth, and as such they cannot be pure reception; they involve hard work.

For Rahner, the "hard work" of a life lived in a world both luminous and hidden is "abstraction." The faculty of this dynamic process is the agent intellect. As Rahner describes, "The agent intellect is the capacity to know the sensibly intuited as limited, *as* a realized concretion, and only to that extent does it 'universalize' the form possessed sensibly, only to that extent does it liberate the form from its material concretion."[21] Yet how is this abstraction possible? How can our finite intellects penetrate the hiddenness of being to bask in its luminosity? Here Rahner returns from the dynamism of the world to that of the self. "In every judgment, and thus in every abstraction, a universal *esse* is simultaneously grasped in a pre-apprehension."[22] In short, like knows like. In some way our intellects

21. *Spirit in the World,* p. 142.
22. *Spirit in the World,* p. 179.

participate in the luminosity of being, which is the goal of knowledge. Thus, when the wine taster reaches for a new term, a new phrase or analogy to describe the bouquet of a fine claret, such a move is possible because the conversation about wine is already saturated with a fuller sense of the reality of its taste. For Rahner, the technical way in which he expresses this participation of the intellect in the thing sought by knowledge is the controversial term "Vorgriff auf *esse*." All our knowing is conditioned by a prior determination of the intellect towards the object of knowledge. Cast anthropologically, "Man is *'quodammodo omnia'* ('in a certain way everything'). What this quodammodo expresses has now been shown: he is everything *'in excessus,'* in the preapprehension."[23] This *in excessus* is the fullest form of our participation in Being; it is the point at which the human person is at least proleptically fully integrated into the world. In this way, the pull of questionability is matched by the push of "preapprehension."

Glancing retrospectively over these basic moves, we can see that Rahner attempts to warrant a *primae facie* affirmation of the task of truth-seeking by building a dynamism into the world as such and the human person *qua* intellect. Both dynamisms stem from a push and a pull: the push of identity — mind and being are internally related — and the pull of difference — mind and being are externally related. Both dynamisms seem "required" (in the limited transcendental sense) if we are to take seriously the idea that human life is fundamentally conditioned by an impulse toward truth. Both seem "grammatical" necessities if we are to speak of the human project of truth seeking in which knowledge is both ordinary enough to be a realistic and worldly goal and extraordinary enough to motivate the sacrifice of self-serving falsehood.

In order to clarify the relative independence of Rahner's account of the dynamic structure of knowing from his specific metaphysical vocabulary, we would do well to consider some parallels with H. G. Gadamer's revised version of the early Heidegger.[24] For Gadamer, the possibility of knowledge, which he translates into the problem of interpretation, is conditioned by a two-fold dynamism similar to that which is at the heart of Rahner's position. The knowing subject is shaped by being in the form of "effective history." Through this concept Gadamer expresses the insight that knowl-

---

23. *Spirit in the World*, p. 186.
24. Cf. *Truth and Method* (New York: Crossroad, 1982).

edge is made possible by the fact that the cosmos grasps the knower. But this is not the only force at work; history does not control interpretation. The knower also brings to interpretation a preapprehension, a sense of the totality in which his interpretation might fit — the functional equivalent of Rahner's "Vorgriff auf *esse*." The dynamic of history grasping the knower and the "horizon" which the knower brings to bear in the act of interpretation are historicized forms of Rahner's interpretation of being and constitute the core of Gadamer's hermeneutic.

Substantive differences qualify the formal parallels between Rahner and Gadamer. For Gadamer, history, culture and education constitute the dynamism which drives the act of interpretation. For Rahner it must be otherwise. The *esse* which grasps the knower, the *esse* which stands as the term of our preapprehension, cannot be thus limited. The effective force of the cosmos and the horizon of our knowledge reaches beyond the manifold world of beings to absolute being. Rahner has assigned himself a much more arduous philosophical task than has Gadamer. Rahner writes, "Side by side with the truth of judgment, [we must recognize] the further ontological truth of being itself, an intrinsic illumination of that which is inasmuch as, and to the extent that it is being, an illumination which finds its absolute fullness and ultimate original norm in that absolute being which is the absolute intelligence."[25] A conversation about the aroma of coffee is, it would seem, more than just a debate about how it smells! Gadamer is willing to rest with the truth of judgment. Rahner has a theological agenda.

3. Beyond in the Midst of Life

PURSUING RAHNER'S ARGUMENTS from being, to absolute being, to absolute intelligence, indeed, all the way to absolute mystery, would be beyond my patience and capacity. At this point Rahner's philosophical position is so clearly proto-theological that efforts to untangle various warrants and commitments become extremely difficult. Suffice it to say that the gist of Rahner's argument is that (1) *if* we know that God exists *and* (2) the being which constitutes our world and which is preapprehended by our intellects as conditions for the possibility of knowledge is not deeply intertwined

25. *TI* XIII, p. 16.

with this God, *then* we would either no longer take the world seriously or reject God. We would be either sensualists or other-worldly mystics — attitudes of pure immanence and radical transcendence. The argument at this point depends upon some suppressed premises about God (e.g., that in God we find our ultimate destiny and happiness) as well as some less tenable assumptions about human motivation (e.g., that we both seek our ultimate destiny and happiness and would give up on the question of truth if we felt that it had no ultimate significance).

In spite of the fact that the inference lacks full support, the overall shape of this argument has some persuasive force. Conceptually, it would seem that our relation to God would have to be the ultimate source for the penumbras of significance in ordinary life. However, this persuasiveness has nothing to do with proving the existence of God or providing a rational justification of religious belief. Indeed, the tendency to read Rahner in this way is deeply wrongheaded. For the decisive feature of Rahner's "philosophy" is the way in which it prefigures the possibility of our being real partners in the unexpected miracle of grace, that peculiar mixture of internal and external relations.

The ways in which Rahner's post-Kantian vocabulary is shaped by the relationship between nature and grace are direct. Our epistemic identities are not vested in either purely extrinsic or purely intrinsic relations. Instead, as rational creatures we are conditioned by a world both distant and near. Moreover, like our relation to God, our sense of both the intrinsic and extrinsic is directly rather than inversely proportional. The more seriously we take the world, the deeper our questions. We enter the conversation about the aroma of coffee only if we have taken seriously the sensation in the first place. The paradox of connoisseurship is that our powers of description become more refined and in some sense "abstract" precisely as we pay more and more attention to, or participate in, the subtleties of the aroma. Moreover, the more we explore the luminosity of the aroma of coffee, the more we discover its hiddenness. The connoisseur is less and not more satisfied with his descriptions. The passion for discussion and discovery increases rather than decreases as we enter more deeply into the texture of the world. The closer we.get to the details of life, the greater our sense of the "more" of the human capacity for knowledge. In this way, the practice of truth-seeking goes "all the way down." There is no rest in some mystical insight, no end to the project of knowing in some other-worldly realm in which we can "see as God sees." For Rahner, the pilgrimage of the mind out of falsehood and into truth is the beginning, middle, and end of our epistemic lives; and this pilgrimage, like the whole of the Christian life, is through, rather than away from, *das Leben*.

However, even if we concede that Rahner's philosophy is "grammatical" insofar as it seeks to explicate the logic (e.g., "the conditions for the possibility") of truth-seeking under the assumption that God is, in fact, involved in the world, we may still wonder whether Rahner's account of the "theological event" of knowledge is *intelligible*. The vocabulary which Rahner uses makes this question difficult to answer. Throughout his account, Rahner appeals to our "experience" of thinking, or more problematically still, our "self-consciousness" of ourselves as thinking beings. As Kerr describes, "The picture would thus be that I enjoy immediate non-linguistic knowledge of my own inner experiences, while what I am experiencing at any moment remains necessarily hidden from other people unless I deliberately choose to disclose it."[26] Descartes exploited the advantages of this subjective emphasis in his quest for certainty, and empiricists since Locke have grounded knowledge in the immediacy of experience. In both cases, this extraordinary moment of consciousness grounds the ordinary task of knowledge seeking. It would seem that Rahner is grounding his philosophy in a similar self-reflexive moment. He appears to enjoin a typically Cartesian move where the reader is asked to introspect and anatomize the cognitive act. If this is the case, then a text such as *Spirit in the World* would serve as a phenomenonology of our consciousness of ourselves as thinking beings.

This enterprise has come under sustained criticism since Wittgenstein. Serious questions have been raised as to whether the idea of private and pre-linguistic experience is conceptually possible. At the very least, Wittgenstein convincingly demonstrates that the notion of direct acquaintance has no value as a warrant for truth and falsity. In this respect, the crucial assumptions of foundationalist epistemologies since Descartes seem unsustainable. Knowledge requires the public realm of language. It cannot emerge, *ex nihilo*, out of the interior act of self-reflection. In light of these conclusions, Rahner cannot say anything intelligible about knowledge by appealing to our consciousness. The only way to *know* anything about the act of knowing is to examine the public, outward ways in which people come to know.

26. *Theology After Wittgenstein*, p. 11.

For Kerr, the fact that Rahner begins with the cognitive subject is a sufficient condition to label him a Cartesian, and therefore to cast his differences with Rahner in terms of the question of private experience and direct acquaintance. For example, Kerr appeals to a characteristic Rahnerian passage from the *Foundations of Christian Faith:* "Everyone strives to tell someone else, particularly someone he loves, what he is suffering." This passage illustrates Rahner's general philosophical point about the alienation of the self from the world. Even at the level of intersubjectivity, who we are is not fully integrated into the relations which constitute our social world. Cast in Rahner's peculiar "transcendental" idiom: "The original self-presence of the subject in the actual realization of his existence strives to translate itself more and more into the conceptual, into the objectified, into language, into communication with another."[27]

For Kerr, the emphasis on suffering and its interpretation in terms of original self-presence shows Rahner's investment in a Cartesian model of knowing in which the inward moment is prior to the outward. He writes, "His example suggests that, when I am in pain, I first have the thought that I am in pain, I then put it into words and finally I find someone to whom to communicate it."[28] There is a divison, then, between "consciousness" and the propositional form of communication. Kerr interprets, "It looks as if Rahner might be working on the double assumption that I am in a position to identify my sensations prior to my applying the customary labels to them, and secondly that what I reveal to someone else remains wholly at my command."[29] By translating Rahner's example of suffering to "a little remark about pain" and his concept of original self-presence to direct acquaintance, Kerr feels confident that he can set aside Rahner's approach as "an extremely mentalist-individualist epistemology of unmistakably Cartesian provenance."[30] This would carry over to the basic project in *Spirit in the World.* There, Rahner would be read as proposing the conceptually suspect view that we can gain critical insight into the human activity of knowing by introspecting and identifying some prior "consciousness" of ourselves as thinking beings.

As my exposition of Rahner's reasoning takes pains to show, Rahner is

27. *Theology After Wittgenstein*, p. 10. Quoted from *Foundations*, p. 16.
28. *Theology After Wittgenstein*, p. 11.
29. *Theology After Wittgenstein*, p. 11.
30. *Theology After Wittgenstein*, p. 14.

not committed to the characteristic Cartesian move. In fact, to the extent that Rahner is faithful to the Kantian method, the point of departure for his transcendental deductions will always be ordinary life. The language of "experience" or "consciousness" is intended as an icon for the full texture of our intellectual practices, not some privileged inner moment of insight. We "experience" ourselves thinking in the thick of conversation or experimentation. We are "self-conscious" of ourselves as involved in the project of truth-seeking — debate, inquiry, speculative musing. As a consequence, the striving which Rahner observes as part of love and suffering is not one which moves from inner knowledge to outer communication, from private language to public language. He makes no claim that the self enjoys a privileged access of foundational significance. We do not need special experiences of love or suffering in order to use language. Instead, Rahner is focusing here as elsewhere on a determinate of the human situation (e.g., suffering) which conditions the self prior to our individual, internal self-awareness. Hence, Rahner's approach is not subject to the charge of appealing to the conceptually unintelligible notion of private knowledge or language.

In spite of these qualifications, Rahner is potentially misinterpreted if appeals to consciousness are corrected by substituting a characteristically Wittgensteinian emphasis on language. The texture of life which Rahner hopes to evoke when he appeals to our "experience" includes that which is quite difficult to portray in language. The case of suffering is perspicuous. Conrad and Dostoyevsky stand as witnesses to the fact that suffering is both pervasive and opaque. Does this mean that Rahner thinks that our striving toward communication with others denotes a private knowledge? Rather, he presupposes "the original self-presence of the subject in the actual realization of his existence." To put the matter more plainly, the mental life of the individual is conditioned and motivated by forces, powers, and capacities which do not take the form of language. To be sure, Rahner often uses the terms "pre-reflective knowledge" and "immediate consciousness," but these terms are not systematically decisive.[31] In both

31. Note in this respect Anne Carr's thesis that Rahner's philosophy leads him to shift his emphasis from dogma to experience (cf. *The Theological Method of Karl Rahner* [Missoula: Scholar's Press, 1977]). Though true in its broadest strokes as a characterization of Rahner's desire to move away from the worst excesses of neo-scholastic "Denzinger" theology, Carr's thesis misrepresents the use to which Rahner puts the term *Erfahrung*. Consider, for example,

cases, the philosophically laden notions of "knowledge" and "conscious-ness" are not what interests Rahner. What stands out as important is the claim that the mind, and with the mind the public realm of human communicative interaction, finds its life and vitality in deeper capacities and determinants of the intellect. In a word, communication results from the dynamism of the intellect and the world, a dynamism ultimately realized in the logic of grace, not in some privileged inner life of the mind. As a consequence, the contrast between this position and the substantive vision of human existence propounded by Kerr, and not questions about the conceptual coherence of the foundational project based on privileged access, must be the focus of an assessment of Rahner's picture of human identity.

Here, the contrast is direct and readily intelligible. Rahner envisions the self as dynamic, always reaching for the "more" of the whole in and through the details of life. Kerr regards this dynamism as a pathological urge caused by the bewitchment of the metaphysical language which characterizes western thought. How are we to interpret and assess this contrast?

One point of contact between Kerr and Rahner is a shared assessment of the worldview which shapes modern society. Rahner calls this outlook "skeptical pragmatism," a pinched approach to life which defines truth as usefulness and reduces all other kinds of knowledge to the status of empty opinion. Science in itself does not directly govern this worldview, but the success of scientific investigation and especially the success of the tech-nology which both drives and derives from science shapes skeptical prag-matism. The explanatory power of science casts a dark shadow over other epistemic practices. As a result, "modern man labours under the false impression that only in those cases in which empirical reality is quite

---

the notion of "pre-reflective experience." The very qualification "pre-reflective" is designed to remove the matter from the narrow realm of epistemology. In this way Rahner hopes to stretch his understanding of mind beyond the confines of propositional knowledge. Thus, we should view the term "pre-reflective experience" without the guiles of philosopher on the hunt for a privileged or foundational set of experiences. For Rahner uses the term as little more than a token for the more unwieldy "intrinsic to the human condition," a notion which, as we saw earlier, is central to his theology of grace. "Pre-reflective experience" need mean no more. If we were to rewrite his major works with some less controversial term, it would have little effect, evidence that the concept does not take on the systematic priority which Carr, among others, presupposes.

directly subject to diagnosis and control on man's part is there much chance of gaining any accurate knowledge of such reality."[32] If something cannot be isolated in a laboratory, then it does not exist as a legitimate area of rational inquiry. However, the complexity of our lives is precisely the sort of thing which resists scientific inquiry. Thus, as Rahner observes, "It belongs precisely to the spirit of natural science to see man as a weak and incidental being who is exposed to a nature which is indifferent to him, until he is swallowed up again by a 'blind' nature."[33]

The result of reducing human existence to its "natural" constituents is potentially nihilistic, but few have the courage to choose the results of the laboratory pure and simple. More often, thinks Rahner, we allow science to define what counts as truth, but then in a kind of schizophrenia, reaffirm those aspects of life, be they moral, religious, personal, or political, which science fails to illuminate on its own terms. The problem is that these aspects are affirmed in distorted form, since they must remain extrinsic to the practice of truth-seeking. Under this condition, morality decays into either emotivism or utilitarianism. Religion becomes either privatized or institutionalized. Politics swings between the extremes of empty self-interest and explosive collective myths. These extremes are unified only in their acceptance of the fundamental irrationality of much of what is most central to ordinary life.

In Kerr's view, these perversions constitute the *terminus ad quem* of the Cartesian self. The anthropology of the metaphysical way of thinking funds the drive towards objectivity in science — to see as God sees — and creates epistemic expectations which make archaic and scandalous the ordinary epistemic practices which have for centuries served as the contexts for discussions about politics and morality, religion and society. As a result, the languages of human flourishing in all their rich diversity come untethered from the practice of truth-seeking, and the concepts of right and duty, freedom and responsibility, love and hate, God and creature find either reductively scientific and technological homes (one thinks here of the therapeutic technology of "relationships" which dominates the magazines populating grocery checkout counters) or come to rest in the pure interiority of the self (so many sermons in too many American churches of most denominations on any given Sunday would demonstrate the pervasiveness of this approach). At every turn, we are

32. *TI* VII, p. 230.
33. *Foundations,* p. 188.

distracted from the ordinary realm in which we actually carry on our arguments and make our decisions.

Against this corrosive tendency, Kerr supplies his counter-image. We are to see ourselves as firmly situated in the world. Life is the incomparable thing that it is. The upshot is that we do not take scientific practice as the model for all uses of the term "true." Stripped of the metaphysical pretention of seeing as God sees, we can see knowledge as our cultural inheritance. Truth-seeking is not a project that requires us to leave home and go to a laboratory. Indeed, for Kerr, truth-seeking is not something that requires intentionality. By virtue of being socialized into language use, he suggests, we are already part of the project of living truly.[34] By being who we are, by embracing ordinary life, we are always already "adequating" our minds to reality. Thus the givenness of life, not the dynamism of the intellect, is the key to overcoming the "skeptical pragmatism" which troubles modernity.

To a certain extent the Thomistic tradition of naive realism exhibits some parallels to Kerr's emphasis on the givenness of life. As we have already noted, Rahner affirms the fundamental worldliness of our existence as intellectual beings. Casting the issue in terms of Thomas' treatment of human knowledge, Rahner writes, "It is impossible for our intellect in the present state of life . . . to know anything actually without turning to phantasms."[35] This means that we rightly accept the world and the peculiar functionings of the human mind as the realm in which we seek our destiny, even as our destiny cuts against the grain of worldliness. Thinking along Kerr's Wittgensteinian lines, we do indeed reverence life as constitutive of truth-seeking. As a result, Rahner cannot be read as advocating a view in which we move beyond the ordinary world in any way which would leave it behind.

Though certain parallels exist, a couple of offhand remarks by Rahner set Wittgenstein aside as part of the problem, not the cure (though it is evident that Rahner never gave serious attention to the later writings of Wittgenstein). For Rahner, the key to overcoming the narrowness of late

---

34. As a practical illustration of the way in which Kerr wishes to shift attention away from standard philosophical notions of truth and truth-seeking and towards life and life sustenance, see his discussion of the status of embryos, *Theology After Wittgenstein*, pp. 176-77.

35. *Spirit in the World*, p. 30.

modern culture is not to "own" our finitude with the immediacy advocated by Kerr. Defining the ultimate nature of truthfulness, Rahner writes:

> It is the openness of man as spirit to being in the absolute (that which provides the basis for the being of all that is). It is that feeling, that initial perception, in which we accept with our minds the mystery of which we are conscious as the foundation and support of all reality, and which we call God, the unique truth of truths which bears its own meaning within itself. It is the basic acceptance of this mystery even though it cannot be exploited by technology and cannot be made to contribute to our biological self-assertion, our physical well-being, our diversion or our enjoyment. It is the feeling for truth which is strict and exacting in its claims upon us.[36]

Compared with Kerr's world, Rahner's vision, like his Catholicism, is baroque. We possess transcendent powers and capacities, and we are subject to extraordinary and mysterious forces and realities. The intellectual life which defines us and the world in which we are embedded are structured with a dynamism which makes "owning" our finitude a project which will push us out of *das Leben* even as it draws us into the givenness of the way things are. The luminous hiddenness of the world and our alienated participation sustain a life of pilgrimage out of falsehood and into truth.

Resolving the points at issue between Kerr and Rahner is beyond our limited purposes. It is sufficient that the matter stand exposed at its root. Rahner sees the human condition as fundamentally intellectual in the broadest sense of the term. As human beings we are distinguished from animals by our desire for knowledge, and this desire is intelligible only if we presuppose as the condition for the possibility of knowledge that we are both in the world and not of it. Kerr harbors a deep fear of any acknowledgment of the second part of this formulation. The slightest attempt to express the "other-worldliness" of the self, the slightest gulf between the self and the world (e.g., that we have souls, that truth is representation, that knowledge is to be sought) is met with anathema. The self is nothing, it is a mere ghost, myth, deception, and uncleanliness if its worldliness, its embodied and encultured state, is compromised. Kerr is not alone is entertaining this position. Hegel mounts a criticism against Kant based on the claim that *Sittlichkeit* is the sufficient condition for

36. *TI* VII, p. 233.

moral and intellectual life. There can be no gulf between self *qua* moral agent and self *qua* member of society. Marx radicalizes Hegel's position by firmly historicizing *Geist*. Our moral and intellectual identities are determined by our position within the mode of production. Nietzsche launched his own enigmatic program against "other-worldliness," though it served the forces of chaos rather than the well-ordered world which Hegel was confident would envelope our lives. In the social sciences, Freud finds our mental lives determined by unconscious and instinctual forces, and happy-minded sociologists such as George Herbert Meade provide strictly social etiologies of the self. Kerr adopts elements from all these views. He constantly explains the preponderance of metaphysics in our intellectual history in terms of unconscious drives. He entertains a morbid fascination with anthropological interpretations of the crucifixion which rest upon a Nietzschean presumption in favor of darker personal forces. Wittgenstein is allied with Marx as a fellow traveler in the intellectual movement which locates thought in practice. In each and every case, the picture of existence as out of the world, even as it is in the world, i.e., as amphibious, is "taken to the cleaners."

Can we afford to rid ourselves, as does Kerr, of the peculiar form of life which is alienated while at home in the world and substitute in its place a radically contextualized or immanent view? Kerr's vision of existence is joined with sustained attacks on the idea of truth. Is "truth" a word with which philosophers need concern themselves? Is Kerr right to suppose that the idea of the True, like the Good and the Beautiful, is but a temptation inviting us to imagine that there exists some realm beyond or below language which is the "really real"? Is he right to regard the idea of truth as the cause of a pernicious dualism which leads us into all manner of doubt and scepticism, philosophical discomforts which might well be avoided if the True were set aside as unnecessary? Rahner recognizes the integral role of the extraordinary in the question of truth. Just as Kerr's position may well involve a rejection of traditional conceptions of truth, the amphibious vision presupposes the legitimacy of truth-seeking. If we really wish to enlist in the anti-transcendent position and support a vision of existence as fully integrated into the cultural and linguistic context, then we must reinterpret traditional notions of truth and truth-seeking. Kerr shows us how radical the anti-transcendent position of pure immanence becomes when pushed to its conclusions. Does his picture of human life strike us as at all "truthful" to the human condition?

I cannot settle this question for the reader. I can only relocate the question theologically. In the Fourth Gospel Thomas asks Jesus, "How shall we know the way?" Jesus answers, "I am the way and the truth and the life." Is Thomas's question legitimate, or is he in the grip of a deceptive "metaphysical way of thinking" which prevents him from seeing that knowledge is, as Kerr says, already at his fingertips, that faith is over his left nipple? Is Thomas's question our question? Are we always seeking the way? Are we truly groping in the darkness of our pilgrim state, requiring far more than practices and traditions, *das Leben* in all its texture, to right ourselves? Is Rahner then right to see human existence as conditioned by alienation? Are we in the world but not of it? Is he correct to view reality as inevitably hidden, never bequeathing to us the fully luminous finitude which we might "own" in the unproblematic immediacy suggested by Kerr? Thomas's question and the story in which it occurs, a story full of mistaken identity and hiddenness in which the characters betray and repudiate even as they participate in the form or figure of Christ, suggest that the metaphysics of knowledge articulated at great length by Rahner may be wrong and unpersuasive in all its details, but right and theologically inescapable in the basic tensions which govern the Christian life of pilgrimage.

Of that detail we might observe that Thomas's question seems to cut against Rahner's characteristic philosophical emphases. Thomas does not ask an abstract question about truth; he asks a practical question, one with immediate implications. More decisively, when Jesus says *I* am the truth, can the metaphysical conception of truth remain untransformed? What could it mean to say that a *person* is the truth in a philosophical tradition which understands truth as a function of abstraction? Can we really join Rahner in his concentration on *being* when the gospels unequivocally point toward a person — not to being or even absolute being — who died on a cross in ancient Palestine? Neither Kerr's position nor Rahner's seems to do justice to the passage. Perhaps the cross is the best way of expressing the limits of both emphases. It is the most ordinary and most extraordinary, a banal execution in an obscure Roman province and a cosmic event which transforms both Greek and Hebrew conceptions of the divine. Which direction do we turn, towards Kerr's immersion of the self into the ordinary or Rahner's commitment to transcendence? My intuition is that Rahner's approach may provide the proper architecture for a transformed theological understanding of Thomas's truth-seeking, while Kerr's anti-transcendent position threatens to render Thomas's question otiose. But the goal of this chapter has not been to convince the reader that Rahner's transcendental philosophy is correct. Instead, I only wish to have convinced the reader that Rahner's understanding of philosophy as a whole and transcendental philosophy in particular seeks to serve Thomas's question — a question both obvious and impossible, the most extraordinary of questions which penetrates into the deepest corners of our ordinary lives — even if it fails in all its particulars.

CHAPTER SIX

❧   ❧

Transcendence and the
Christian Form of Life

What we cannot speak about we must pass over in silence.

Tractatus Logico-Philosophicus 7

*"Mystery" is not merely another word for that which for the time
being has not yet been comprehended and perceived; it is both
possible and meaningful explicitly to come to terms with mystery
as such and in itself, so that we precisely do not have to say with
Wittgenstein that we should be silent about anything concerning
which we cannot speak clearly.*

Theological Investigations XI, p. 102

W E HAVE SEEN in brief outline how the mixed form of the human
condition which emerges from Rahner's account of the relationship
between nature and grace shapes his account of philosophy's relation to
theology, as well as the basic content of his metaphysics of knowledge. I
hope that the reader is now at least open to the possibility of treating
Rahner's philosophical works as *explications* of a material commitment to
the pilgrimage of the Christian life. By reading Rahner this way, I have
tried to show that the "transcendental" vocabulary is not decisive. Instead,
as the contrast with Kerr illustrates, the crucial core of Rahner's philosophy,

like his theology as a whole, is the vision of human existence as a dynamic
interplay of the ordinary and extraordinary, of being at home in and
alienated from the world. And as the concluding remarks of the last chapter
indicate, this anthropological commitment, in spite of whatever limitations obtain in Rahner's transcendental expression, may be indispensable
to the Christian way of thinking.

In his account of the relationship between nature and grace, Rahner
has already outlined the reasoning by which the mixed view of human
existence as both natural and supernatural is entailed by the basic Christian
proposition that God is love. Given this reasoning, the dynamic tensions
of alienation and participation, hiddenness and luminosity would seem
fitting expressions in a different, now philosophical, key. However, the
propositional point of departure in the arguments concerning nature and
grace yields an overly formal theological account of our situation, and that
formalism tempts us to think that the real substance of Rahner's thought
is to be found in his transcendental philosophy. Faced with the challenge
posed by Kerr, we need to enrich the senses in which the Christian way
of thinking cannot escape the dynamic view of Christian pilgrimage even
as it remains rooted in the diverse texture of the Christian form of life.
We need to *see,* then, the "necessity" of pilgrimage not only within the
"what" of the propositional core of theology, but also within the "where,"
the "how," and the "whither" of theological reflection.

1. The Ironies of Community

HOW ARE WE to understand the context of our theological efforts? Rahner
consistently returns to the observation that the contemporary person has
lost direct and trouble-free access to a homogeneous and uncontested
linguistic world. At the most basic level, the proliferation of the sciences
has made large segments of our culture *de facto* alien. Consider this broad
contrast:

> In previous ages (until roughly the end of the nineteenth century) an
> educated person could *himself* have at least an approximate over-all view
> of the whole field of insights and questions relevant to a worldview and
> given or imposed as tasks on his age; he was thus able, as it were at first
> hand, to form more or less adequately *direct* judgments about worldview

questions. Nowadays, however, the number of such questions has grown to such an extent that no individual can personally enter into direct contact with the *whole* mass of such questions, methods, insights, difficulties, and so on.[1]

Anything which might be called "western culture" has become unmanageable, even inhuman, in complexity. Current political struggles over the very purpose and content of education are evidence that no cultural consensus prevails. In more ways than one, we seem to have lost the ideal of the "educated man," a victim of the very success, perhaps, of the western intellectual project.

The post-modern view furthered by Kerr accepts this analysis of contemporary culture. The Promethean ambitions of the Enlightenment ideal of rationality have, ironically, led to the decay of the conditions for the "comprehensive view." Consider Thomas Nagel's characterization of the modern scientific drive towards objectivity. The ideal of objectivity involves "a position that regards life in detachment from specific or general human purposes." This detachment is needed as a way "to counter the egocentric distortion of a purely internal view, and to correct the parochialism engendered by the contingencies of [our] overspecific nature and circumstances."[2] The goal of this process of detachment is to attain the most comprehensive point of view, one which is independent of a particular time and place in the universe. Nagel focuses on the difficulties which emerge when the logic of objectivity collides with the irrepressible claims of subjectivity (e.g., the problems of free will and personal identity). However, problems internal to the quest for objectivity itself emerge. When we enter into the disciplines of science in order to attain the most objective and comprehensive possible view of reality, we must radically narrow the scope of our attention. This is so because we adopt very abstract forms of notation and representation as tools for discerning reality at the most objective possible level. The more we seek the stance of objectivity the more deeply we must immerse ourselves in the particular language of our specialty, and therefore, the more difficult becomes our capacity to attain a comprehensive vision of reality. As a result, in the practice of science,

1. *TI* VI, p. 22.

2. Both quotes from *Mortal Questions* (Cambridge: Cambridge University Press, 1979), pp. 196-97.

objectivity cannot be linked to comprehensiveness and instead takes the form of expertise. The goal of objective science may be the comprehensive point of view, but in the actual practice of science, our detachment from particularity is bought at the price of narrowness of vision.

Socially we are rendered rootless by the triumph of expertise. Rahner observes that to find out who we are we must arrange endless consultations with biologists, sociologists, psychologists, philosophers, literary critics, theologians. The complexity of the modern disciplines insures that no Goethe who has achieved the degree of expertise necessary in all the culturally authoritative fields will emerge to create an interpretive synthesis. The consequences of this rootlessness can be serious. As expertise comes unhinged from a broad sense of human nature and purpose, our identities are subjugated to the imperatives of efficiency, the "logic" of organization, the goal of mental "health." The danger of a "soulless" society committed to comfort, growth, and security grows out of our loss of a sense of the proper ends and purposes of human existence. We have no point at which to stand in order to argue against the conclusions of economists, psychologists, sociologists. "What is good for General Motors is good for America" — we are tempted to raise the legal artifice of the corporate person to the highest normative level because we have so lost a sense of the normative significance of real persons.

More troubling than the banalities of late industrial life are its various "remedies." Whether the strategies of interiority and authenticity or the radical rerooting of oneself in political commitment or charismatic authority (or the perverse combination of both), the cure is worse than the disease.[3] For some critics, we need to escape the antinomies of modernity by a re-formation of traditional identities. The public square can be covered by a new post-Enlightenment tent. Our need for roots can be addressed only by smaller communities which enjoy the rich texture of traditional practice. A "new St. Benedict" will save us from the dilemmas of modernity.[4] In spite of important differences, Kerr's ideal of "owning" our finitude would seem to lead in the same direction. The meaning of life is supplied

3. For a stunning integration of rooted political commitment and unhinged charismatic authority see Frantz Fanon, *The Wretched of the Earth* (New York: Grove Press, 1963).

4. For a trenchant assessment of the social and ethical consequences of the modern quest for objectivity and a proposed solution, see Alasdair MacIntyre, *After Virtue* (Notre Dame: University of Notre Dame Press, 1981).

by the practices of communities of language users. Our lives, therefore, become more meaningful to the degree that we more fully identify with these practices.

The neo-scholastics were metaphysicians to the last, holding a particularly potent version of the metaphysical way of thinking which would seem to detach them from the cohesive whole of their linguistic community just as the aspirations of Enlightenment objectivity have undermined the comprehensiveness of its vision. Yet the neo-scholastics functioned in a manner similar to that advocated by Kerr. Rahner writes, the "theologians of the generation before our own went about their work in a theological territory which was already defined for them, one with which they were familiar." They enjoyed a hermetic worldview, clearly circumscribed and well defined. All developments and insights were controlled by the logic of the system. Rahner describes the situation: "As little as thirty years ago [writing in 1969] the state of Catholic theology was that of a system closed in upon itself in such a way that any further developments that took place within it took place according to laws which were already given within it." New insights had to either fit into the logic of the system or were reinterpreted as issues on the periphery. Hence the proliferation of theses on Mariological topics. The worldview of neo-scholasticism was so cemented into place that, as Rahner notes, "It was hardly possible to imagine that the substantial nucleus of faith could once more be thrown afresh into the arena of theological questioning." The upshot was the phenomenon which Rahner labels "Denzinger Theology." Not only did the neo-scholastics have great confidence in the adequacy of their philosophical conceptualities, "they were convinced that they had at their disposal . . . a sufficiency of clear, exegetically unassailable 'dicta probantia', and at the same time a sufficiency of assured knowledge from the history of dogma and theology to confirm their own propositions as the outcome of a permanently valid tradition."[5] In this respect, the milieu of Rahner's intellectual and spiritual formation, a milieu which was deeply invested in the metaphysical way of thinking, comes as close as imaginable to satisfying Kerr's quest for context. Yet, ironically, the very immediacy of the linguistic context seems to have nurtured the metaphysical ambitions of neo-scholasticism. The radical transcendence implied in the neo-scholastic desire to "see as God sees" seems to have been intimately linked

5. All four quotes from *TI* XI, pp. 70-71.

to their "owning" their finitude in the sense of taking the neo-scholastic worldview for granted.

Rahner appreciated the comprehensive embrace of a shared and unquestioned linguistic community. His teachers, the priests and theologians who populated the Church of his youth, shared the neo-scholastic habit of thought and expression. As Rahner comments, "They spoke a common language." We misunderstand if we think that Rahner's predecessors all said the same thing. Sharing a common language does not necessarily lead to agreement on substantive matters. The kind of univocity which Rahner identifies involves a shared set of concepts, rules of expression, patterns of thought. Concretely, for the neo-scholastic Church, the consensus about the common language of faith facilitated understanding, and as a consequence, served as a lubricant for the necessary influences of magisterial authority. As Rahner notes, "If [the neo-scholastics] disagreed, they did so in a manner that each of them knew why and in what respect they did disagree, and that in these respects they actually could disagree without the teaching authority of the Church being invoked against them."[6] This does lead to some of the darker, authoritarian possibilities which others have suspected lurk beneath the surface of some forms of the communalist agenda.[7] There is nowhere to hide in a community which shares a broad consensus. However, the results of the neo-scholastic consensus were, in many respects, very positive.

The shared linguistic world of the nineteenth century Church allowed individuals to form firm judgments about any number of central issues. Neo-scholasticism was a very efficient communications system for the territory of faith and beyond. So, as Rahner observes, theologians could discern the requirements of the community for their own theological reflection. A lack of religious identity can be as painful to the believer as an overbearing institutional authority. At least, for the neo-scholastics, one knew what it meant to be a Catholic. One had a firm, institutionally supported identity. Intellectually, tasks were clearly defined. Scriptural exegesis involved a translation of biblical material into neo-scholastic terminology. Church history led to a recapitulation of the doctrinal decisions

---

6. Both quotes from *TI* XI, p. 70.

7. See Sabina Lovibond's extended engagement of the question of the potentially repressive quality of the Wittgensteinian view in *Realism and Imagination in Ethics* (Minneapolis: University of Minnesota Press, 1983), pp. 94ff.

of Popes and Councils as they culminated in the comprehensive vision of the modern Church. Even beyond the strictly theological, neo-scholasticism provided a clarity of vision sufficient to secure firm judgments about philosophical and political matters. As Rahner notes with chagrin, Pius XII felt that the neo-scholastic worldview had sufficient interpretive power to give guidance on topics in astronomy and psychoanalysis.

The clear sense of identity created by the common language of neo-scholasticism created a combination of solidarity and freedom. Spiritually, the theologian could determine the conformity of his reflection with the teaching of the church. Since he spoke the same language as the magisterium and was largely convinced that this shared language was the best and most precise way to interpret both Scripture and the authoritative formulations of the tradition, the theologian could grasp with a high degree of accuracy the requirements of faith. Moreover, the authorities could readily detect dissent and impose conformity. The individual was, in short, quite conscious of his solidarity with the Church and its traditions.

This solidarity had the salutary effect of confirming believers in their calling. One could see oneself as contributing to the upbuilding of the community. Rahner focuses on the intellectual tasks of theology, but the same would hold true for other vocations. There need be no anxiety about the core of commitment, and this could, in turn, free the believer to take up his special task within the community. Rahner notes the way in which so much of neo-scholastic theology was work at the fringes of doctrine, fine tuning the neo-scholastic synthesis or exploring the byways of Mariology. It was very much a time of "normal science" and one was freed, then, from responsibility for beginning with radical questions about the heart of the matter. In an interesting aside Rahner observes that freedom from this responsibility may have freed the earlier generation for a very direct, personal and subjective engagement with faith. That the matter was given and settled allowed one to concentrate on the distinctive particularity of one's own relationship with God. In this way, then, a strong sense of rootedness in which the most important matters are taken for granted — again, precisely the sort of context I imagine Kerr to desire as a home for the self — may have contributed to the privatization of religion. Yet, ironically, this emphasis on the subjective is part of the disease which the vision of contextualized life is designed to cure!

In the broader cultural context, neo-scholasticism's common language provided a comprehensive point of departure for judgments about secular thought and practice. The individual was free to leap into the public square, secure that his judgments were, indeed, Catholic. There need be no hesitation, no dithering on the sidelines unsure of the proper attitude or course of action. The consensus shifted from time to time. For example, communism took over for liberalism in the twentieth century as the great evil to be fought on the world stage. Some believers were caught in the wheels of change, but what is important for the sense of communal integrity is that the rationale for change was clearly intelligible to all. Those who left the fold knew with accuracy what it was that they rejected and understood why they were pilloried in the anti-modernist backlash. One knew where one stood, and that had the effect of creating a whole generation of Catholics who felt confident that they could responsibly affirm their Christian identity.

In this respect, the neo-scholastic consensus sustained a further irony insofar as the limitations of its worldview, the closure and insularity of its intellectual life, created the preconditions for something very much like the capacity for objectivity which Nagel describes. Fully integrated into a community which was accepted as absolute, the neo-scholastics were in a position to articulate what Bernard Williams calls "the absolute conception of reality." In this way, then, a deep immersion in the linguistic practices of the nineteenth century Church had exactly the opposite effect than that which Kerr's theory would predict. Instead of "owning" their finitude in any conscious or intentional way, the neo-scholastics entertained the most Promethean of ambitions. The very practices of the neo-scholastic language led to the position which Russell sought — "to see as God sees."

The homogeneity of neo-scholasticism seems to have given rise both to private and subjective emphases and at the same time to the Promethean ambition of the absolute conception of reality. Both seem to go hand in hand with an immersion in a clearly defined form of life. Rahner points to both and, like the neo-scholastic consensus as a whole, rejects them. And not surprisingly, for the intensely personal and the absolutely objective correspond to the logic of immanence and radical transcendence. Just as Demea and Philo are practical allies in spite of their opposite conception of human destiny, so also the subjective/objective contrast seems to be joined by a shared form of life. For Rahner, however, neither allows for the real pilgrimage of Christian transcendence. The privatization of faith renders the ordinary outward world extrinsic to the pilgrim life. The absolute conception of reality presents the goal of the pilgrim life as a metaphysical abstraction already accomplished, or worse, as a profoundly narrow form of "spiritual expertise." Neither takes seriously the full scope of the adventure of faith.

2. A Fractured Form of Life

RAHNER HOPES to revive the drama of confessional engagement, discovery and pilgrimage in the lives of believers. The language of theology must serve as more, thinks Rahner, than the technical language of description and explication. For the Christian community, the grammar of faith, if you will, has a kerygmatic function which requires us to entertain the central doctrines of Christianity ever anew. Just as he is exercised by a legitimate worry about the domestication of grace in his technical formulation of its relationship to nature, Rahner is also concerned to avoid a certain suffocation of doctrine under the stifling blanket of theological "normal science."

The reality of pluralism is an inescapable challenge to the contemporary Church. As we have seen, Rahner adopts a historical outlook which identifies the proliferation of the sciences as the most important constitutive factor of the intellectual situation today. There is a vast complex of subject matters, pressing questions, methods of inquiry and bodies of hypotheses facing us. Even single academic disciplines have so expanded that applied physicists, for example, have no intercourse with their more theoretical brethren. More significantly, in the humanities, scholars with differing and sometimes antagonistic methods can deal with common texts and questions with no apparent overlap. As a result, notes Rahner, "Today one can at most know something in one discipline or in one small sector of a subject; only in this sense can one be a specialist today who is able to appreciate seriously the questions and answers of a particular discipline and who can take part in its discussions and pass critical judgments."[8]

Intellectual pluralism is felt in the theological sciences. One of Rahner's favorite examples is the "primacy text" of Matthew 16:18. The example serves as a point of contact between biblical study, fundamental theology, and ecclesiology. As a systematic theologian, asks Rahner, "How can I possibly . . . form an independent, competent judgment with the prin-

8. *TI* VI, p. 114.

ciples and methods of modern exegesis — a judgment which I have myself critically examined and proved?" The answer is, of course, that one cannot, and as a consequence, "in modern scientific work and its methods, it is no longer possible for the young theological student [or even the venerable professor] to construct a fundamental theology for himself for which he could be held responsible before the tribunal of his knowledge of the truth."[9]

Rahner is mute as to where, exactly, this impossibility is located in the present cultural context. Is it the result of intra-academic machinations of the Fachmeisters who have a vested interest in restricting access to their specialties and retaining control over their disciplines? Is the impossibility a result of larger social forces which have led us to abdicate responsibility for interpreting human life to the experts? Or is the overwhelming plurality a function of the legitimate constraints and demands of two centuries of explosive intellectual growth? Consider Rahner's observation about the study of theology:

> Theology is becoming more and more "scientific"; it develops in accordance with the immanent laws of science "in itself"; it branches off into ever new subjects and is concerned with many matters which previously were left to practice and experience; it proliferates its subject matter so that it can no longer be taken in by one person on its own.[10]

What are we to make of the quotation marks? Is the prevailing pluralism legitimately required by the dictates of responsible inquiry, or are our conceptions of responsibility being corrupted by a false professionalization of the intellect? In general, Rahner floats above these questions. He discerns a deeper, continual cause of pluralism.

This deeper cause is "gnoseological concupiscence." Incorporating his broader understanding of the concupiscent state of humanity into his analysis of our epistemic situation, Rahner concludes that we are seriously restricted in our capacity to attain intellectual synthesis. He writes, "Concupiscence in the theological sense means that despite an original unity of man there is a pluralism of his faculties and impulses which in practice can never be integrated into an absolute unity surveyable and controllable

9. Both quotes from *TI* VI, p. 115.
10. *TI* VI, p. 122.

from a single point." This holds true for the faculty of reason and the impulse towards truth. As a result, one "has to allow for an irreversible pluralism of sciences."[11] This carries over into the individual sciences. The lack of noetic integration yields differences of emphasis, a pluralism of approaches, a diversity of technical vocabularies. Pluralism both intra- and extra-disciplinary is an ineliminable phenomenon. It is built into the concrete structure of human life.

For Rahner, then, no concrete instance of human identity is free from the tension between and within practices and language games. The Wittgensteinian native language user — the shopkeeper, the bridge builder — is an image which appeals to our sense of and desire for original unity. But attractive and powerful though that image may be, even a romantic such as Rousseau knew that we could never return to such a state of affairs. The shopkeeper may have no trouble with "five," "red" or "apple," but he may very well be agitated by "Whig" and "Tory" or "Labour" and "Conservative." And supposing that he is fully depoliticized, or so ardently loyal that questions of identity never arise, he might spend a good deal of time wondering about "High Church" and "Low Church" or "Evangelical" and "Laditudinarian." The fact that these types of questions cut through our forms of life testifies to the reality of gnoseological concupiscence, and more importantly for our concerns, such questions open up a space between who we are as individuals (am I a Tory or Whig? High or Low?) and the social world of language use. The self-understanding of theology, i.e., its "method," must take this *gulf* between the individual and the community of language and practices into account.

The gap between the individual's faith and the linguistic structure of the community is, for Rahner, salutary. Of all the qualities which theological science seeks to cultivate and communicate, the most important is "that it devotes itself to the reality in question with that passionate sympathy which this unique reality can demand more than any other, and without which it does not become truly accessible." When Rahner applies this criterion to the neo-scholasticism of his day he finds that the very fruitfulness of its homogeneity, the positive results of its common language, the institutional support which its descriptive precision lends, is the leading cause of its downfall. The neo-scholastic consensus had been held together by the suppression of inevitable pluralism, and the price which it had paid

11. Both quotes from *TI* XIX, p. 18.

was steep. Rahner notes in 1959, "Dogmatic theology today is very orthodox. But it is not very alive." The closure of the neo-scholastic theological consensus could not motivate or sustain the passion which Rahner
feels is an absolute prerequisite. The results are various heresies of complacency:

> Once the danger of explicit and theoretically formulated heresy appear-
> ing *within* the Church and seeking to spread *within* it has been largely
> excluded by a very high degree of reflective precision concerning the
> formal principles of faith and theology, then heresy can appear in just
> two forms: as "cryptogamic" heresy, merely lived out existentially and
> avoiding self-expression in a theoretical reflexive form, and as dead
> orthodoxy, which may be true to the letter because it is fundamentally
> uninterested in the whole buisness.[12]

The closed options of communal consensus can create the illusion of
orthodoxy because the very precision of its formulations dissuade the
heterodox from attempting to reshape the intellectual forms of the tradition for their own purposes. For Rahner, the petrification of doctrine is a
distinct liability. The contest of disputants in the theological arena — an
arena with boundaries, but an arena of contest nonetheless — is integral
to the development and renewal of church life.[13] "Orthodox" formulations
need to be subjected to the discipline of dissent.

This does not mean that the community of faith must abjure from
condemnation and rejection of heresy. Rahner defends the proper authority of the magisterium in church life. The need for openness is not
translated into neutrality or pure tolerance for any opinion. The point of
Rahner's remarks is rather that the church needs to accept the riskiness of
theological diversity and exploration, and must live with the ambiguity of
a pluralism of theological languages rather than seek the security of a single
official set of concepts. This conditions Rahner's assessment of authority
in the Church. He recognizes that falsehoods and distortions of doctrine

---

12. All quotes in this paragraph from *TI* I, pp. 13-14.

13. Of heresy Rahner writes, "Heresy is the means which 'must be' by which the Church
is led into all truth. . . . It is only by hearing contradiction and rejecting it as repugnant
to her truth and her (still evolving) understanding of herself that the Church acquires a
clearer grasp of her own truth" (*Dictionary of Theology* [New York: Crossroad, 1981],
p. 207).

will slip through a net made more porous by the acknowledgement of pluralism. Theological experimentation may do more harm than good when the dust settles. Yet these are risks worth taking.

Making theology a matter of open contest rather than closed description does more than revitalize theological sciences. It also reforms theology as an arena for the whole range of religious concerns. The "dead orthodoxy" to which Rahner alludes results from an acceptance of neo-scholasticism as the final word. There is no drama of discovery because the issues have been settled with definitions written for all to simply lend their assent. In this context, faith threatens to descend into unreflective reiteration. In the neo-scholastic world, Rahner is worried that Christian faith has too much been (to echo Wittgenstein) at the fingertips of believers. For Rahner, the life of faith must have a reflective, intentional dimension, and theology must be so constituted as to draw believers into the intellectual demands of the pilgrimage of faith.

Thus, the fact that Kerr relies so heavily on cultural-linguistic practices as epistemic ballast means that Rahner's observations about the inelimi-nable reality of pluralism and the dangers of false closure cut deeply into Kerr's contextual position. All forms of life, in Rahner's view, have splinters and fissures. This is especially true for the Christian form of life. To a large extent, neo-scholasticism was able to sustain its consensus and the high degree of ecclesiastical homogeneity because it diverted attention away from central linguistic and symbolic forms of the tradition. Rahner, then, joins Kerr at least at the primary level of criticizing a facile imposition of abstractions onto the texture of tradition, abstractions which coerce the particularities of the Christian form of life into a preestablished mold. The difference is that Rahner comes away with a more accurate assessment, I submit, of the role and status of transcendence in the project of epistemic attention to the particularity which both he and Kerr seek.

To the degree that one is attentive to the texture of tradition, the rips and tears in the fabric of belief take on greater significance and become more recalcitrant in their dissonance with respect to other elements in the tradition. In light of this plurality we have difficulty seeing the reflective task of making sense out of our lives as a quest for immersion in a common or ordinary language. Attention to particularity as a precondition to sys-tematic thought means, thinks Rahner, that "today it is no longer so easy for [the theologian] as it formerly was to think of himself as a worker on a common building site on which a single building is being erected according to a plan which has been worked out and is known to all."[14] Take as an example the gospel stories. If we give a close reading of the Gospels of Mark and John, then we cannot help but be struck by how very different the narratives are. And yet, they do, at the same time, seem to fit into a larger whole. However, explicating the "fittingness" in terms which do justice to the particular art of the two narratives is a deeply challenging task. There is guidance from the tradition, especially as to formulations of "fittingness" which are ruled out, but no theological position settles the issue in what Rahner would call a direct or "positive" fashion. The gulf remains between who we believe ourselves to be as Christians (i.e., as believers in the "larger whole"), and what we take to be central linguistic and symbolic forms of the authoritative Christian tradition. Recalling Kerr's ideal of faith, we cannot "inhabit" or "own" our finitude in the sense of directly identifying ourselves with the particularities of the Christian form of life. In our reflective mode we are constantly trying to bridge the gulf between Gospel and gospels, Word and words, Confession and confessions, Church and churches, Tradition and traditions, Authority and authorities, Truth and truths with an explication of the relationship between the diverse particularities of the tradition and the singular Object of faith. If we accept that there is a gulf to be bridged, then we are admitting that there can be no first-order identification with *das Leben*. Something more enters into the equation, and this something more always draws us out and pushes us into new and different directions with respect to what we have taken for granted. The fractured condition of the ordinary is porous to the extraordinary.

3. The Indirect Method

IN LIGHT OF the pluralism which characterizes the church as well as the world, Rahner describes as "indirect" our efforts to bridge the gulf between diverse Christian particularities and the unity of faith. The indirect method acknowledges fragmentation and pluralism as its territory of reflection. There is no attempt to escape from the diversity of Christianity. However wide and deep might be the cleft between the faith of believers and the polymorphous language of the church, the latter remains, for Rahner,

14. *TI* XI, p. 17.

indispensable and decisive. Though we cannot escape the difficulties of bridging the gulf by Kerr's imperative to "own" our form of life, neither can we "solve" the problem by eliminating the troublesome particularities which resist easy synthesis. Further, this method does not draw the conclusion that no synthesis or synoptic view is possible. For all his attacks on the dangers and failures of neo-scholasticism, Rahner preserves its quest for an intellectual grasp of the totality of the Christian faith. A significant portion of his energy was devoted to a series of theological encyclopedia, precisely the instruments for forging a new overarching consensus. In addition, Rahner served as the editor for a number of editions of Denzinger's *Enchiridion Symbolarum.* Here, as in so many other places, Rahner cleaves to the Christian vision which eschews the pure solutions of immanence and radical transcendence and seeks a peculiar mixture.

For Kerr, Rahner cannot do justice to the complex form of life which is Christianity because Kerr assumes that the *Foundations of the Christian Faith,* Rahner's one attempt at synthesis, is overdetermined by an "obsession with epistemological preliminaries."[15] This obsession, reasons Kerr, commits Rahner to the classic foundationalist project in which abstract or universal principles, and not the texture of ordinary life, dictate the shape of rational assent. In the case of Christian faith, this would mean that the fragmentation and pluralism of the Christian language is subordinated to foundational principles. Kerr regards Rahner as invested in a foundational phenomenology of experience, but whether the foundational project is driven by a phenomenology of religious experience, principles of reason, or rules of evidence is not decisive. The point, for Kerr, is that in each case the particular details of the Christian life are assumed to be a troublesome realm ("wrapped in cellophane") in which we might be misled and hindered in our relation to God. To overcome the limits of ordinary Christian language, these details must be carefully judged by the prior and more basic foundational principles. Only under the justification of something more basic, according to the foundationalist impulse, can we be confident that the Christian pilgrim life moves in the right direction.

For Kerr, the consequence of such an impulse is devastating for Christian identity. The foundationalist assumption that the ordinary forms of Christian life stand as ambiguous and uncertain, needing the clarity and support of epistemological justification, "only obscures and excludes the

15. *Theology After Wittgenstein,* p. 10.

membership of a community and a tradition."[16] The foundational approach obscures because foundational thought creates an inevitable pull away from the troublesomely uncertain and pluralistic (the details of the Christian form of life) and impels us towards the font of certainty and unity (the foundational principles). The upshot is an intensification of our universal identities as experiential (or rational or intentional) beings while suppressing our particular identities as Christians. For the scrupulous, the foundational approach also excludes. For if the religious life is a matter of ultimate significance, and if the ordinary forms of traditional Christian practice do not enjoy a perfect "fit" with the foundational principles which justify them, then it would be irrational to risk one's ultimate destiny with an unqualified affirmation of the Christian form of life. In both cases, if a phenomenology of experience justifies Christianity, then our Christian identity is absorbed into, if not excluded by, our deeper and more decisive identity as experiential beings.

If Rahner does indeed pursue a foundational project as Kerr assumes, then he would be turning his back on the solution which he provided to the problem of the relationship between nature and grace. For the anthropology of pure nature and the supernatural existential is coherent only within the logic of divine love. And in that logic, the general form of human existence, e.g., who we are as experiential beings, is absorbed into the particular Christian claim that God has offered himself in love, not the other way around. Thus, it is very important for us to see whether Kerr is correct in his presumption that the foundational language of Rahner's *Foundations of the Christian Faith* expresses a classical foundational approach. To do so we need to examine the different senses in which Rahner uses the term "foundational" in his exposition of the indirect method in general and in his application of that method in his *Foundations*.

1. The most evident and natural sense of "foundational" pertains to the imperative of intellectual honesty. Given the fact that the terrain of contemporary epistemic life is highly pluralistic, Rahner notes that we are all theological amateurs, *rudes*. The traditional proofs of fundamental theology, regardless of their "scientific" validity, have little purchase on the modern mind. For example, one can no longer accept Jesus' conferral of the keys to Peter as "proof" of the apostolicity of the papacy, as was the case in the manual tradition. We cannot assume "that all difficulties could

16. *Theology After Wittgenstein*, p. 8.

be overcome positively and in a way which the individual could understand by means of a frontal attack upon them."[17] Historical criticism, sociological analysis, insights into the political valences of ecclesiastical structures of the Church, and so much more crowd in upon any determinate and scientifically grounded judgment about the ultimate status of the current shape of the Catholic Church. In light of the proliferation of expertise, we are unable to come to "scientific" judgments about historical questions such as papal primacy and apostolic succession. Moreover, these historical questions swerve away from the larger question of the "absoluteness" of Roman Catholicism, the terminus of traditional fundamental theological compendia of historical claims about the Church. Proofs of the existence of God, another crucial element of traditional fundamental theology, also comes into question. Linguistic philosophy, stucturalist and post-structuralist theories block appeals to the naive realism of traditional Thomism. The epistemological debates of recent decades stand in the way of a definitive position with respect to natural knowledge of God. Therefore, as intellectual beings we stand alienated from the web of Christian beliefs.

However, the fact that diverse critical perspectives compete for our attention and, more importantly, resist definitive synthesis, does not excuse us, says Rahner, from the responsibility of forming some judgments about the basic shape of our Christian faith. Rahner takes it as a matter of faith, if you will, a matter of the logic of belief, that Christian identity entails at least some degree of internal intellectual assent. And, reasons Rahner, since internal intellectual assent is required by the logic of belief, and since the possibility of belief is promised to us, then it must be possible to attain an intellectually responsible affirmation of Christian claims, even if "scientific certainty" is ruled out. We must be able to transcend the limits of "positive" knowledge in order to make an all-things-considered judgment about basic Christian claims.

This affirmation is made at what Rahner calls a "first level of reflection." What, exactly, this entails is by no means clear. Rahner appeals to Newman's "illative sense." "There is," writes Rahner, "a convergence of probabilities, a certainty, an honest and responsible decision which is knowledge and free act together." In other words, the individual fashions a personal synthesis which stands at the foundation of his personal faith. The community cannot "give" us this synthesis. It is something which we must

17. *TI* XI, p. 76.

achieve. This honest and responsible decision is, however, not a private
affair. It is subject to analysis and scrutiny. In spite of the fact that it is
not directly and systematically subject to the criteria of the various sciences
which now constitute the diverse spectrum of theological approaches,
Newman's illative sense is a human dynamic which, though subjective in
the sense that it is not person, time, and place independent, is scrutible.
The "first level of reflection" may be personal, but it is also intersubjective.
There is, in other words, a logic to the legitimately unscientific nature of
the first level of reflection, a "science" which might rightfully be pursued
and which can deepen and aid the imperative of honest and responsible
decision. And for Rahner, "it is this first level of reflection that is intended
in a foundational course that is the first step in theological studies."[18] The
term "foundational" designates, then, the fact that these sorts of reflections
could serve as the foundations or impetus for a personal act of faith.

2. The above account emphasizes the need for an intellectually honest
form of assent within the Christian life. However, we are mistaken if we
view this assent as a simple reception and acceptance of existing theological
propositions. The challenge of intellectual honesty is, thinks Rahner, one
of the primary ways in which the believer comes to see the worldliness of
grace. Christian claims cannot be given special exemptions. Rahner intends
to bring all doctrines to the bar of honest and responsible decision. Pressing
for justification, in the limited sense which Rahner intends through the
indirect method, involves transcending the immediacy of rote confession
and is one of the ways in which grace is made intrinsic. The result of
affirmation is that theological propositions are woven into our world of
experience, reflection, and action.

In this way, the indirect method is the "foundation" of the individual's
efforts to live a faithful life. Rahner warns, "The title 'foundational course'
very easily gives the false impression that we are dealing with an introduction which cheaply absolves the beginning theologian of any rigorous
thinking. However, [we] should and must recognize that it is trying to
help the *beginner* to get his start in theology as a whole."[19] The *Grundkurs*
is no simple means for justifying assent; the indirect method also involves
a substantive engagement and re-formation of basic theological commitments. Not only does the first level of reflection address the general cultural

---

18. Both quotes from *Foundations,* p. 10.
19. *Foundations,* p. 6.

need for intellectual honesty, but it also serves as the basis for a specifically Christian spiritual formation. Moreover, as the individual integrates Christian beliefs into his life, the conceptual shape of those beliefs may change. The Christian language is not a reified object. For Rahner, the foundational engagement with the logic of Christian faith may issue in new conceptualizations, new formulations, new insights. The capacity of the individual to sustain a new synthesis contributes, then, to the objective structure of the Christian community.

That Rahner intends his text to be foundational in both ways — as a basis for affirming one's faith and as a basis for interpreting one's faith — reveals an important unity in his approach. Rahner presupposes "an intrinsic unity between fundamental theology and dogmatic theology." Theological commitments are wrapped into our interpretation of their plausability. We have just seen above how Rahner "argues" that intellectual justification must be possible since the logic of Christian faith requires intellectual assent. This is a direct expression of "the good Thomistic presupposition that fundamental theology is done under the 'light of faith,' and is a justification of faith by faith."[20] The warrant for this circularity is internal to the logic of Christianity. Rahner writes, "Given the structure of man as seen in divine revelation, the concrete, a posteriori experience of salvation and the historical facts of salvation cannot be turned into a purely transcendental, formal stucture without Christianity ceasing to be Christianity."[21] In other words, the egocentric forces of the Cartesian project are avoided by Rahner because instead of isolating the criteria for justification from the substantive issue to be justified, he weaves them together. As a consequence, there is no danger that the particular shape of the Christian tradition will be reduced to privileged internal experiences, or for that matter, eternal and incorporeal forms.

This kind of circularity was already evident in the *analogia gratiae* which informs his analysis of the logic of divine love, and such circularity is anathema to the Anglo-American sense of "foundational." Were Rahner attempting to show that Christianity involves a set of propositions which command our assent as justified true beliefs based upon a given set of criteria independent of Christianity, then the unity of the fundamental and dogmatic moments, the circularity of his justification of faith by faith,

20. Both quotes from *Foundations*, p. 12.
21. *Foundations*, p. 14.

would have to be rejected. However, this is not the case. The indirect method involves a virtuous circularity. The patterns of justification illumine dogmatic claims as the defense of the "idea" of Christianity is intertwined with a presentation of it. Rahner explains, "When we apply indirect methods of the kind of which we have been speaking these can very well serve to yield insights into the actual matter itself which is being treated of in the concrete."[22] Here, a parallel with Kerr's Wittgensteinian proposal emerges. Rahner approaches fundamental theology in much the way that Wittgenstein insists that we must "show" the deepest commitments of our form of life. However, the decisive difference is that Rahner builds the entire edifice of the *Foundations* upon the assumption that we exist in a pilgrim state, legitimately concerned with our general cultural identities as well as the distinctive and particular world of faith. As a result, central to Rahner's indirect method is a twofold transcendence: the capacity of the individual *qua* believer to penetrate Christian particularity in the quest for intellectual justification, and the possibility of the individual *qua* rational being to overcome the limitations of sin and concupiscence to say the "Yes" of Christian faith. As is the case at every turn for Rahner, however, this transcendence cannot be radical. It cannot leave behind either Christian particularity or the limitations of the distinctively human point of view without, at the same time, leaving behind the grammatical consequences of the proposition that God is love.

3. The third sense of "foundational," in Rahner's use of the term, intensifies the circularity of fundamental and dogmatic theologies. The analysis pursued in the *Grundkurs* is foundational because it attempts to grasp the basic or fundamental logic of Christianity. This is what Rahner means when he subtitles the text, "An Introduction to the Idea of Christianity." The metaphor of foundations is appropriate because the "idea" of Christianity does not involve a synoptic overview of Christian doctrine. Instead, the goal is to expose the interconnections which run through the loci of faith, God, sin, grace, Christ, and the Eschaton. He hopes, to steal a metaphor from Wittgenstein which is particularly suitable, to show the "river beds" through which the Christian linguistic practices flow. And in the *Foundations* in particular, but also in nearly all of Rahner's theological writings, the deepest channel is the dynamism of the Christian view of transcendence.

22. *TI* XI, p. 76.

Commenting on the fact that brief presentations of the essence of Christianity are perennial, Rahner indicates why he finds himself led back to the task already executed by St. Augustine, St. Bonaventura and St. Thomas, to name only the most exalted efforts. It would seem that we cannot rest in the linguistic inheritance of the tradition in any direct and immediate fashion. Rahner writes:

> There must always be new attempts at reflection upon the single whole of Christianity. They are always conditioned, since it is obvious that reflection in general, and all the more so scientific theological reflection, does not capture and cannot capture the whole of this reality which we realize in faith, hope, love and prayer. It is precisely this permanent and insurmountable difference between the original Christian actualization of existence and reflection upon it which will occupy us throughout. The insight into this difference is a key insight which represents a necessary presupposition for an introduction to the idea of Christianity."23

A permanent and insurmountable difference: this is precisely the sort of dualism which pries the believer out of a direct and immediate relationship to the particularities of the Christian community. The life of faith cannot simply "own" the single whole of Christianity. Our relationship to God is not equivalent to our ecclesial identities. "Ordinary" Christian ways of talking are not sufficient. Everything must be said again and anew, but not in a way which, like radical transcendence, treats the ordinary as the problem to be overcome. New attempts of theological reflection are always a transformative embrace of the same old gospel stories. For Rahner, seeking the "foundations" for faith, the bedrock of belief, the Alpha and Omega of our destiny in God, takes the form, then, of the Christian view of transcendence. It is a project of transcendence through, rather than above or beyond or behind, the givenness of the Christian form of life.

Rahner's own "foundations," his "idea of Christianity," may not do justice to the givenness of the Christian form of life. The particular philosophical idiom of the *Foundations* may deflect us away from rather than allow for transformative embrace. Rahner's judgments about the decisive logic of the Christian "whole," his assessment of the challenges facing the contemporary believer, his assumptions about the limitations

23. *TI* XI, p. 2.

and possibilities of modernity, all these may be misguided and judged mistaken. Nonetheless, even if Rahner is wrong in every respect regarding *what* expression Christianity might take within the life of the believer, his account of *how* we inhabit the particularities of Christianity preserves the amphibious transcendence which follows from the proposition that God is love. Within that mixed form of transcendence, the intellectual project of faith entails finding ways to "put on" rather than "put off" the distinctive Christian form of life. In this way, our rational transcendence, our sense of the "whole," should bathe us in the warp and woof of the tradition rather than cleanse us of its particular shape and purpose. Our transcendence in the judgment of intellectual assent should transform the confusing details of the Christian faith into a lived conviction rather than suspending or subordinating the distinctive creed and confession of the tradition to some higher epistemic or religious principle. Whether Rahner succeeds is another matter altogether.[24] Our goal here is to recognize how

---

24. Rowan Williams characterizes Balthasar's fundamental objection to Rahner on precisely this point. Williams observes that Balthasar's "objection is an objection not so much to one contemporary theologian (for whom, in fact, he has enormous respect) as a protest against the whole tradition of European 'mainstream' philosophy between Kant and Heidegger . . . a tradition which he sees as negating the 'sense of belonging in the world' by its obsession with subjectivity and the self-constitution of the subject" (*Analogy of Beauty*, ed. John Riches [Edinburgh: T & T Clark, 1986], p. 23). Williams may, perhaps, overstate Balthasar's protest. Balthasar does not reject or condemn modernity and its singular philosophical expressions. When Balthasar engages major modern figures, the specific structure of their thought often becomes an occasion for recapitulating a theological truth. (Cf. *Karl Barth*, pp. 12-13, for an account of the need to speak the "languages" of modernity.) His complaint is more nuanced. He protests against a too irenic and comfortable use of the specific "languages" of modernity. For Balthasar, Rahner's "idea of Christianity" — Rahner's strategy for infusing epistemic significance into faith — is not mistaken as a theological aspiration. Rather, Rahner's fulfillment of this aspiration suffers from insufficient attention to the limitations of the characteristic "languages" of modernity. For Balthasar, these limitations are essentially two-fold. On the one hand, modern concerns about subjectivity and self-consciousness alienate us from the world and make the ordinary uninhabitable for those who take existence "seriously." In other words, modernity tempts us toward a stance of radical transcendence. On the other hand, with all the gestures toward the "abyss," the "absolute mystery of existence," the "pre-thematic" which characterize radical transcendence, a dismissive attitude develops toward the written and preached, present and quite thematized *Ernstfall* of Christ's death and resurrection. Modernity translates the particular shape and structure of God's extraordinary grace into an appendage of subjectivity and self-consciousness. In other words, what begins as radical transcendence with respect to "spirit" becomes pure immanence with respect to Christ. In short,

Rahner views the "foundational" task of theology, not to evaluate his particular proposal.

4. Strangeness, Depth, and Mystery

FOR RAHNER, the central task of theology, the goal of the Christian life, and the purpose of revelation, is *reductio in mysterium*. And in that task, goal, and purpose we can see the final and enduring form of the Christian vision of transcendence. Throughout his work, Rahner exercises himself to parry superficial interpretations of the *reductio* which trade on the impulse towards radical transcendence. Mystery is not another name for an unfortunate obscurity which is caused by human finitude or corporeality. Rahner joins Kerr in setting aside the dualism implicit in an explanation of mystery as the temporal form of something which is, in principle, comprehensible. There is no compulsive contrast between human knowledge and variants of the platonic forms, where mystery covers the inevitable "slip" between the two components. As a result, Rahner sets aside both rationalism and idealism as approaches which trade on this false view of mystery: "Man is not a being who employs the *idea clara et distincta* (in the sense of Cartesian rationalism), nor is he the subject of an absolute system in which he alone and reality in general attain their conscious identity definitively (in the sense of German Idealism)."[25] It is not the case, then, that the perennial need to rethink the foundations of Christian faith rest in the ambiguity or uncertainty of ordinary Christian claims which creates the need to move beyond the mere "representations" of Christian language to the deeper truths of faith.

The dangers of a false view of mystery involve more than the temptations of radical transcendence. For Rahner, there is a peculiar link between the false view of mystery as obscurity and the neo-scholastic tendency to

---

Balthasar finds typically Rahnerian formulations inadequate to the amphibious Christian vision, even as the architecture of Rahner's thought gives that vision striking centrality (the key to Balthasar's deep respect for Rahner's project). Here, then, we might agree with Balthasar and set aside Rahner's use of the distinctively modern language of transcendence, while at the same time commending the amphibious vision of transcendence, the very vision to which Rahner seeks to bend, perhaps unsuccessfully, modernity's characteristic preoccupations.

25. *Sacramentum Mundi* IV (New York: Herder and Herder, 1969), p. 135.

become complacent in Christian language use. When discussing past conceptions of mystery, Rahner detects the tendency to cast mystery in terms of the inadequacy of the human intellect. Mystery is presented, in this view, only under a negative aspect. God is deemed incomprehensible because of the limitations placed on human existence. In this model, "the measure and ideal of knowledge that is applied to knowledge of mystery is that which comprehends and thoroughly sees into the object known."[26] The ideal, then, is that thorough comprehension will occur in the perfection of the intellect in the beatific vision.

The upshot of the flawed view of mystery is the extrinsicism which is the focus of the debates about nature and grace. By characterizing mystery as the temporal hiddenness of God, and by explicating this hiddenness in terms of the idea of perfect comprehension in the age to come, the neo-scholastics generated a central dichotomy. In our pilgrim state, God is radically inaccessible *in se,* and is only available *ad extra* in the negative guise of incomprehensibility. As we saw from the very outset in our consideration of Demea's position in the *Dialogues,* in temporal life, then, the most that we can hope to achieve is some participation in God which is simply given in a verbal profession of faith, while we hope for actual union with God at some later point. The model which emerges is that ordinary life is radically discontinuous with our extraordinary life in God. The only connection between the two is established by the divine decree which establishes the Church. Rahner, like Kerr, finds this dichotomy spiritually debilitating. The "real" God is divorced from ordinary life, rendering the drama of human existence a mere play of shadows.

Rahner's rejection of this facile view of mystery establishes a distance from the Enlightenment turn to the subject which he otherwise embraces. Kerr's analysis of the Cartesian legacy gains its polemical edge from the destructive tendencies which he detects in the contrast between ordinary knowledge and the privileged knowledge which secures truth and certainty. The human condition, in this view, is characterized by striving from deception to understanding, confusion to comprehension. The result of this view, thinks Kerr, is that we develop a discomfort with our created condition, we begin "wrapping ordinary life in cellophane." Like neo-scholastic extrinsicism, the Cartesian legacy tends to portray common features of human existence as superfluous at best, debilitating and destructive at worst.

26. *TI* XI, p. 103.

As we have seen, Kerr's solution to the tendency to compulsively contrast our current state with some perfect state above and beyond ordinary
life is radical. In effect, he denies that there is anything beyond the
givenness of *das Leben*. There is no need to strive from deception to
understanding, confusion to comprehension, because we already grasp
things as well as we need. Immersing ourselves into our form of life is the
beginning, middle, and end of our search for truth. As he observes, "The
depth of the world is on the surface."[27] With respect to the specific
question of divine mystery, Kerr would seem to be saying that in our
immersion in the givenness of Christian language, we grasp the divine
nature as well as we need. There is no divine comprehensibility or incomprehensibility. Both terms cast us back into the dualisms which fund radical
transcendence. Instead, we either are or are not part of the practice,
linguistic or liturgical, which constitutes Christianity. To rephrase his
remark about the depth of the world: the depth of God is on the surface.

As has been the case throughout, Rahner adopts neither the "beyond"
of radical transcendence nor the givenness of pure immanence. Unlike the
view so common in neo-scholasticism, mystery is not something to be
overcome. Yet, at the same time, the depth of God is not on the surface.
Though mystery is not to be viewed as an impediment, a denotation of
the gap between our current flawed ways of talking about God and the
actuality of God behind the language, we must still view mystery as a
project. God has a depth which must be penetrated even as we immerse
ourselves in Christian ways of talking and acting. Indeed, for Rahner, we
enter into the depths of mystery precisely as we gain expertise in the
Christian language. Like a taste for coffee, the more one knows the aroma
and its inner complexity, the harder one pushes for the right taste. So,
though the depth of God is not *on* the surface of the Christian form of
life, that depth is very much *in* the givenness of the tradition.

In this sense, then, comprehensibility and incomprehensibility are not
rejected as debilitating concerns. Instead, Rahner yokes them together.
"We must understand," he writes, "that this *reductio* [*in mysterium*] constitutes not a regrettable imperfection in theology, but rather that which
is most proper to it of its very nature."[28] The speechlessness of wonder
before the divine offer of love is the *terminus ad quem* of theological

27. *Theology After Wittgenstein*, p. 188.
28. *TI* XI, p. 101.

scholarship. Here, then, we find a project of transcendence in which the goal is not the pure intelligibility of clear and distinct ideas, nor is it the systematic unity of the Absolute Idea. Instead, Rahner claims that for the Christian, the direction of transcendence is through what we know so well and so clearly, the Christian form of life, to what we cannot possibly understand, the God for us. And if this is the structure of Christian transcendence, then the depth of mystery is infinite and the project of transcendence eternal. For the more we know and understand, the more clearly we grasp the "surface," the more extensive becomes the depth; the more clearly we see God, the more hidden he becomes.

The pervasiveness of mystery cuts against the grain of Kerr's purely immanent vision of the Christian life. Rahner interprets mystery as the most basic warrant for the alienation of the believer from the Christian linguistic community: "Theological statements only authentically become such in a process in which they reach out to a point radically beyond themselves."[29] The more that we immerse ourselves in the Christian form of life, the more skilled we become in the practices which constitute the Christian community, the *less* familiar, the *less* immediate, the *less* comfortable becomes our faith. For Rahner, the Christian "grammar" has a propelling depth, and transcendence names the mode of existence by which we enter into those depths.

The "grammar" of Christianity is structured by the strangeness of grace. We are confronted by the divine self-offer in our creaturely state, in our ordinary lives; but the reality of this offer is anything but ordinary. It is not as though the linguistic structures of the Christian community are odd or skewed. Instead, for Rahner, the Christian community speaks the most ordinary language of stories and parables. But the content of the Christian language is odd — "God so loved the world that he gave his only begotten Son." To the degree that we "inhabit" this sentence, to the extent that we learn the practices which constitute the basis of worship and service, Rahner claims that we cannot help but raise fundamental questions about God, love, world, and gift. We cannot help but recognize that the enabling language of revelation is not transparent and ordinary in a way which we might easily inhabit. Instead, that language issues the most extraordinary demands. *Credo!* For Rahner, it should be at our fingertips in a way which cuts to the quick of our souls.

29. *TI* XI, p. 112.

Index

223